Foundations o Educational Technology

An engaging book for professional educators and an ideal textbook for certificate, masters, and doctoral programs in educational technology, instructional systems, and learning design, *Foundations of Educational Technology, Second Edition* offers a fresh, interdisciplinary, problem-centered approach to the subject, helping students build extensive notes and an electronic portfolio as they navigate the text. The book addresses fundamental aspects of educational technology theory, research, and practice that span various users, contexts, and settings; includes a full range of engaging exercises for students that will contribute to their professional growth; and offers the following four-step pedagogical features inspired by M. D. Merrill's *First Principles of Instruction*:

- TELL: Primary presentations and pointers to major sources of information and resources;
- ASK: Activities that encourage students to critique applications and share their individual interpretations;
- SHOW: Activities that demonstrate the application of key concepts and complex skills with appropriate opportunities for learner responses;
- DO: Activities in which learners apply key concepts and complex skills while working on practice assignments and/or projects to be created for their electronic portfolios.

The second edition of this textbook covers the core objectives addressed in introductory educational technology courses while adding new sections on mobile learning, MOOCs, open educational resources, "big data," and learning analytics along with suggestions to instructors and appendices on effective writing, professional associations, and journals and trade magazines.

J. Michael Spector is Professor and former Chair of the Department of Learning Technologies at the University of North Texas, USA. Dr. Spector has served as Executive Vice President on the International Board of Standards for Training, Performance and Instruction (ibstpi), on the Executive Committee of the IEEE Learning Technology Task Force, and as past-President of the Association for Educational and Communications Technology (AECT). He was lead editor on the third and fourth editions of the *Handbook of Research on Educational Communications and Technology*, edited the *Encyclopedia of Educational Technology*, and has more than 150 journal articles, book chapters, and books to his credit.

Interdisciplinary Approaches to Educational Technology

Series Editor: J. Michael Spector

Current and forthcoming series titles:

Foundations of Educational Technology

Integrative Approaches and Interdisciplinary Perspectives

Second Edition

J. MICHAEL SPECTOR

Routledge
Taylor & Francis Group

NEW YORK AND LONDON

Second edition published 2016
by Routledge
711 Third Avenue, New York, NY 10017

and by Routledge
2 Park Square, Milton Park, Abingdon, Oxon OX14 4RN

Routledge is an imprint of the Taylor & Francis Group, an informa business

First edition published by Routledge 2012

Library of Congress Cataloging in Publication Data
Spector, J. Michael.
    Foundations of educational technology: integrative approaches and interdisciplinary perspectives/
J. Michael Spector.—Second edition.
    pages cm
    Includes bibliographical references and index.
    1. Educational technology. I. Title.
    LB1028.3.S6295 2015
    371.33—dc23
    2014046337

ISBN: 978-1-138-79027-8 (hbk)
ISBN: 978-1-138-79028-5 (pbk)
ISBN: 978-1-315-76426-9 (ebk)

Typeset in Minion Pro, Helvetica Neue and Copperplate Gothic
by Florence Production Ltd, Stoodleigh, Devon, UK

Printed and bound in the United States of America by
Edwards Brothers Malloy on sustainably sourced paper

This volume is again dedicated to those who shaped my understanding of educational technology: Walter Davis (a computer scientist and mathematician), Robert M. Gagné (an educational researcher and psychologist), David H. Jonassen (an educational researcher and instructional design theorist), M. David Merrill (an instructional engineer and technologist), and Robert Tennyson (an educational psychologist). In addition, I have several of my philosophy professors to thank for training me to think more clearly and to write more coherently: Edwin B. Allaire, Oets K. Bouwsma, John P. Murphy, and Stuart Spicker.

Contents

Preface

This is a revised second edition of the introductory volume in the Routledge series entitled "Integrative Approaches to Educational Technology: Interdisciplinary Perspectives on Technology in Support of Learning, Performance, and Instruction." This book introduces the topics to be covered in more detail in subsequent volumes in the series. In addition, this volume establishes a general four-part, problem-centered framework that will be used in all volumes in this series.

Part I of this volume provides an overview and introduction to the field of educational technology. Chapter topics include an elaborated definition of educational technology, a foundations and values perspective on educational technology, a discussion of learning and performance as well as teaching and training, issues pertaining to technology support, and integrative approaches to planning and implementing educational technologies.

Part II provides an elaboration of some of the theoretical perspectives informing the profession. Theories of human development, learning and performance, information and communications, instruction, and instructional design are reviewed. Leading researchers and scholars associated with the most influential theories are briefly discussed.

Part III provides a more detailed elaboration of practical perspectives and prominent technologies associated with the profession. Issues involved in implementing pilot efforts on a larger scale, the diffusion of innovation, and change agency are introduced along with the challenges of teaching with technology and implementing educational technologies in workplace settings. Principles of design and lessons learned with regard to integrating technology successfully are discussed in this part of the volume. Prominent technologies are also highlighted in this part of the book. In addition, many variations in professional practice are noted, along with how professional practitioners are being prepared in various university and enterprise settings.

Part IV is entitled "Broadening the Context" and contains an initial chapter that discusses some of the factors relevant to successful design and implementation of educational technology in K-12, higher education, business and industry, governmental agencies, and nonprofit and nongovernmental organizations. Emphasis is placed on the recruitment and training of professional practitioners in these various settings, including recommendations for professional development. There are three new chapters included in this part of the book that round out the concept of a broadened context: (a) Professional Preparation and Training, (b) Scalability, and (c) Emerging Technologies.

Each of the chapters is structured to provide introductory remarks followed by a discussion of the major points covered. In some cases, there are classroom and online discussion forum activities suggested, and occasional quizzes are spread throughout. Each chapter also includes an end-of-chapter test that can be used as an assignment, self-test, or discussion thread. After the test of understanding, there is a representative educational technology challenge intended to provide students and other readers with a sense for the kinds of complex problems that educational technologists and instructional designers are expected to solve. Following the representative educational technology challenge, there is a suggested learning activity that is most often tightly connected with the representative problem. References, links, and other resources are also included at the end of every chapter.

This is by no means a definitive treatise on educational technology. It is intended to be a useful textbook to help orient those new to the profession and discipline to the many dimensions of complexity with which educational technologists and instructional designers work. There are some discussions of theory and principles that might be regarded as scholarly tidbits, but there are also discussions of practical issues that are encountered in everyday practice. The intent is to blend theory and practice based on the notion that well-informed practitioners and well-grounded researchers are the kinds of people who contribute the most to the advancement of the broadly defined enterprise of educational technology.

A particular challenge in writing this book was to introduce technology-enhanced examples and discuss some general aspects of various types of technologies while limiting elaboration of specific technologies. The reason for this approach is that specific technologies come and go at an alarming rate, and new technologies emerge and evolve quite rapidly. If a great deal of detail were provided on specific technologies, the volume would probably be out of date before it was even in print. However, there is a discussion of emerging technologies (e.g., massive open online courses (MOOCs), mobile devices, and personalized learning) that are likely to influence the future of educational practice toward the end of the book.

There are, of course, other good books in this area, and several of these are referenced herein. Because research, development, and teaching involving educational technologies are inherently complex domains of inquiry and practice, one should always consider alternative perspectives and approaches.

Acknowledgments

I wish to thank my editor at Routledge, Alex Masulis, for his guidance and patience in putting together this textbook series and encouraging me to get this second edition in print. I have to thank many people who provided feedback on the first edition, and who, as a result, have helped me think more clearly about the foundations of the complex enterprises of educational technology and instructional design.

part one

INTRODUCTION AND OVERVIEW

one
Defining
Educational
Technology

"We shape our tools and afterwards our tools shape us"
(from Marshall McLuhan's Understanding Media*)*

Technology

Consider refrigeration as a technology. Refrigeration has changed a great deal over the years. People have known for thousands of years that food stored in cool places or packed in snow would last longer than food not kept cool. Refrigeration is not a new technology. There were not many advances in refrigeration until it was discovered (perhaps in the 1500s) that the temperature of water could be lowered by the addition of certain chemicals such as sodium nitrate. Icehouses became popular in the 1800s and various insulating techniques for slowing the melting process were devised. Mechanical refrigeration took off in the middle of the nineteenth century as methods to compress a gas, such as ammonia, methyl chloride, or sulfur dioxide, circulate it through radiating coils, and then expand it were devised in America, Australia, France, and elsewhere. In the early part of the twentieth century, chlorofluorocarbons such as Freon replaced the more toxic gases that had been in use. Fifty years would pass before it was discovered that chlorofluorocarbons had a harmful effect on the atmosphere (ozone depletion) and indirect toxic effects on humans. Technology is usually considered to be the disciplined application of knowledge to benefit mankind, but technology can also have harmful effects.

The means used to control the vaporization and condensation of the gases used in refrigeration have also changed over the years. A gas or propane refrigerator is able to control these processes by simply heating a gas such as ammonia that first vaporizes, and then dissolves and condenses in water. This process involves no motor and is quite simple. However, gas refrigerators did not do as well in the marketplace as electric refrigerators that used a motor to control expansion and compression. In modern electric refrigerators there are automatic defrosters, ice-makers, and many other features. When my grandmother passed away in the 1980s at the age of 94, she had four refrigerators in her farmhouse in Alabama. One was an icebox that had an upper compartment to hold a block of ice and a lower compartment to hold food. She also had a propane refrigerator and two electric refrigerators, one of which had an icemaker and automatic defroster. All four refrigerators were in working order and in use. She used the icemaker in the newest refrigerator to keep the icebox supplied. She was fascinated by the technology of refrigeration and used the technology to preserve the food she produced on her farm. Her use of refrigeration technology definitely benefited our family.

Why begin a book about educational technology with this short history of refrigeration? There are several reasons. First, this example will be used to develop a definition of technology. Second, this example emphasizes a key aspect of technology—namely, change. Third, the example suggests that technology by itself is neither good nor bad; rather, it is how technology is used that is good or bad. Finally, there are effects on society and the marketplace to be considered when planning and evaluating technology.

Defining Technology

From the refrigeration example, one might be inclined to say that technology involves a tangible thing such as a block of ice or a refrigerator. However, such a definition would omit the processes used in evaporation and condensation, the various gases involved, techniques for insulating ice, methods for producing the gases used, and more. Some refrigeration units were fully specified on paper but never manufactured. Is the detailed specification for a refrigerator a technology? Is the process used in propane-powered absorption a technology? These are good questions to discuss in class, by the way. The word 'technology' is derived from two Greek words—*techne* (art, craft, or skill) and *logia* (words, study, or body of knowledge). The etymology of 'technology' suggests knowledge about making things, which would seem to include the specification for a refrigerator as a technology.

The classical view of a definition involves the essence of the thing being defined— that which makes it what it is and not something else. One might be tempted to ask about the essence of technology, perhaps in the form of necessary and sufficient conditions or characteristics. However, a modern view of a definition also considers how the term is used. It is true that many people use the word 'technology' to refer to manufactured objects such as computers, telephones, and refrigerators. If one listens carefully, one will also hear people talk about the means of transmission used by different kinds of telephones as technologies or the different generations of computer technology. Those uses of 'technology' refer to something more abstract than a particular telephone or computer. What seems to run through most uses of the word 'technology' is the application of knowledge for a practical purpose. My grandmother used the icebox to preserve food; she wanted to feed her family (the practical purpose), and she knew the icebox would help make the food last longer (the knowledge).

Let us agree that a *technology involves the practical application of knowledge for a purpose*. One way to make this notion concrete is through the concept of a patent. Nearly everything that is or could be patented represents a technology according to this definition. This broad definition also will allow us to focus on different kinds of knowledge and different purposes to which that knowledge might be applied. Of course, the general purpose with which we are concerned is education, but this is also a broad area that is examined in the next section.

Before moving on, though, it is worth noting that this definition of technology allows for change. In fact, change might be considered a basic aspect of technology since knowledge is generally progressing and the goals and intentions of people are dynamic. *Technology changes.* Just as refrigeration technology has changed dramatically over the years, most technologies tend to change. As technology changes, what people do changes. People preserve food for longer and longer periods of time and start to eat things grown in one season or in a different part of the world in a different season or region of the world. *Technology changes what people do and what they can do.* Technology can also influence what people want to avoid doing. Can you think of examples? That which a technology makes possible is called an *affordance*. Refrigeration technology affords us the opportunity to eat things grown elsewhere or out of season.

Test Your Understanding

Which of the following is/are (is/are not) a technology and why (why not) (refer to specific knowledge and purpose involved)?

1. a. White sand on the beach at Gulf Shores, Alabama.
   b. Sand poured into a hollowed box container large enough for a block of ice.
   c. Sand glued to a piece of sturdy paper.
   d. White sand in the desert near Tularosa, New Mexico.
   e. A procedure to turn sand into glass.

2. a. A laptop computer.
   b. A mobile telephone (cell phone).
   c. The Internet.
   d. A wireless network.
   e. An electric toothbrush.

3. a. A procedure to sort items into ascending alphabetical order.
   b. An algorithm for determining the standard deviation of a set of scores.
   c. A blueprint for a digital design studio.
   d. The pictographs and petroglyphs at Hueco Tanks, Texas.
   e. Picasso's painting entitled "Guernica."

Education

Education, like technology, is quite broad in terms of what it encompasses. The word 'education' comes to us from Latin *educare*, which means upbringing, training, or support based on the combination of *ex* or more simply *e* (from, or out of) and *ducere* (to lead, to guide). The derivation of the modern term is informative as it suggests that education involves a purpose or a goal, and a process of support or guidance toward the achievement of that goal.

However, to be sure we do not deviate too much from common sense and popular usage, it is worth noticing how the word 'education' is used. It is not uncommon to hear someone say of another person that he or she is well educated (or not). I have been told that my education is lacking in some areas—notably the arts. The word 'education' is often combined with a modifier to indicate a subject area or general approach, as in 'engineering education' or 'liberal education.' Occasionally, one might hear someone sum up a particularly unusual or unexpected experience by saying "that was certainly educational." In these uses of 'education' we again see the notion of a purpose and some kind of knowledge involved. There is typically the suggestion of a person or institution involved in the educational experience, although the person doing the educating might be oneself (as in 'self-educated'). Often, the word 'education' is used in a résumé to indicate the institutions attended and degrees earned by an individual.

It would seem that both knowledge and a process of learning are involved in an educational experience. Rather than dig a deeper and deeper hole and fill it with more words, let us agree that learning involves a change in what a person is able or inclined to do or believe. Why introduce the notion of change here? Well, 'education' already has knowledge and purpose in common with 'technology.' Perhaps the notion of 'change' is a third common element. Indeed, if one claims that learning has occurred, then it would seem reasonable to ask "How do you know?" The answer could be that before the educational process occurred, the person could not do X but now that the person has learned something, he or she is able to do X (Gagné, 1985). Note that there is no attempt here to make fine distinctions between being educated and having learned, nor is there an effort to distinguish education from training, as many others have done. Rather, the intention is to maintain a broad definition of education that is closely associated with learning and that encompasses training.

It is possible to make a distinction between learning well-defined and fully specified tasks and procedures (often called training) and learning more open-ended kinds of knowledge, such as historical interpretations of events or philosophical principles (a broader kind of learning than training). In our view, many things to be learned by humans involve a mixture of things that could be considered best learned by training (e.g., a routine procedure to determine the acidity of a fluid) and things that can be best learned by a broader kind of education (e.g., environmental planning). The concept that things to be learned involve multiple kinds of knowledge linked together can be found in a landmark journal article by Robert M. Gagné and M. David Merrill (1990; see www.ibstpi.org/Products/pdf/chapter_5.pdf for the reprinted article in *The Legacy of Robert M. Gagné*) and also in an important book by Jeroen van Merriënboer (1997).

Defining Education

Drawing on this discussion of the etymology and general use of the term 'education' we can now define education as a process of improving one's knowledge, performance, and understanding through a systematic and sustained effort. While one use of the term 'education' implies that education can be unplanned and incidental (as in "my unexpected inability to perform was both enlightening and educational"), most uses of the term involve an intentional and effortful activity. Learning and knowledge are associated with education. While education is sometimes differentiated from training, in the view presented here education includes training as one supporting type of instruction appropriate for well-defined, recurrent tasks. Typically, education includes a broad range of learning activities and instructional sequences aimed at a broad goal, such as becoming a computer scientist, an engineering designer, a lawyer, a nurse, a refrigeration technician, or a teacher. Being an educated professional implies a certain level of competence in solving problems and performing tasks as well as a high level of knowledge about the subject area.

Educational goals, as reflected in universities around the world, can be clustered around the following: (a) develop productive workers (emphasized in the Industrial Age and now being re-emphasized in the competitive global economic era); (b) develop effective problem solvers (emphasized in many disciplines and increasingly important in the Digital Age); (c) develop analytical and critical thinkers (long emphasized in engineering and management programs and increasingly important in the Information Age); (d) develop responsible citizens (a hallmark of a liberal education dating back at least to Dewey, 1907, 1916 and probably much further back in history); and (e) develop life-long learners (mostly a tacit educational goal until the twentieth century when lifespans increased and people began to have multiple careers and leisure time to pursue other interests). The point here is that education certainly involves change, as reflected by the use of 'develop' in each of the above goal clusters, those goal clusters themselves have been relatively stable over the years, although emphasized differently at different times and in different circumstances, as suggested in the parenthetical remarks above.

In summary, our definition of education is broad and involves intentional and systematic study, guidance and support from others and often from an institution, along with changes in one's ability and knowledge. Education involves learning, instruction and performance, all of which are addressed in this volume. Education, like technology, involves change in addition to being purposeful and specific to a subject domain.

Test Your Understanding

Which of the following involve (or not) education and why (why not) (refer to specific knowledge and purpose involved)?

1. a. Learning to repair the compressor on a refrigerator.
   b. Moving a nonfunctioning refrigerator to a garbage collection site.
   c. Learning about the Jornado Mogollon people who lived around Hueco Tanks, Texas.
   d. Reading about the conversion of gypsum into dry wall used in construction.
   e. Memorizing common phrases in a foreign language prior to visiting a country where that language is spoken.

2. a. Getting a driver's license.
   b. Obtaining a high school diploma.
   c. Having a transcript from a four-year university.
   d. Getting an award for outstanding performance in sports.
   e. Winning a prize in a school-sponsored raffle.

3. a. Sorting items into ascending alphabetical order.
   b. Determining the standard deviation of a set of scores.
   c. Developing a blueprint for a digital design studio.
   d. Drawing replicas of the pictographs and petroglyphs at Hueco Tanks, Texas.
   e. Searching the Internet for a restaurant that serves fresh fish.

Educational Technology

Having established broad boundaries for technology and education, we are now in a position to consider the general subject area of this book—educational technology. It is almost impossible to think of education without also thinking about the many different kinds of technology used to support education. A common technique used to teach children concepts is to provide an example, state the rule that makes it an example, point at more examples and also at some nonexamples explaining how the nonexamples violate the rule, and then allow the child to test his or her understanding on new examples, providing feedback on the child's performance. To teach the concept 'fruit,' one could point at a banana, an orange, and an apple and say of each one that it is an example of a fruit. When one then introduces a common definition of a fruit as the edible, seed-bearing portion of a plant, a teacher is likely to encounter all sorts of questions from children, such as "where are the seeds in a banana?" or "are tomatoes and squash fruits since they are edible and have seeds?" or "what about seedless watermelons?" Definitions are such fun and children are wonderful at finding counterexamples and problematic cases. We ought to preserve that talent. Next come the nonexamples such as nuts of various kinds, potatoes, sesame leaves, and turnip greens. Such a lesson might involve more than the concept 'fruit.' It might, for example, involve multiple concepts (fruits, nuts, vegetables) and the higher order concept of a balanced or nutritious diet. Nonetheless, basic concepts and terminology are important in many cases and for many learners—not just young children. One might say that one step in becoming an educated professional in a particular domain is learning to speak the professional language associated with that domain. This book is about learning to speak the language of educational technology.

What happens when we try out that four-part technique (examples, nonexamples, categorizing rule, practice) of concept learning with 'educational technology.' Well, here are some examples of things people call educational technologies: (a) a computer tutorial introducing a new user to the use of a particular computer program; (b) an interactive whiteboard on which a computer screen is projected and then touched to activate a particular menu selection; (c) a discussion forum in an online learning management system; (d) a computer program that converts a formula into a curve; and (e) a database that contains detailed historical information about politicians and their votes.

What rule might we generate that would help a novice correctly characterize these examples as educational technologies? Suppose we try out a simple rule such as this: a technology that can help a person learn something is an educational technology. These examples might all satisfy such a rule. Then we might try adding more examples such as (a) a handheld calculator; (b) a procedure for converting Farenheit to Celsius; (c) a formula for determining the volume of a sphere; (d) a Web-based tool to introduce, illustrate, and solve the Towers of Hanoi problem for an arbitrary number of disks (for an example, see www.mazeworks.com/hanoi/index.htm); or (e) a slide rule.

A slide rule is an educational technology. Really? Really. It is one of the most effective educational technologies ever devised. A slide rule allows one to perform division and multiplication by simply adding and subtracting logarithms. A very nice introduction to the slide rule and a self-guided tutorial on its use can be found at the website for the International Slide Rule Museum: http://sliderulemuseum.com/SR_Course.htm (see Figure 1.1). This website integrates history, procedures for performing calculations, and mathematical knowledge quite nicely.

So, how is a slide rule an educational technology? One can learn about logarithms using a slide rule. One can perform calculations used in many mathematical and engineering enterprises with a slide rule. In short, a slide rule can support learning and performance and has many educational affordances, so it qualifies as an educational technology.

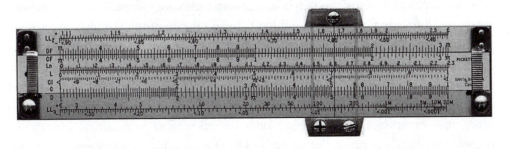

FIGURE 1.1 A slide rule (see http://sliderulemuseum.com/SR_Course.htm)

What makes a slide rule an exceptionally effective educational technology, however, is the fact that it requires very careful use of the sliders and scales. A very minor error in moving the sliding cursor and reading the scale with the hairline indicator can result in a major error. This forces slide-rule users to understand the problem being solved in advance well enough to formulate a range for what a reasonable answer would be. If the slide rule does not yield something in the anticipated range, the user would first suspect user error and perform the calculation again. In other words, what made the slide rule so effective was that it forced users to think about the problem being solved—users would typically reflect on the problem and formulate a rough answer prior to using the technology. While the slide rule has been replaced by powerful handheld calculators and computers, it reminds us that *a powerful affordance of an educational technology is to get one to think about the problem* one is trying to understand. The educational principle here is that reflecting on the nature of the problem being solved is often effective in promoting learning and understanding—a principle well worth remembering.

We shall omit providing nonexamples of educational technology to teach the concept of educational technology to someone new to the field. Such an activity might prove to be insightful in a classroom setting. As soon as a nonexample is postulated, I would expect someone to think of an educational application, however. That might prove to be fun to try in a classroom setting or discussion forum. When implementing concept learning in a classroom setting, the notion of practice with timely and informative feedback is important. Simply stating the rule and providing a few examples may be expedient but can easily result in misconceptions.

Defining Educational Technology

The prior discussion implies that one could define educational technology using an intersection of technology and education. How would that look?

Figure 1.2 depicts a Venn diagram with two intersecting ovals: education and technology, creating four areas: (1) neither education nor technology; (2) education but not technology; (3) technology but not education; and (4) education and technology.

Clearly, area 4 is the general focus of this book. However, while there is a certain logical appeal to such a figure, it creates the task of identifying examples in each area, which is not so easy—give that a try as a class discussion activity or as a personal project.

We still require a usable definition of educational technology to guide our explorations and further discussion. Here is a definition based on the common elements of purpose, knowledge, and change: *Educational technology involves the disciplined application of knowledge for the purpose of improving learning, instruction, and/or performance.* The notion of disciplined application of knowledge is included here to reflect the view that educational technology is an engineering discipline in the sense that principles based on theory, past experience, and empirical evidence guide what professional educational technologists do. These principles are derived from basic science and empirical research in such areas as cognition, cybernetics, information science, human factors, learning

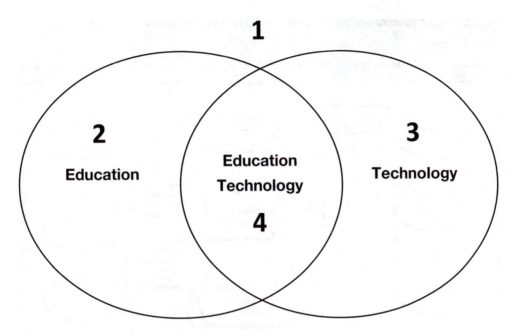

1

2
Education

Education
Technology

4

3
Technology

FIGURE 1.2 Educational technology Venn diagram

theory, mass communications, message design, organizational theory, and psychology. Educational technology is inherently an interdisciplinary enterprise. The principle of encouraging problem solvers to reflect on the nature of the problem first can be traced to research in cognitive psychology (perhaps it goes back much further).

Educational technology draws on the work of multiple disciplines. Because multiple disciplines are involved and because problems in educational technology are often complex and challenging, it is especially important to think about what one does (and of course how and why) in a disciplined and systematic manner. A systems perspective has long been a hallmark of educational technology. The systems perspective involves (a) a long-term view of the problem and solution (from imagination through implementation to interment); (b) a broad and holistic view of relevant factors (from the immediate context to incidental and unanticipated activities); and (c) a dynamic view of the problem space (things are likely to change).

Educational technology involves multiple disciplines, multiple activities, multiple people, multiple tools, and multiple opportunities to facilitate meaningful change. There are a number of principles drawn from different disciplines that guide what educational technologists do. Many tools and technologies have been developed to help educational technologists perform their responsibilities. Figure 1.3 is a notional concept of educational technology created using a knowledge modeling tool called *MOT plus* developed at the LICEF Research Centre affiliated with the University of Montreal, Canada (see www1.licef.ca). In Figure 1.3, rectangles represent concepts, ovals represent procedures or processes, hexagons represent rules or principles, and octagons represent facts. Connections of various types exist, such as components (steps) of procedures,

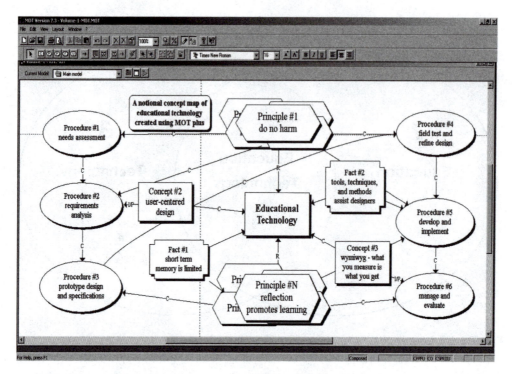

FIGURE 1.3 A notional concept map created with MOT plus

principles that influence concepts and categorizing decisions, and concepts and facts that affect procedures and other concepts. This obviously incomplete representation of educational technology is focused on the knowledge involved rather than on those who implement that knowledge to promote learning or on how the knowledge will be acquired, mastered, and applied.

In addition to multiple disciplines and tools, educational technologists have different perspectives on the various processes and activities with which they are involved. Using technology to promote learning, instruction, and performance is far from a formulaic enterprise. There are many approaches, methods, and tools to inform good solutions for the challenging problems educational technologists confront. Figure 1.4 represents a way to view educational technology in terms of support for learning and instruction, especially with regard to instructional objects (see Spector, 2014b).

In addition to offering support for instructional objects and others aspects of learning and instruction, new forms of technology are appearing that are referred to as smart technologies (Spector, 2014a). Smart technologies are those that exhibit characteristics of intelligent human behavior (e.g., selecting an appropriate alternative among multiple choices based on past knowledge and experience). Table 1.1 reflects the characteristics that might be considered necessary, desirable, or likely for a smart technology.

We close this chapter with an illustration of a representative complex problem and suggested activities to work toward a solution. This example is used to inform two

A Hierarchy of Components to Support Learning and Instruction

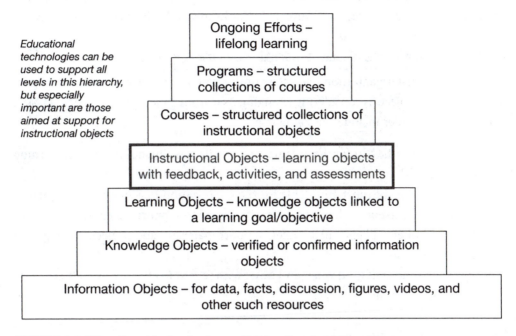

Educational technologies can be used to support all levels in this hierarchy, but especially important are those aimed at support for instructional objects

Ongoing Efforts – lifelong learning

Programs – structured collections of courses

Courses – structured collections of instructional objects

Instructional Objects – learning objects with feedback, activities, and assessments

Learning Objects – knowledge objects linked to a learning goal/objective

Knowledge Objects – verified or confirmed information objects

Information Objects – for data, facts, discussion, figures, videos, and other such resources

FIGURE 1.4 Educational technologies and instructional objects

TABLE 1.1

Elaboration	
Necessary characteristics	
Effectiveness	An intelligent tutoring system with evidence of improved learning
Efficiency	A tool that automatically assesses student inputs and provides feedback
Scalable	A technology that can be easily implemented on a large scale in multiple contexts
Desirable characteristics	
Engaging	An interactive game linked to a learning objective
Flexible	A tool or environment that automatically reconfigures itself to accommodate the current situation
Adaptive	A technology that automatically adapts itself to a specific learner and that learner's profile
Personal[izable]	A technology that responds to an individual with an awareness of that particular individual's history or situation
Likely characteristics	
Conversational	A system that interprets and responds with natural language
Reflective	A technology that prompts the learner to reflect on a particular aspect of a responsive
Innovative	A system that effectively integrates a new technology to support learning and instruction

activities associated with this chapter: (1) discussing the example in small groups and collaboratively developing a more elaborated solution approach; and (2) initiating a portfolio which may be used for future activities in this and subsequent courses.

A Representative Educational Technology Challenge

A large educational organization that offers online courses and provides online support for courses and projects is considering changing its learning management system (LMS). Questions to consider include the following:

1. Which LMS is the best for the organization and its constituency in terms of learning effectiveness?
2. Which LMS is the most affordable for the organization to acquire and maintain?
3. What issues exist or are likely to arise with regard to support, acceptance, and use?
4. How and when will existing courses, support materials, and projects be migrated to the new system?
5. Who will train staff (and when and how) with regard to effective and efficient use of the new system?

Learning Activities

1. Develop a plan that addresses the first three issues in the representative educational technology challenge. Share the plan with your colleagues and ask them to provide a critique; critique one or more of their plans in exchange for the feedback.
2. Develop a plan that addresses the last two issues in the representative educational technology challenge. Share the plan with your colleagues and ask them to provide a critique; critique one or more of their plans in exchange for the feedback.
3. Investigate several Internet sources pertaining to educational technology and develop a list of activities and responsibilities typically associated with instructional designers and educational technologists. Indicate the knowledge and skills associated with these activities and responsibilities. Share your findings with your colleagues and ask them to provide a critique; critique one or more of their findings in exchange for the feedback.

Links

The article entitled "Integrative Goals for Instructional Design" by Robert M. Gagné and M. David Merrill that appeared in *Educational Technology Research and Development* in 1990 was reprinted with permission in *The Legacy of Robert M. Gagné*, a volume sponsored by the International Board of Standards for Training, Performance and Instruction (www.ibstpi.org) and is freely available at the following URL: http://eric.ed.gov/?id=ED445674.

A nice example of a Web-based tool to help students learn about exponential functions in the context of the Towers of Hanoi game can be found at www.mazeworks.com/hanoi/index.htm. There are many more such examples of the Towers of Hanoi game available online. It is worthwhile to have a look at these and see how different examples might be used to teach different aspects of the Towers of Hanoi problem.

An introduction to the slide rule and its use can be found at the website for the International Slide Rule Museum: http://sliderulemuseum.com/SR_Course.htm. This website integrates history, procedures for performing calculations, and mathematical knowledge.

A powerful knowledge modeling tool is freely available from the LICEF Research Center in Montreal, Canada—www.licef.ca/Home/tabid/36/language/en-US/Default.aspx.

Another powerful concept mapping tool is called CMAPS developed by the Institute for Human and Machine Cognition (IHMC) affiliated with the University of West Florida—http://cmap.ihmc.us/conceptmap.html.

Other Resources

The Association for the Advancement of Computing in Education (AACE)—www.aace.org

The Association for Educational Communications and Technology (AECT)—www.aect.org

The International Board of Standards for Training, Performance and Instruction (ibstpi)—www.ibstpi.org

The New Media Consortium (NMC)—www.nmc.org (look for the Horizon Report)

Spector, J. M. (Ed.) (2015). *The encyclopedia of educational technology*. Thousand Oaks, CA: Sage.

Spector, J. M., Merrill, M. D., Elen, J., & Bishop, M. J. (Eds.) (2014). *Handbook of research on educational communications and technology* (4th ed.). New York: Springer.

References

Dewey, J. (1907). *The school and society*. Chicago: University of Chicago Press.

Dewey, J. (1916). *Democracy and education: An introduction to the philosophy of education*. New York: Macmillan.

Gagné, R. M. (1985). *The conditions of learning* (4th ed.). New York: Holt, Rinehart & Winston.

Gagné, R. M., & Merrill, M. D. (1990). Integrative goals for instructional design. *Educational Technology Research and Development, 38*(1), 23–30.

Spector, J. M. (2014a). Conceptualizing the emerging field of smart learning environments. *Smart Learning Environment, 1*(2), 1–10.

Spector, J. M. (2014b). Remarks on MOOCs and mini-MOOCs. *Educational Technology Research & Development, 62*(3), 385–392.

van Merriënboer, J. J. G. (1997). *Training complex cognitive skills: A four-component instructional design model for technical training*. Englewood Cliffs, NJ: Educational Technology Publications.

two
Values, Foundations, and a Framework

"Everything changes and nothing remains still"
(attributed to Heraclitus by Plato in the Cratylus*)*

Values

Given that technology changes and that what people do and can do changes, how are
we to maintain a solid foundation and maintain our values? This challenge is put best,
perhaps by Bob Dylan in his song "Forever Young" ("may you have a strong foundation
when the winds of changes shift"), but is also evident in the writings of many, dating at
least as far back as Heraclitus, a pre-Socratic philosopher. In the previous chapter, the
claim was made that educational technology could be either beneficial or harmful,
depending on its use. While the general intention is to use educational technologies for
the good of one or more persons, unanticipated consequences can occur that are harmful.
It is not logical to build the concept of ethics into the definition of educational technology,
just as it would be inappropriate to build the concept of ethics into the definition of
medical surgery. However, it is clear that ethics are part and parcel of medical practice,
as exemplified by this portion of the classical Hippocratic Oath:

> Whatever houses I may visit, I will come for the benefit of the sick, remaining free
> of all intentional injustice, of all mischief and in particular of sexual relations with
> both female and male persons, be they free or slaves.
>
> (Edelstein, 1943: 1)

Just as practitioners of medical technology are and should be guided by ethical principles, practitioners of educational technology are and should be guided by ethical

16

principles. An *Educratic Oath* inspired by the Hippocratic Oath was proposed by Spector (2005) for educational technologists:

1. Do nothing to impair learning, performance, and instruction.
2. Do what you can to improve learning, performance, and instruction.
3. Base your actions on evidence that you and others have gathered and analyzed.
4. Share the principles of learning, performance, and instruction that you have learned with others.
5. Respect the individual rights of all those with whom you interact.

The classical version of the Hippocratic Oath was selected rather than the modern version so as to introduce the notion of culture into the discussion. Ethical principles and values are closely connected with culture. Our culture is generally free from slavery, but there are many disadvantaged persons in our society. One of the unfortunate aspects of educational technology is that it can be unwittingly used in a way that creates additional disadvantages for those already being left behind economically and educationally. The first principle of this *Educratic Oath* implies that contributing to the widening of the so-called digital divide would be wrong. *Do not create disadvantages for one population while creating advantages for another population.* This is a difficult ethical principle to uphold, but it is our obligation to do so.

The practice of educational technology does not occur without consideration of all sorts of values, including ethical principles. Some communities place particular value on the esthetics of learning spaces and environments. Others emphasize the openness of the learning community to alternative points of view. Some put economic considerations first while others put learning outcomes first. One cannot say that one group or one values perspective is right or wrong. One should be able to identify the values perspectives of all those involved and do one's best to respect those values—or decide to go elsewhere.

For additional information on ethics in educational technology, visit the Websites of the Association for Educational Communications and Technology (www.aect.org) and the International Board of Standards for Training, Performance and Instruction (www.ibstpi.org).

Skepticism

Within the context of values pertaining to educational technology, it is perhaps worth mentioning the value of a skeptical predisposition with regard to the application of educational technology to improve learning and performance. There is a substantial history of educational technologists promising that the introduction and use of a particular technology will yield dramatic improvements in learning and instruction (Spector & Anderson, 2000). That has not happened, yet the promises of dramatic improvements on account of technology continue to be put forward. One ought to have a skeptical attitude with regard to such promises and predictions. A skeptical attitude is

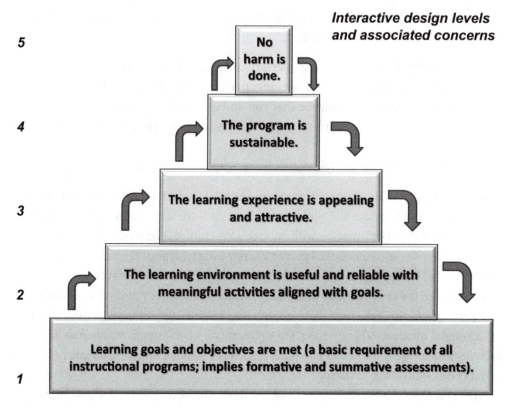

FIGURE 2.1 Design levels and association concerns

essentially a questioning attitude, which is to say that one is engaged in trying to find out and willing to consider alternatives. *Skepticism implies doubt along with a desire to know.* Admitting that one does not know but wants to understand and is willing to investigate various explanations of something is the hallmark of skepticism, and it is also an important value to keep in mind for educational technologists.

Another way to emphasize this point about skepticism is to say that one role of an educator and one use of educational technologies is to encourage students to *have questions* and to support activities resulting from having those questions. To have a question is to (a) admit to not knowing or understanding something, (b) commit time and effort to find out and understand, and (c) be open to explore and consider alternative explanations. That is to say, an educator is someone who gets others to have questions; an educational technology is something that supports finding answers. Of course, both characterizations are too narrow, but they can serve as useful guideposts.

Levels of Design

Figure 2.1 emphasizes the position of values in this educational technology framework and serves as a transition to the discussion of foundations. This figure also introduces the notion of design levels, which will be discussed later.

The emphasis in the current discussion is on the top part of this pyramid—do no harm. Additional components and the notion of levels of design depicted in Figure 2.1 will be introduced in subsequent chapters in this volume.

Test Your Understanding

Identify potential harmful outcomes of each of the following scenarios.

1. Students are introduced to the graphing calculator and taught how to use it to reason about the relationships of variables in an algebraic expression. Calculators are available for all students at the school, and students are encouraged but not required to purchase their own calculators.
2. An update to the ejection procedure in a fighter aircraft has been introduced. Formerly, this aircraft ejected the pilot out the bottom of the aircraft, requiring the pilot to invert the aircraft when ejecting at low altitude. The new version of this aircraft now ejects the pilot out the top, like most other fighter planes. Pilots had received extensive training in the former procedure. The new procedure is announced and each pilot is sent a paper copy of the new procedure with no additional training.
3. A school has decided to give teachers merit pay based on the aggregated average performance of their students on state-mandated, standards-based tests. The school is supporting this effort by making available to all teachers new software that can be used to test students to see how likely they are to perform well on those tests and to identify particular trouble spots in terms of standards-based topics causing many students problems.
4. A massive open online course (MOOC) developed for graduate computer science students in the area of artificial intelligence offered at a top university is made a requirement for all graduate computer science students enrolled in a new artificial intelligence course offered at a small, regional university. Evidence of completing the MOOC is a requirement for attaining a grade of B in the new course. Additional tasks are required to attain an A. All those failing to complete the MOOC will receive a C, which is considered a failing grade for a graduate course at the small, regional university.

Foundations

Recognizing that values permeate and inform what educational technologists (and others) do, it is now appropriate to look at the underlying disciplines upon which educational technology rests. The traditional treatment of foundations is to show pillars upon which something rests, as in Figure 2.2.

Various authors have depicted a variety of foundation pillars for educational technology. The six pillars in Figure 2.2 represent a composite summary of what others have identified (for example, see Richey, Klein, & Tracey, 2011). These particular pillars

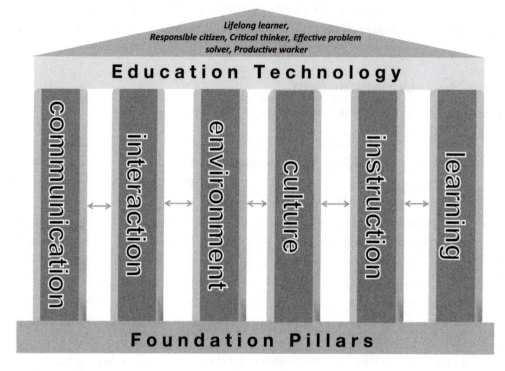

FIGURE 2.2 Foundation pillars of educational technology

were selected because they also represent clusters of things that people do or that strongly influence what people do when in instructional situations. The six foundation clusters (pillars) are: communication, interaction, environment, culture, instruction, and learning. Each of these six pillars will be briefly discussed prior to offering an alternative view of foundations.

Communication

Communication skills are important to everyone in almost every profession. Educational technologists, whether they are developers, designers, instructors, or technology specialists, have a need to communicate clearly and effectively with others, and particularly with persons having different backgrounds and training than their own. The International Board of Standards for Training, Performance and Instruction (ibstpi; see www.ibstpi.org) found that the most critical skills for instructors as well as instructional designers were communication skills (see Klein et al., 2008) rather than skills in using or integrating technology. Communication skills include writing, speaking, and listening skills, in the context of the ibstpi studies.

Communication skills are especially important in the world of educational technology as persons with different backgrounds and interests are involved (learners, managers, sponsors, technical specialists, designers, etc.). In addition, many communications occur in a digital form not involving face-to-face interaction (design specifications, instructional messages, learning content, etc.). Being clear, precise, coherent, and focused are crucial for success. Avoiding unfamiliar terminology, defining key terms, and providing meaningful context and rationale are at a premium in the world of educational technology.

From a foundations perspective, communication theories and principles form key aspects of the effective use of educational technology. For the purpose of this discussion, communication theory is broadly defined to cover theories, models, principles, and formats for representing, transmitting, receiving, and processing information.

An example of a communication theory with implications for education is Paivio's (1991) dual coding theory. Although it is often considered a cognitive processing theory, Paivio argues that the human mind has evolved in such a way that it can simultaneously process and interrelate verbal (e.g., text) and nonverbal (e.g., images) information. For a person designing a representation of something complex and desiring to minimize the cognitive load on the learner, a graphical representation along with text might be effective, according to dual coding theory. This notion is further reinforced by cognitive flexibility theory (Spiro & Jehng, 1990), which is also generally considered a cognitive theory rather than a communication theory. Given the definition of communication suggested above, both can be considered communication theories, and both have strong implications for the effective planning and implementation of materials to support learning and instruction.

Two additional comments round out this brief discussion of communication as a foundation pillar of educational technology. First, all of us are by nature language users and message designers. When we talk with our neighbors about politics or the weather, we are constructing messages for a particular purpose. Sometimes the purpose is to present simple information, in which case we might construct a purely descriptive message. On other occasions, the purpose might be to persuade, in which case we might make use of metaphor and hyperbole. Those who construct and deliver messages to support learning and performance need to think carefully about the purpose and the intended audience in order to design effective instructional messages.

Second, while the ability to share information and exchange ideas with others is a characteristically human trait, a more fundamental but related characteristic is the ability to create internal representations of things we experience. Every human is a constructor of these internal representations, called mental models by cognitive psychologists (Johnson-Laird, 1983). The ability to create these internal representations is the essence of a constructivist epistemology. While most cognitive scientists and educational technologists accept epistemological constructivism as a common point of departure, there is a great deal of misunderstanding surrounding mental models and constructivism. People are naturally and continually constructing these internal representations, which are completely hidden from view. One never sees a mental model—not even one's own. What one can see is a representation of a mental model, and these representations come in many forms (spoken and written text, pictures, crudely drawn images, and so on). These representations can be effective (or not) in showing or eliciting information about what a person knows and understands about a particular situation. Eliciting and evaluating such representations is a critical component of meaningful feedback in many situations.

It should be obvious by now that the communication foundation pillar itself has underlying foundational theories, principles, and knowledge (e.g., cognitive science, epistemology, and media theory). This notion of related theories and principles is true of the other foundation pillars as well.

Interaction

Just as it is natural for people to talk about their experiences and create representations of their mental models, it is natural for people to act—to do things. M. David Merrill has said publicly in many of his presentations that people learn what they do. This is not so surprising. From a behavioral perspective, if an action is recognized as successful, it is thereby reinforced and likely to be repeated in similar circumstances. From a cognitive perspective, a person naturally seeks to be successful and, as a consequence, is likely to monitor actions taken, evaluate consequences, determine success, and then formulate an expectation of repeated success when similar decisions and actions are taken. From a neuronal perspective, neural connections and synaptic associations are reinforced in the brain with repetition.

Those who plan and implement instruction typically seek to support the recognition of success and associated decisions, actions, and factors influencing success. Typically, this occurs through formative feedback mechanisms that help learners develop their own skills in monitoring progress (self-regulation). Timely, informative feedback is a key factor in supporting learning and improving performance. There are many technologies that can be used to support formative feedback.

Instructional support often occurs with computers and other instructional devices. Some feedback naturally occurs through the computer interface itself. Designing supportive educational interfaces is a demanding skill that is informed by research in several areas, including human-computer interaction. Selecting and configuring a technology appropriately is an important educational technology skill. More importantly, designing and sequencing appropriate learning activities is a fundamental task for every teacher and instructional designer. Interactions that are designed to help learners develop confidence and competence and succeed in accomplishing increasingly complex tasks are a critical aspect of effective educational technology applications.

As was the case with the communications pillar, there are multiple supporting pillars for interaction. These include behaviorism, cognitivism, neural psychology, perception research, human-computer interaction, feedback, and formative assessment theories and principles, expertise theory, human development, and more.

Environment

The environment includes the physical, social, and psychological context in which learning and instruction takes place. Some authors call the physical context the *learning place* and the social-psychological context the *learning space*. The environment pillar includes both as well as such concerns as the organizational atmosphere (e.g., hierarchical, trusting, rigid, democratic, etc.), economic factors, technology life-cycles, support personnel, and so on.

With regard to this pillar, the primary theoretical perspective is systems theory. Education typically occurs within the context of a system. An educational system contains many interrelated components, including learners, instructors, learning goals, instructional materials, learning activities, formative and summative assessment tools and technologies, and other such things (see Figure 1.3 in Chapter 1 and Figure 2.4 in this chapter). Educational systems are often quite complex, containing many interrelated components, multiple stakeholders with different priorities and values, dynamic and nonlinear relationships among multiple components, and delayed effects (e.g., the impact of introducing a new technology to support learning often does not become obvious for some time). The effects of a technology intervention are rarely immediate and often quite difficult to detect and report accurately. Moreover, the diffusion of a new educational technology within an organization or school is notoriously slow.

Systems thinking, then, is an important educational technology skill. What is it to be a systems thinker? According to Peter Senge (1990), a systems thinker is someone who (a) has achieved mastery of relevant skills (e.g., designing and developing instruction, facilitating learning environments, integrating technology into teaching, etc.), (b) has well-developed mental models that can be brought to bear to resolve complex problems, (c) is able to listen to and exchange ideas with others to develop a shared understanding of challenging problems, (d) can work well with others who have different backgrounds, and (e) is able to develop a holistic view of the task environment and appreciate the many interrelated factors and their dynamic relationships.

While systems thinking is a critical component of the environment foundation, developing a systemic understanding of an educational system and the diffusion of technology throughout that system is a serious challenge. According to Dörner (1996), we are inclined to take a partial view of a complex problem rather than try to think about the entire system. In addition, we do not reason well with regard to nonlinear relationships and delayed effects; we tend to expect immediate results and are inclined to think that the future state of system components and their relationships will closely resemble the current state in relevant ways. In short, we are creatures who are inherently inclined to simplify. The inclination to simplify is possibly a result of a long evolutionary process and in part a result of the fact that we are constructors of knowledge—we create internal models of external situations. Models by their very nature are simplifications. In summary, while developing the skills of a systems thinker is an important task for an educational technologist, this is an ongoing task—one can become more inclined to think systemically, but the task is never done.

Culture

Culture might well be considered one part of the environmental foundation. However, because learning is becoming increasingly globalized and because cultural differences are important considerations in designing effective learning environments, culture is treated here as a separate foundation pillar. Technology innovations that work well with one group may not work at all with a culturally different group. For example, imagine an online exercise in which students are asked to critique the instructor's argument and present an alternative in a discussion forum posting. In a hierarchical culture that has a long and strong tradition of master teachers who are highly regarded and never publicly challenged, such an exercise may not be very effective, whereas it might prove to be highly effective in a different cultural context.

In the spirit of the theme that technology changes what people can do, here is another example. A teacher in a private Catholic school in Louisiana was teaching advanced placement English and decided to introduce Web-based support for the class. In relation to one of the books that was assigned, the subject of abortion arose. The classroom discussion was quite restrained and consistent with the standard Catholic position in opposition to nearly all abortions. However, the teacher had activated discussion forums in the online support environment; with no active prompting from the instructor, a very lively discussion about all aspects of abortion took place with most of those participating now expressing something other than the canonical position they had expressed in the classroom. Why the online forum was perceived as more open to expressing alternative views is not exactly clear, but this suggests that the classroom culture was quite different from the online culture in this case. It is well beyond the scope of this volume to try to define culture and treat its many nuances and complexities. For an in-depth treatment of cultural considerations in the context of e-learning, see Carr-Chellman (2005).

Instruction

Instruction is that which facilitates learning and performance, broadly and simply stated. Instruction is a goal-oriented enterprise. The instruction foundation encompasses various instructional approaches, models, and strategies, as well as models, principles, and theories pertaining to the design of instruction. Instructional approaches and design models exist at different levels, ranging from the level of a specific interaction to the unit of instruction to a course module or course, and then to a degree. Considerations and emphases are different, depending on the level being addressed (see Figure 2.3).

An example of an instructional approach at the module level is mastery learning in which learners are provided support and time to achieve mastery of the module's content. Typically, learners are not allowed to progress to the next module until mastering the current module. Mastery approaches are often mentioned as desirable but not commonly

Planning Levels	Representative Concerns
Global	Culture, economics, politics
Institutional	Mission alignment
Program	Evaluation, accreditation
Curriculum	Professional requirements
Course	Requirements, goals, evaluation
Module	Coherence, sequencing, context
Unit	Content, context, control, relevance
Lesson	Objectives, context, assessments

FIGURE 2.3 Planning levels and representative concerns

implemented in school and university settings. In some cases, the distinctions between modules, units, and lessons are somewhat different than that represented in Figure 2.3. The main point, however, is that there are different planning considerations for different levels of planning. Consistency across levels is highly desirable and requires a great deal of communication to achieve.

As Reigeluth (1983) points out, instructional design is a prescriptive enterprise rather than a descriptive enterprise as would be the case for learning theory. Whereas learning researchers are generally concerned to identify and describe the factors that are involved in learning, instructional designers and instructional design researchers are generally concerned with identifying the conditions (e.g., environmental factors and technologies) and methods (e.g., instructional approaches and strategies) that will optimize learning outcomes for learners. As a consequence, instructional design research and educational technology practice are inherently more complex and challenging than learning research.

The complexity of instructional design is evident in the Fourth Generation Instructional Systems Design (ISD-4) model developed by Tennyson (1993; see Figure 2.4). Tennyson's ISD-4 model is based on a synthesis of what instructional designers

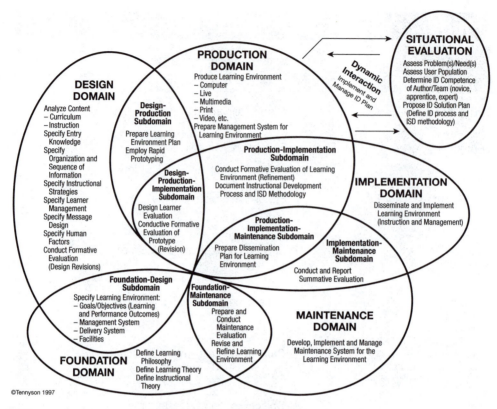

FIGURE 2.4 Tennyson's ISD-4 model (used with permission)

actually do. It suggests many of the foundation areas represented in this chapter. It also emphasizes the notions of a situational evaluation and the fact that instructional designers do not always start with analysis; the specific situation and circumstances determine to a large extent what designers actually do.

Learning

Educational technology is primarily concerned with improving learning and performance. Whereas performance involves observable actions and is not especially problematic, learning involves processes occurring within a person that are not directly observable. As noted in Chapter 1, learning involves stable, persisting changes in an individual's (or group's) abilities, attitudes, beliefs, knowledge, and/or skills. Educational technology is aimed at fostering and facilitating cumulative and productive changes that result in the development of expertise and understanding.

Learning theory in general is aimed at identifying and describing the mechanisms and processes involved in the development of expertise and understanding. The progressive development of robust mental models is one such process, as indicated earlier. The facile storage and retrieval of information is another relevant learning process. Researchers have found that individual differences (prior knowledge and training, representation preferences, gender, age, etc.) can impact learning outcomes (Jonassen & Grabowski, 1993).

As suggested for the other foundation pillars, the learning foundation pillar has links to the others along with strong links to both cognitive and noncognitive aspects of human thought and behavior. For example, the beliefs a person holds with regard to the nature of the subject to be learned or his/her ability to learn that subject have an influence on learning, as do the emotional states of a person during a learning experience (Kim & Keller, 2010). The small arrows between the columns in Figure 2.2 are meant to suggest that there are many relationships between and among the foundation pillars.

Alternative Foundation Metaphors

As mentioned earlier, the selection of these six foundation pillars is somewhat arbitrary, based partially on a clustering of foundation components mentioned by others. The reality is that educational technology rests on multiple bodies of knowledge and is inherently an interdisciplinary enterprise. Each of the foundation pillars briefly characterized above has its own set of supporting disciplines and bodies of knowledge, which are also interrelated and which will be discussed in subsequent chapters of this volume.

This aspect of educational technology foundations leads to an alternative metaphor for a foundation. Rather than separate but obviously interrelated pillars, one might consider *cement*. Cement has long been used in construction for foundations and for binding together various kinds of building blocks. Cement is, in fact, a blend of substances used as a binder in construction. The components of the blend (e.g., lime, gypsum plaster, etc.) are perhaps analogous to our foundation pillars. Values might be considered analogous to water in mixing the blend—values permeate all that educational technologists do. The particular blend and amount of water involved depends on the aggregate (gravel, bricks, etc.), the context (above ground, under water, etc.), the climate, and the structure to be built. This is analogous to taking into account characteristics of the learners, the learning environment, the local learning culture, and so on. Construction engineers often consider the likelihood of unusual circumstances and add components or adjust the blend in order to be able to build a robust structure that will withstand extreme conditions and the many tests of time. This practice reflects a *values-orientation*—that is to say, that what matters most is the integrity of the structure and its ability to be maintained and sustained for long periods of time.

Likewise, a values-orientation in educational technology would be to place particular emphasis on creating learning environments that work well for different learners with a wide variety of individual differences and that are easily modified and sustained for a long period of time. Just as surely as technologies will change, the circumstances in which technologies are used will change. For this reason, a cement metaphor may serve well to remind us that (a) values are significant and part of a strong foundation for success, (b) the educational technologies that are developed and deployed should produce desirable outcomes, and (c) the educational technologies we choose to implement require support and are likely to be used in ways that the developers did not foresee. "May you have a strong foundation when the winds of changes shift" (from Bob Dylan's "Forever Young"—see www.bobdylan.com/#/songs/forever-young).

Yet another foundation metaphor is that of an arch—a structure that is formed by blocks that form a semicircle or a parabola. The top-most block is called the keystone. Arches have been used in construction for thousands of years, in part because they required no cement or mortar, but were quite strong and self-supporting. With regard to the arch metaphor, the keystone might represent learning, with the supporting blocks on either side being the other pillars mentioned here or by others. The arch metaphor is particularly enticing because it introduces the notion of self-support. Educational technologies, when properly implemented, should be more or less self-sustaining, requiring little maintenance and training once deployed throughout an organization.

Test Your Understanding

1. Which of the following might provide evidence that a person has learned to replace a component in an electronic device?
   a. The person is able to state the function of the component.
   b. The person is able to show where the component is located.
   c. The person is able disassemble the device, remove the component, instal a new component, and reassemble the device.
   d. The person is able to test the component to determine if it is functioning properly.
   e. The person can identify incorrect steps in a replacement procedure.

2. Jean Piaget (1929) argued that children naturally pass through four major stages of cognitive development (sensorimotor, pre-operational, concrete operational, and formal operational). Indicate in which foundation pillar(s) you believe Piaget's work (called genetic epistemology) best fits and why:
   a. communications;
   b. interaction;
   c. environment;
   d. culture;
   e. instruction;
   f. learning.

3. Lev Vygotsky (1978) introduced the notion of the zone of proximal development (ZPD), which represents the gap between what a learner can do unassisted and what that learner can do with the support and assistance of peers and/or a teacher, tutor, or instructional system; Vygotsky argued that social interaction and communication (with peers, parents, teachers, and others) were essential for cognitive development and growth. Indicate in which foundation pillar(s) you believe Vygotsky's work best fits and why:

a. communications;

b. interaction;

c. environment;

d. culture;

e. instruction;

f. learning.

A Representative Educational Technology Challenge

An innovative private school has decided to redo its high school mathematics and science curriculum in response to recent emphasis on the integrated nature of science and mathematics, and strong interest in having more graduates pursue college majors in science, mathematics, and engineering disciplines. However, to maintain the school's accreditation, its students must perform acceptably on standardized tests that have been developed to test knowledge on traditional science and mathematics topics, rather than assess skills in putting that knowledge to practical use. There are at least two fundamental issues to address:

1. How should the new curriculum be designed in order to achieve both goals—(a) encouraging more students to pursue further studies in math, science, and engineering, and (b) ensuring that students will generally perform well on the existing standardized tests?

2. What kinds of formative assessments will help students and teachers maintain steady progress toward both goals?

Learning Activities

1. Develop a general framework with guidelines and a notional high-level curriculum to respond to the first issue in the representative educational technology challenge.

2. Develop a formative assessment scheme along with a suggested schedule for assessments, guidelines (rubrics) for use of assessments by students and teachers, and one specific assessment and accompanying rubric (assessment guideline with expectations) to illustrate the scheme.

Links

The Theory into Practice (TIP) online database developed by Greg Kearsley is an excellent way to gain a short introduction the various theories mentioned in this and subsequent chapters—see http://tip.psychology.org

Brent Wilson's (University of Colorado at Denver) Learning and Instructional Technologies—http://carbon.ucdenver.edu/~bwilson/index.html

Other Resources

ICT Mindtools—http://ictmindtools.net

Learning Theories (Capella University)—www.learning-theories.com

The Handbook of Research on Educational Communications and Technology (3rd and 4th eds.)—available at no cost to members of AECT—www.aect.org

The Mitre Corporation site on Engineering Complex Systems—see www.mitre.org/sites/default/files/pdf/norman_engineering.pdf

References

Carr-Chellman, A. A. (2005). *Global perspectives on e-learning: Rhetoric and reality.* Thousand Oaks, CA: Sage.

Dörner, D. (1996). *The logic of failure: Why things go wrong and what we can do to make them right* (Trans. R. Kimber & R. Kimber). New York: Metropolitan Books.

Edelstein, L. (1943). *The Hippocratic Oath: Text, translation, and interpretation.* Baltimore, MD: The Johns Hopkins University Press.

Johnson-Laird, P. N. (1983). *Mental models: Towards a cognitive science of language, inference, and consciousness.* Cambridge: Cambridge University Press.

Jonassen, D. H., & Grabowski, B. L. (1993). *Handbook of research on individual differences, learning, and instruction.* Hillsdale, NJ: Erlbaum.

Kim, C., & Keller, J. M. (2010). Motivation, volition, and belief change strategies to improve mathematics learning. *Journal of Computer Assisted Learning, 26*(5) 407–420.

Klein, J. D., Grabowski, B., Spector, J. M., & de la Teja, I. (2008). Competencies for instructors: A validation study. In M. Orey, V. J. McLendon, & R. M. Branch (Ed.), *Educational media and technology yearbook 2008.* Portsmouth, NH: Greenwood.

Paivio, A. (1991). *Mind and its evolution: A dual coding theoretical approach.* Mahwah, NJ: Erlbaum.

Piaget, J. (1929). *The child's conception of the world.* New York: Harcourt Brace Jovanovich.

Reigeluth, C. M. (Ed.) (1983*). Instructional-design theories and models: An overview of their current status.* Hillsdale, NJ: Erlbaum.

Richey, R. C., Klein, J. D., & Tracey, M. W. (2011). *The instructional design knowledge base: Theory, research and practice.* New York: Routledge.

Senge, P. (1990). *The fifth discipline: The art and practice of the learning organization.* New York: Doubleday.

Spector, J. M. (2005). *Innovations in instructional technology: An introduction to this volume.* In J. M. Spector, C. Ohrazda, A. Van Schaack, & D. A. Wiley (Eds.) (2005), *Innovations in instructional technology: Essays in honor of M. David Merrill* (pp. xxxi–xxxvi). Mahwah, NJ: Erlbaum.

Spector, J. M., & Anderson, T. M. (Eds.) (2000). *Integrated and holistic perspectives on learning, instruction and technology: Understanding complexity.* Dordrecht: Kluwer Academic Press.

Spiro, R. J., & Jehng, J. (1990). Cognitive flexibility and hypertext: Theory and technology for the non-linear and multidimensional traversal of complex subject matter. In D. Nix & R. Spiro (Eds.), *Cognition, education, and multimedia* (pp. 163–205). Hillsdale, NJ: Erlbaum.

Tennyson, R. D. (1993). A framework for automating instructional design. In J. M. Spector, M. C. Polson, & D. J. Muraida (Eds.), *Automating instructional design: Concepts and issues* (pp. 191–214). Englewood Cliffs, NJ: Educational Technology Publications.

Vygotsky, L. (1978). *Mind and society: The development of higher mental processes.* Cambridge, MA: Harvard University Press.

three
Learning and Performing

"We become just by performing just acts"
(from Aristotle's Nichomachean Ethics)

Learning

The learning foundation pillar (see Figure 2.2) deserves emphasis and individual elaboration, because learning represents the bottom line in the use and integration of any educational technology (see Figure 2.1). The purpose of education is to develop understanding and competence, and the goal of instruction is to promote the learning that informs understanding and underlies competence.

As indicated in Chapter 1, learning is defined as a change in one's abilities, attitudes, beliefs, knowledge, and/or skills. In this definition of learning, there are clearly both process and outcomes involved. The outcomes involved the resulting changes that have occurred. In order to establish that changes have occurred and that goals and objectives have been met, there is clearly a need to conduct both pre- and post-tests. In some cases, a learner may do well on the post-test but may not have learned anything if that same learner would have done as equally well on the pre-test. There are many technologies to support testing of this kind. Objective measures for testing factual knowledge have a very strong theoretical and empirical foundation. One example of a well-established educational technology to support objective testing is item response theory (IRT; see van der Linden & Hambleton, 1997), which is a mathematical method to determine the probability of an individual's likelihood of responding correctly to a particular test item.

Learning processes are somewhat more complicated. First, there are both cognitive and noncognitive factors involved in learning. Motivation—the interest and willingness of a learner to commit time and effort to achieving desired outcomes—involves cognitive aspects (e.g., an awareness of a learning goal and the ability to determine how well one is doing to achieve that goal) and noncognitive aspects (e.g., emotions concerned with the topic, the learning task, and one's ability to succeed) (see Keller, 2010; Kim & Keller, 2010). Formative assessment and learner feedback are critical factors in promoting effective learning processes.

There are technologies that can support formative assessment, just as there are technologies to support summative assessment. Moreover, when the learning tasks are more open-ended and somewhat ill-structured, as in solving complex problems, there are technologies that can provide formative assessments and feedback to learners. For example, one can ask a learner to create a representation of the problem space associated with a particular problem scenario and then compare that response with an expert response or reference model (see Pirnay-Dummer, Ifenthaler, & Spector, 2010). It should be obvious that assessment, especially formative assessment, is critical in determining learner progress. Moreover, assessments of learning outcomes represent a central aspect of course and program evaluation. Note that the term 'assessment' is used to refer to persons, as in 'assessing students', while the term 'evaluation' is used to refer to programs and projects, as in 'evaluating courses.'

Critical Distinctions Pertaining to Learning

There are several critical distinctions pertaining to learning, including the difference between intentional and incidental learning situations. A story may serve best to illustrate and animate these distinctions.

This story is taken from Leo Tolstoy's *Confession*, which is based on his journal and personal reflections. *Confession* was written in 1879 when Tolstoy was 51—after he was already well known and highly respected for *War and Peace* and *Anna Karenina*; it was first published in Russian in 1882. Tolstoy already had fame and fortune, and was enjoying the benefits of his success when he happened to visit Paris, France, around the year 1865, when these events occurred. At the time, Paris was regarded by Tolstoy and others as the intellectual center of the universe and a showcase for progress in a civilized society. Tolstoy was regarded as one of the leading lights of modern civilization.

He had gone to Paris to meet friends and have a good time. While cavorting in Paris, he chanced upon a public execution. At the time, France applied the death penalty for serious crimes and the form of execution was the guillotine. Executions were public, perhaps based on a belief that the horror of such executions would deter crime.

In any case, Tolstoy records in his journal something like the following (loosely translated): "When I saw the heads divided from the bodies and heard the sound with which they fell separately into the box, I knew with my whole being that this was a bad thing."

This unplanned and unexpected event marked a turning point in Tolstoy's life. It is marked by the following words recorded in his journal (again the same rough translation): "When I saw the heads divided from the bodies and heard the sound with which they fell separately into the box, I knew with my whole being that this was a bad thing." (The repetition is intentional.) He goes on to reflect about his prior beliefs with regard to civilized society, with regard to Paris as the cradle of civilization, with regard to progress proceeding from Paris throughout the rest of the world, and so on. He writes that his belief in progress included a faith that society was moving in a positive direction and that Paris was leading this movement.

Then he recalls the event: "When I saw the heads divided from the bodies and heard the sound with which they fell separately into the box, I knew with my whole being that this was a bad thing." (The repetition is intentional.) He knew with his whole being— he was fully engaged in this moment. He saw, he heard, he thought. As a result, he could no longer hold on to his prior belief in progress and faith that Paris was the cradle of civilization. He could no longer regard himself as one of the leaders of civilized society if this was what civilized society represented.

His faith in progress was shattered. He changed his life entirely based on this event. He gave away his fortune. He declared all of his writings public property. He began writing short moral tales for the common people rather than writing for the educated elite. He began advocating for the reform of peasant schools. He changed his life on account of having witnessed by chance a public execution in Paris.

He learned something that day in Paris. That he learned something is marked by the fact that changes occurred that persisted through other events and for the remainder of his life. These changes included how he thought as well as what he did; the changes are observable in his subsequent writings and in how he lived his life after witnessing the execution. What he learned was not planned. He was not explicitly directed toward a goal nor guided by a plan to achieve a goal. What he learned might be characterized as incidental to his having witnessed the execution.

By contrast, the kinds of education primarily discussed in this volume involve intentional learning where a particular goal is involved. It is worth noting that the goals of a learner might not always coincide with the goals of an instructor. In formal learning environments, which generally involve intentional learning in school settings, it is optimal when the learner's goals and those of the instructor are closely aligned.

What did Tolstoy learn? (Do you recall the sentence from his journal that was repeated three times? Why do you suppose I repeated it three times?) Perhaps this is difficult to say without knowing more. He learned that not all social practices in Paris were good. He learned that he could not accept a society that publicly executed criminals as a civilized society—this reflects a values perspective, which is essential in education and in the application of technology to support education, according to the framework presented in this volume. He probably learned a lot more, and that learning event might well be regarded as a process that only began that day in Paris in 1865; perhaps it began earlier.

This story provides a concrete way to think about learning—learning is marked by stable and persisting changes in attitudes, behaviors, beliefs, knowledge, mental models, skills, and so on. Learning may be planned or unintentional. Learning in which an individual is fully engaged is especially effective. Full engagement often involves perception, cognition, and emotions. Technology can be especially useful in promoting active engagement.

What about memory? Memory is clearly a relevant and essential aspect of learning. We recall facts. We retrieve visual images from memory. Cognitive psychologists often distinguish word-based memory from image-based memory (see Anderson, 1983). Cognitive scientists also distinguish working memory from long-term memory and have documented the limitations of working memory—seven plus or minus two (Miller, 1956). How to leverage the limitations of working memory? One method is to tell stories. Stories may represent a form of chunking that allows more to be recalled in a single chunk. Moreover, it may be the case that stories are encoded in long-term memory in a form different from other word-based items. The term for this kind of memory is *episodic memory* (Tulving, 1983), and it may involve both words and images together.

If one accepts these distinctions, it is possible to imagine using the story for multiple purposes—for developing a definition of learning, for explaining the difference between incidental and intentional learning, for elaborating the notion of engagement in learning, for explaining different kinds of memory, and so on. There might also be multiple audiences—students in a psychology course, instructional design students, high school students learning about Tolstoy, and so on. One might include multimedia items in a presentation of the story—pictures of Tolstoy, an audio file telling parts of the story, a movie of a guillotining if one is inclined to depict such horror, and so on.

Here are a few basic points of emphasis about learning:

1. Learning fundamentally involves change.
2. Relevant changes can be directly or indirectly observed as evidence that learning has occurred.
3. Learning is a holistic concept that involves both cognitive (e.g., memory, mental constructs, language, associations) and noncognitive (e.g., emotional states, attitudes, and physical conditions and constraints) aspects.
4. We have extensive knowledge about human physical development, but more limited knowledge with regard to other aspects of human development (e.g., cognitive, emotional, and social development).
5. Much learning is unplanned and incidentally associated with a variety of activities; much of the learning that occurs in educational programs is planned and intentional with specific goals and objectives.
6. Planned learning activities typically occur in complex environments (e.g., class-rooms, online settings, workplace locations) with many things that can enhance or inhibit learning.
7. Determining the extent to which learning has occurred involves the analysis of measures or indicators of change (before, during, after, and long after the learning activities); determining why learning occurred to the extent measured or observed is even more challenging.

Test Your Understanding

Which of the following situations involve learning and why/how?

1. Memorizing dates associated with certain historic battles.
2. Watching a video of a person disassembling a particular device.
3. Using an ohmmeter to test the level of resistance at a certain point in an electrical circuit.
4. Figuring out how to cut several pieces of wood in order to fit together in a prescribed pattern.
5. Practicing a particular piece of music on the piano.
6. Telling a student that a particular sentence is incomplete.
7. Asking a student why a particular calculation was done in the course of solving a problem.
8. Asking the reader why something was repeated three times.

Indicate which of the following involve intentional learning and which involve incidental learning and indicate why/how.

1. Accidentally touching a hot stove.
2. Practicing solving various quadratic equations.
3. Confusing someone's name with the name of someone else.
4. Asking a teacher to explain the rationale for something one does not understand.
5. Exploring a virtual reality world.
6. Developing an electronic portfolio to illustrate one's work.
7. Playing a flight simulator game.

Performance

A performance of some kind represents an outcomes aspect of learning. A performance might also be involved in various learning activities and practice exercises. Performance in general refers to a learner's observable activity in response to a problem-solving situation, a test item, a challenge activity, and so on. Performances are observable and measurable. Ideally, performances are linked directly or indirectly to desired learning outcomes. As mentioned in the previous section, assessment is a core aspect of learning. Unless one has pre- and post-assessment data, one cannot say with confidence that learning has occurred. (Pop quiz: Can you explain why that is the case?)

Measuring or assessing performance has an additional aspect—namely, performance measures can help learners and teachers develop a sense of learning progress and problematic areas. Moreover, letting learners know what the expectations are with regard to satisfactory performance is likely to help learners identify and accept learning goals and objectives, which is especially critical in formal learning situations. A principle to consider in this regard is the following: What you measure is what you get (WYMIWYG, pronounced *whim-ee-whig*). As already mentioned, an instructor does not know what learning has occurred without having some measures or indicators of changes in performance or ability. These measures could be test scores, problem-solving results, responses to specific survey questions, and so on. In addition, students are likely to perform to the expected level, but not much beyond in many cases. The reason for this is quite simple—students are rational and busy with other lessons and activities. Many students will simply do what is expected and move on to another task, activity, or course.

Two conclusions follow once one accepts WYMIWYG. First, it is important to let students know the specific expectations of a unit of instruction or course or program. This is best accomplished using targeted learning outcomes and representative test items or problems that include the level of expected performance (e.g., correctly solve quadratic equations, correctly identify an unknown substance), the conditions in which the performance will be elicited (e.g., in a closed-book exam, in a laboratory with no assistance, etc.), and how that level will be assessed (the criteria). Second, measurements, which can be quantitative or qualitative, can and should be used to help students identify problematic areas deserving more attention. The most useful performance measures are those which directly contribute to improved performance. Withholding the outcomes of the measurement from students is not likely to help them improve their performance or their understanding. Timely and informative feedback is a vital aspect of learning progress.

There are many technologies that can help with regard to measuring and assessing performance, and these technologies are continually becoming more sophisticated and powerful. A key issue to keep in mind is to link the performance to be assessed to the intended learning outcome. If one wants to improve a student's ability to solve complex problems, simply measuring factual knowledge is not likely to be especially supportive of that goal. Providing many problem-solving opportunities along with timely and informative feedback is much more likely to build competence and confidence.

Developing Expertise

Dreyfus and Dreyfus (1986) identify five levels along the way to highly skilled, expert performance depicted in Figure 3.1.

While others may offer different levels of expertise, this account has the advantage of helping to focus the level targeted by a program of instruction. In general, as one progresses through an instructional program or curriculum, it is reasonable to say that one is or ought to be moving through these various stages of expertise. One can apply these levels of expertise to specific skills and sets of knowledge at almost any educational level. For example, with regard to mathematical skills, students in elementary school might be typically at the novice level. As students move to middle and high school, with regard to specific mathematical skills, they are likely to progress to higher levels. At the college level, there are typically survey courses to introduce beginning level students to a particular discipline level. These are followed by more specific courses elaborating the

Expertise Level	Characteristics
Novice	Just beginning a program of study without knowledge of basic terms and rules
Advanced Beginner	Able to follow basic procedures and guidelines with some situational awareness
Competent Performer	Able to act independently with minimal guidance and little supervision
Proficient Performer	Able to consistently perform with skill and accuracy in a variety of situations; see problems holistically
Intuitive Expert	Able to immediately grasp a problem-solving situation and produce an appropriate solution response with ease

FIGURE 3.1 Levels of expertise (Dreyfus & Dreyfus, 1986)

topics covered in the survey course, hopefully helping to move students to the stage of advanced beginners or possibly competent performers in such areas as chemistry, environmental planning, history, and so on. In graduate school, students are typically expected to develop competence and perhaps proficiency in an area, and some programs of study have certification exams that are used to demonstrate that competence has been achieved.

Proficient performance is not so easily acquired or developed through formal schooling. A great deal of practical experience is required to develop proficiency of the kind described by Dreyfus and Dreyfus (1986). Ericsson, Krampe, and Tesch-Römer (1993) have studied the development of superior performance in many different domains and consistently found that about ten years of deliberate and focused practice is required to develop high levels of performance of the sort that might be called highly proficient performance or possibly intuitive expertise.

One difference between Dreyfus and Dreyfus (1986) and Ericsson et al. (1993) is that the former believe it is somewhat unknown how intuitive expertise develops whereas the latter believe that with sufficient deliberate practice anyone can become an intuitive expert. While it is enticing to believe that anyone could become a highly superior performer, the reality is that appropriate educational goals are more likely to target the levels of advanced beginner, competent performer, and proficient performer.

Here are a few basic points of emphasis about performance:

1. Performance is something that can be observed and assessed, measured, or rated against a standard or other point of reference.
2. Change in performance, especially improvement in performance, is of particular interest to educators and trainers.
3. Providing feedback on performance very soon after the actual performance is often effective in improving performance, especially if the feedback is specific and constructive.
4. Developing an individual's ability to monitor and assess his or her own performance is often a desirable and measurable goal for advanced learners.
5. Performance is a holistic concept that typically involves cognitive as well as noncognitive activities; performance may vary with an individual's mood or with other events happening that impact that individual at a particular time.
6. Our understanding of human performance is reasonably well developed but far from complete; many variations in performance across different individuals and tasks are not predictable based on current evidence, knowledge, and theory.
7. Performance and learning are closely coupled concepts; performing tasks and activities can result in learning, and as learning develops in a particular domain, performance on tasks in that domain is likely to improve.

Test Your Understanding

Which of the following might be appropriate performance measurements aligned with the learning goal of understanding the causes of World War II and why?

1. Identifying the countries associated with the allied and axis powers.
2. Naming the heads of states of the major countries involved.
3. Summarizing the contents of Hitler's *Mein Kampf*.
4. Describing the economic conditions in Europe, North America, and Asia in the 1930s and 1940s.
5. Naming the generals who led the major armies involved.
6. Analyzing the conditions in Europe following the end of World War I.
7. Describing the League of Nations and its activities in the 1930s.

A Representative Educational Technology Challenge

A populous developing country in Asia with rich natural resources and a culture that values education has passed a law requiring all primary and secondary teachers to have four-year college degrees with teacher certification through a demanding national examination within the next ten years. At present, approximately 10 percent of the 2 million teachers involved have four-year degrees and another 15 percent have two-year degrees. There are 35 universities spread throughout the country, of which seven offer teaching degrees, plus a large open and distance learning university that also offers teaching degrees. The communications infrastructure is such that the Internet is available in larger cities but it is relatively expensive for the average citizen. Rural areas have little or no access to the Internet. Mobile phones are in widespread use throughout the country and are not prohibitively expensive. The open and distance learning university has 35 regional centers, all of which have computer laboratories with reliable and free Internet access for students. The challenge is for the country to live up to its commitment to increase the training of its teachers and quality of instruction in the given time frame without compromising the quality of education and training. (Note that this problem can be scaled and modified to fit many local circumstances.)

Learning Activities

1. Identify and describe the key barriers to success involved in achieving the goal stated in the representative problem above.
2. Identify and describe the key factors that are likely to become part of an implementation plan for this problem situation.
3. Indicate and describe the relationships among the key factors that have been identified.
4. Indicate what things are likely to change in the period involved in implementing the plan.
5. Create an annotated concept map that reflects the things indicated in response to the previous four tasks.
6. Reflect on your responses and your concept map, and then describe the assumptions you have made and what resources would be required to implement the solution you have in mind.

Links

A website focused on John Anderson's ACT-R Theory and the architecture of cognition— http://act.psy.cmu.edu/

Other Resources

The entire translation of Tolstoy's *Confession* is available online at http://flag.blackened.net/daver/ anarchism/tolstoy/confession.html

The Learning Development Institute is dedicated to human learning and has developed extensive resources freely available to the public. Of particular relevance to this chapter is *The Book of Problems*—see the list of resources for 2002 at www.learndev.org

References

Anderson, J. R. (1983). *The architecture of cognition.* Cambridge, MA: Harvard University Press.

Dreyfus, H., & Dreyfus, S. (1986). *Mind over machine: The power of human intuition and expertise in the era of the computer.* New York: Free Press.

Ericsson, K. A., Krampe, R. Th., & Tesch-Römer, C. (1993). The role of deliberate practice in the acquisition of expert performance. *Psychological Review, 100*(3), 363–406.

Keller, J. M. (2010). *Motivational design for learning and performance: The ARCS model approach.* New York: Springer.

Kim, C., & Keller, J. M. (2010). Motivation, volition, and belief change strategies to improve mathematics learning. *Journal of Computer Assisted Learning, 26,* 407–420.

Miller, G. A. (1956). The magical number seven, plus or minus two: Some limits on our capacity for processing information. *Psychological Review, 63*(2), 81–97.

Pirnay-Dummer, P., Ifenthaler, D., & Spector, J. M. (2010). Highly integrated model assessment technology and tools. *Educational Technology Research & Development, 58*(1), 3–18.

Tolstoy, L. (1882). *Confession* (Trans. D. Patterson, 1983). New York: Norton.

Tulving, E. (1983). *Elements of episodic memory.* Oxford: Clarendon Press.

van der Linden, W., & Hambleton, R. K. (Eds.) (1997). *Handbook of modern item response theory.* New York: Springer.

four
Teaching and Training

"The teacher is the voice that encourages, the ear that listens, the eye that reflects, the hand that guides, the face that does not turn away" (adapted from a sermon by Rabbi Joseph Spector)

Instruction

In the previous chapter, the related topics of learning and performance were discussed. Previously, it was noted that instruction is that which supports learning and performance. In addition, the notion of separating training from education was mentioned, although they are perhaps more appropriately considered together (Gagné & Merrill, 1990). In this chapter, training and education (also referred to as teaching in what follows) will be discussed separately, but it is wise to consider them as merely different sides of the same coin. The coin itself might be called *learning* while the heads side of the coin might be called *education* with the other side being called *training*. In what follows, some distinctions will be made that will help designers and instructors determine appropriate instructional approaches, methods, and technologies.

Typically, teaching is associated with school-based learning and formal curricula (e.g., K-12 and higher education), whereas training is often associated with focused learning for adults pursuing professional recognition or certification (e.g., refrigeration specialty training, network engineer programs, professional athletics, etc.). It is tempting to associate training with developing skills in performing recurrent tasks and to associate teaching with developing more general knowledge and complex cognitive skills.

However, common usage of 'teaching' and 'training' suggests a much less clear distinction. For example, it is not uncommon to hear parents talk about 'potty training' for infants learning to use the toilet. Moreover, many academics refer to their graduate programs as professional training even though these programs are situated in a higher education context. Additionally, university programs to prepare teachers for the classroom are often called teacher training programs. Also, much early childhood education involves mastering recurrent tasks (e.g., adding numbers, spelling words, etc.).

When one considers what teachers and trainers do, there is also a significant amount of overlap. Coaches and exercise specialists are often called trainers. Quite often these trainers pay close attention to individual learners, and adjust methods and approaches to suit the individual needs of those involved. However, many teachers also pay close attention to individual differences and adjust methods to meet individual needs, as in differentiated or personalized instruction. Trainers often have clear performance targets for trainees and frequently test to see determined progress toward those targets. However, as noted in the previous chapter, this is also true with regard to teachers, which is why the notion of formative assessment was so strongly emphasized.

Finally, when one considers the technologies that can be used to support teaching and training, many of the same technologies are mentioned. For example, simulation-based environments are often used in what many would call training situations (e.g., flight training, medical training, etc.); these kinds of environments are also found in academic settings associated with teaching (e.g., economic modeling, environmental planning, etc.). The use of the Internet and mobile technologies (e.g., social networking, e-portfolios, information repositories, pictures, recordings, text messages) can be found in both training and teaching situations.

In what follows, brief comments are made about teaching and training separately, although it is the analysis of learning goals, learners, the learning situation, and other such factors that are critical in determining appropriate approaches, methods, and technologies.

Teaching

Figure 4.1 depicts the knowledge and skills expected of instructors, according to the International Board of Standards for Training, Performance and Instruction (Klein et al., 2004).

One can find similar sets of knowledge and skills in a variety of places (publications, professional association websites, etc.). The ibstpi instructor competencies are reasonably representative of others and appropriate for the context of teaching effectiveness (these competencies also apply to trainers). According to ibstpi, a competency is a set of closely related knowledge, skills, and attitudes required to successfully perform a specific task or job function (Klein et al., 2004). It should be noted that the items in the left column represent competency clusters—closely related sets of competencies. These clusters were established empirically rather than notionally, which is to say that an analysis of responses to the criticality and frequency of instructor competencies revealed these clusters. The items in the right column represent individual competencies. In each case, there are

The 2003 IBSTPI Instructor Competencies

Professional Foundations	Communicate effectively.
	Update and improve one's professional knowledge and skills.
	Comply with established ethical and legal standards.
	Establish and maintain professional credibility.
Planning and Preparation	Plan instructional methods and materials.
	Prepare for instruction.
Instructional Methods and Strategies	Stimulate and sustain learner motivation and engagement.
	Demonstrate effective presentation skills.
	Demonstrate effective facilitation skills.
	Demonstrate effective questioning skills.
	Provide clarification and feedback.
	Promote retention of knowledge and skills.
	Promote transfer of knowledge and skills.
Assessment and Evaluation	Assess learning and performance.
	Evaluate instructional effectiveness.
Management	Manage an environment that fosters learning and performance.
	Manage the instructional process through the appropriate use of technology.

FIGURE 4.1 Instructor competencies (see www.ibstpi.org)

supporting performance statements which can be used to determine if a person has attained that competency. In addition, ibstpi (Klein et al., 2004) suggests a third level of elaboration beneath the performance statements that would be appropriate for the context (e.g., online vs. classroom instruction). One can additionally imagine a level of elaboration pertaining to the teaching-training context (e.g., K-12, higher education, professional training, etc.), although ibstpi has not attempted such an elaboration.

It is obvious that the instructional methods and strategies cluster occupies the largest portion of this set of instructor competencies, and this is not at all surprising. If one imagines where a teacher spends most of his or her time, it is likely to be in activities pertaining to this cluster.

These instructor competencies are neutral with regard to whether the individual is considered a teacher or a trainer, and this is intentional. It is the specific activities associated with these competencies that distinguish teachers from trainers. The specific methods and strategies that one develops are likely to be different for contexts normally associated with teaching from those normally associated with training. For example, many training activities integrate hands-on activities and performance tasks from the very beginning of an instructional sequence, whereas many teaching activities first develop and demonstrate basic concept learning prior to engaging students in performance tasks. This is a very rough over-generalization as many problem-based learning environments are structured much like training environments and some training environments are quite similar to many traditional educational approaches that begin with concept learning.

With regard to teaching children, there are certainly developmental considerations that should be taken into account (Piaget, 1929; Vygotsky, 1978). Here is a personal example that exemplifies differences in children's understanding dependent on their developmental stage. While traveling through the Blue Ridge Mountains in Virginia with two of my children who were 6 and 10 at the time, we chanced upon some unusually large icicles. It was late spring, but we were at some altitude and there had been a recent freeze and snowfall. We were on our way back to Texas where the weather was much warmer. My kids were fascinated by these large icicles. The youngest said that we should take one back to Texas. The older one said that it would probably melt before we got back (a two-day drive). The younger one prevailed, arguing that such a large chunk of ice (it was about a meter in length) could not possibly melt that fast, and besides it was cold. I decided to take the opportunity to create a subsequent teachable moment and broke off the icicle and put it in the trunk of the car. It was 3 or 4 centimeters in length when we arrived home in San Antonio. My younger one simply did not have the experience or abstract reasoning ability to think through things such as the temperature at which water freezes or melts, the likely temperature in Texas, and the length of time it would take to get there. My older one understood those things immediately.

A good teacher (also a good trainer) can recognize relevant differences in learners and make appropriate adjustments. We did check the icicle several times on the drive back, since my youngest really wanted to show it to her friends. She saw that it was getting smaller and smaller, but held out hope for some being left when we arrived home. We did take a picture at the beginning of the long drive back, so she could at least show that to her friends. In this instance, I figured that my son made a much better teacher than I did, and I had confidence that my daughter's experience of the slowly evolving evidence would be highly instructive.

Training

The competencies required of a trainer are very similar to those required of a teacher, as suggested by ibstpi. However, as mentioned earlier, the contexts may differ. It is not uncommon to discover that effective trainers in a corporate environment had prior experience as classroom teachers. Likewise, those with corporate training experience often seek advanced degrees in areas related to educational technology and end up in university faculty positions.

There are two particular aspects to which trainers and training designers need to pay particular attention when planning educational technology solutions for training contexts—namely, characteristics particular to adult learners in a particular learning situation and the type of tasks to be trained. Each of these two concerns are discussed next.

Andragogy

According to Knowles (1984), adult learners are typically self-directed and like to take responsibility for their own learning. This means that adults in advanced educational contexts and training situations are inclined to be oriented to the learning task and want to know at the outset why and how the task is relevant to their concerns. This is increasingly the case with adolescents and young adults in many contexts as well. However, while adults may want to know the relevance to specific job tasks and performance requirements, adolescents typically lack that context and have general beliefs that much of what is presented in a school context is not relevant to careers they want to pursue.

Adults often bring to a learning situation a wide variety of backgrounds and experiences with the expectation that some of it will be acknowledged and useful when learning something new. Adults are especially interested in planning their own learning trajectories and negotiating particular learning goals insofar as that is possible. As a result, adults are likely to appreciate realistic problem-solving situations that are perceived to be relevant to their lives. Such characterizations are less likely to be true of adolescents. All such generalizations are subject to many exceptions and limitations, however.

The developmental stages that apply to children do not apply to adults, although the five stages of expertise development mentioned in Chapter 3 are generally relevant to adults. One might say that adults are just big kids with wrinkles—the wrinkles being a strong sense of self, a desire to control their own learning, and an inclination not to waste time and effort on tasks perceived as irrelevant or nonproductive. While those three characteristics (strong sense of self, desire to control learning, inclination not to waste time) might also be true of adolescents, the reasons are likely to be quite different. For example, an adult might want to focus on learning tasks that are likely to improve performance, productivity, and chances for promotion, whereas an adolescent might want to focus on learning tasks that leave lots of time to pursue other activities.

However, the other side of this overgeneralization could be that adult learners are often quite similar to adolescent learners. One often hears adult learners as well as adolescents say things like "just tell me what I need to know to do this right" or "don't waste my time with your life's stories—get to the point." Additionally, it is easy to assume that adult learners are self-motivated and that Gagné's (1985) first few events of instruction (gain attention, inform learners of the goal, recall prior knowledge) might not be needed for adults in a training situation. However, overlooking those events in an adult training situation could easily result in suboptimal learning outcomes, just as it would be likely to result in suboptimal learning if overlooked in a teaching situation with adolescents.

Complex Cognitive Skills

A second aspect that is typically prominent in adult training situations concerns the tasks being trained. These are often procedural in nature and may require decision-making and problem-solving skills, which are often the target of a training regimen.

Van Merriënboer (1997), with the encouragement and guidance of his former professor at the University of Twente, Sanne Dijkstra, developed a four-component model (4C/ID) for the design of instruction for such tasks. A major distinction in the 4C/ID model is the difference between recurrent and nonrecurrent tasks that might be the target of training. Recurrent tasks are those that are performed frequently with very little variation in how they are performed given variations in the surrounding circumstances. An example of a recurrent task would be replacing a memory chip in a computer or solving a quadratic equation. Such tasks can be trained to the level of automaticity such that a learner could learn to perform the task without much thought or effort.

Nonrecurrent tasks are performed differently depending on variations in the task situation. An example of a nonrecurrent task would be directing a plane in a flight pattern to land at an airport. The air-traffic controller needs to take into account particular characteristics of the plane to be directed, other planes in the landing pattern, planes taking off, and the situation on the ground at the airport. Such a task is representative of a class of learning tasks requiring complex cognitive skills. Complex cognitive skills also occur in educational contexts, including engineering design, environmental planning, ethics, instructional design and development, historical analysis, medical diagnosis, organizational management, technology integration, and many more.

Training designers and instructors involved in supporting the development of complex problem-solving skills need to recognize the kind of task to be learned and use appropriate methods, strategies, and technologies. For nonrecurrent tasks, it might be useful to include a heuristic to guide decision-making and problem solving, and to use a simulator so as to provide learners with the wide variety of variations with which they need to develop competence. Other possibilities clearly exist.

Test Your Understanding

Which of the following are nonrecurrent tasks and why?

1. Parallel parking.
2. Preparing a sauce for pasta.
3. Troubleshooting a computer malfunction.
4. Designing classroom instruction for school children.
5. Determining the average score on a set of tests.
6. Finding misspelled words in a text.
7. Looking up an entry in an online encyclopedia.
8. Planning a vacation.

Rank order the following ten skills in terms of their criticality to effective teaching and then to effective training; discuss your rankings with your peers and the instructor.

- Updating one's professional knowledge and skills.
- Establishing one's credibility.

- Communicating effectively.
- Finding appropriate instructional materials.
- Planning appropriate instructional methods.
- Selecting appropriate instructional technologies.
- Presenting information effectively.
- Providing appropriate feedback.
- Assessing learning and performance.
- Managing the learning situation effectively.

A Representative Educational Technology Challenge

A large educational organization that previously only offered classroom training for adult learners—specifically, in-service classroom teachers—has decided to move its entire curriculum online, primarily in an effort to reduce travel costs and lost teaching time for school districts. Many of the targeted teachers have never taken an online course. School administrators want to have reliable and convincing evidence that teachers are learning relevant skills that will improve their teaching performance.

Learning Activities

1. Identify and describe the key barriers to success involved in achieving the goal stated in the representative problem above.
2. Identify and describe the key factors that are likely to become part of an implementation plan for this problem situation; include in the description of each key factor any recurrent and nonrecurrent tasks likely to be involved.
3. Indicate and describe the relationships among the key factors that have been identified.
4. Indicate what things are likely to change in the period involved in implementing the plan.
5. Create an annotated concept map that reflects the things indicated in response to the previous four tasks.
6. Reflect on your responses and your concept map, and then describe the assumptions you have made and what resources would be required to implement the solution you have in mind.

Links

The Association for Educational Communications and Technology (AECT) website has extensive resources for instructors and the use of technology to support instruction—www.aect.org

The American Society for Training and Development (ASTD) website has extensive resources for professional trainers—www.astd.org

The International Society for Performance Improvement (ISPI) website has extensive resources pertaining to training and performance improvement—www.ispi.org

Other Resources

The Association for Psychological Science website with many resources pertaining to various disciplines within psychology, including educational psychology—http://psych.hanover.edu/APS/teaching.html

childstudy.net website with extensive treatment of classic theories of child development—http://childstudy.net/tutorial.php

K. H. Grobman's website for resources and links pertaining to developmental psychology—www.devpsy.org/sitemap.html

References

Gagné, R. M. (1985). The conditions of learning (4th ed.). New York: Holt, Rinehart & Winston.

Gagné, R. M., & Merrill, M. D. (1990). Integrative goals for instructional design. *Educational Technology Research and Development, 38*(1), 23–30.

Klein, J. D., Spector, J. M., Grabowski, B., & de la Teja, I. (2004). *Instructor competencies: Standards for face-to-face, online and blended settings.* Greenwich, CT: Information Age Publishing.

Knowles, M. (1984). *Andragogy in action.* San Francisco, CA: Jossey-Bass.

Piaget, J. (1929). *The child's conception of the world.* New York: Harcourt Brace Jovanovich.

van Merriënboer, J. J. G. (1997). *Training complex cognitive skills: A four-component instructional design model for technical training.* Englewood Cliffs, NJ: Educational Technology Publications.

Vygotsky, L. (1978). *Mind and society: The development of higher mental processes.* Cambridge, MA: Harvard University Press.

five

Technology Support for Learning, Instruction, and Performance

"Technologies should not support learning by attempting to instruct the learners, but rather should be used as knowledge construction tools that students learn with, not from" (from David Jonassen and colleagues in TechTrends *in 1998)*

Supporting Learning and Instruction

There are many different opinions with regard to how technology can and should be used to support learning, instruction, and performance. First, it is obvious that there are many different kinds of technologies that might be used to support various educational goals and activities. Second, there are many different aspects of learning, instruction, and performance that might be supported with the various tools and technologies now available. It would be foolish to decide at the outset that there is only one kind of relevant technology and only one way that it should be used in support of any particular educational goal with a group of learners. In fact, deciding which technologies are relevant and how they are best deployed is a complex and challenging task. This chapter is an attempt to explore the landscape of that general task.

A starting point for this exploration is to consider the many different kinds of educational activities and tasks that might be supported, and then the available technologies that might be pertinent to those activities and tasks. In previous chapters, the activities in which teachers and learners are engaged were discussed somewhat informally. A definition of instruction as that which supports learning and performance was provided. Who supports learning and performance, and what activities are commonly involved in such support?

Who Supports Learning and Performance?

It is obvious that teachers and trainers support learning and performance directly. However, others are involved as well—namely, instructional designers, training managers, media and technology specialists, evaluators, and many more. Any and all of those involved in supporting learning and performance may make use of technologies to make their support more effective, to make their efforts more productive, and perhaps to make better use of their time and expertise. Table 5.1 is not comprehensive. Students are omitted as the focus is on support. Individuals may be in more than one role.

It may seem that some of the roles in Table 5.1 are only marginally relevant to learning, instruction, and performance. In some cases, this may well be the case. Nonetheless, it is worth noting that there are typically many individuals involved in supporting learning, instruction, and performance in schools, business settings, military training settings, and so on. If any of these persons fail to perform tasks effectively or adequately, it is likely that there will be a negative impact on learning and performance (e.g., diminished improvement). If the facility is unavailable, for example, a class session might be missed with an impact on subsequent sessions. Moreover, each of these roles and representative activities has associated technologies which can assist those involved. Most treatments of educational technology focus only on the first category and the associated

TABLE 5.1 Supporters of learning and performance and associated activities

Individual role	Representative activities
Teacher, trainer, coach	Implement lessons and activities, present information and feedback, administer quizzes and exams, report outcomes (i.e., tells, asks, shows, and helps do)
Instructional designer	Determine needs, design lessons and activities, identify relevant materials and technologies, create storyboards
Training manager	Select and support instructional designers and training developers
Media specialist	Advise on media tools and formats, and develop particular media items for instructional purposes
Technology specialist	Advise on relevant technologies, assist in using particular technologies, provide training, and implement the technology in the context of use
Instructional developer	Develop specific instructional materials, lessons, and courses
Assessment specialist	Advise on relevant assessments and assist in implementing and analyzing assessments
Evaluator	Develop and implement formative and summative evaluation plans for courses, curricula, and programs
Equipment specialist	Ensure that relevant equipment is in good condition, maintain the various technical systems involved
Program manager	Oversee the implementation of an instructional system
Facility manager	Ensure that facilities are maintained in good condition

learners. While there are clearly powerful technologies to support teachers and learners, there are also powerful technologies to support others in Table 5.1. Finally, recognizing the many people involved in supporting learning, instruction, and performance is likely to contribute to a systems perspective on education and training, which is often critical for program success and which is discussed in the next chapter.

Activities to Be Supported

It was noted earlier in this volume that technologies change. Because technologies change so much in a short period of time, the focus in this volume is not on particular technologies. It is worth reviewing the New Media Consortium's *Horizon Reports* in various contexts over a period of years to see how much and how rapidly technologies change (see www.nmc.org). In 2012, the integration of mobile devices, in learning, instruction, and performance, and tablet computers were the top two near-term educational technology developments for K-12 settings. Just two years later, in 2014, the top two near-term technology developments for K-12 settings were BYOD (bring your own device) and cloud computing.

As a consequence of rapid changes in technology, the focus in the *Foundations* volume is on what someone might do to improve instruction, learning, and performance with technology, considering technologies that are (or soon will be) available. Table 5.2 depicts some of the activities from Table 5.1 plus a few student-oriented activities along with some representative technologies that might be considered for use. An interesting class exercise would be to expand this table to include additional technologies now available. For a comprehensive list of cloud-based authoring tools, see http://elearningindustry. com/the-ultimate-list-of-cloud-based-authoring-tools. HTML5 is the emerging standard for authoring Internet-based applications. In Table 5.2, content management systems (CMSs) and learning management systems (LMSs) are grouped together. While there is a great deal of overlap between CMSs and LMSs, a CMS is generally aimed at support for academic classroom use (including hybrid and online courses), and, as a result, is often more narrow in scope than an LMS. An LMS is typically aimed at corporate training, adheres more closely to industry standards, and is more easily adapted for informal learning settings.

There are a number of things to consider when selecting a technology to support a particular activity. First and foremost should be the suitability of the tool for the intended task to be performed by specific individuals. While a particular tool might be the best one recommended for a particular task, its use by those involved might be problematic for a number of reasons. The recommendation here is to consider the tool's capabilities and functionality together with the tasks to be performed and a representative sample of persons who will be performing the task. This applies to technologies to be used by students, teachers, designers, developers, managers, and others who might be involved.

TABLE 5.2 Instructional activities and representative technologies

Instructional activity	Representative technologies and tools
Implement lessons and activities	• A learning or course management system (LMS; CMS) such as BlackBoard, Litmos, Mindflash, Moodle, Sakai, or TOPYX
Create storyboards for lessons and activities	• An authoring tool such as Adobe Creative Suite, Articulate, DigitalChalk, Powerpoint, Shotbox
Sequence and assign people to design activities	• Project planning software such as Basecamp, Microsoft Project, OpenProject, Projectplace, Prong, and Visionera VisionProject
Develop educational apps	• GoMo Authoring Tool, Hot Lava, ZebraZapps
Develop a variety of media items for instructional purposes	• Authoring tools such as Audacity, Blender 3d, DreamWeaver, Flash, PhotoShop, SoftChalk as well as animation tools such as EWC, Go!Animate, and Prezi
Develop computer-based or web-based tutorials	• Adapt Learning, Camtasia Studio 8, Captivate 7, Digital Chalk, Jing, Litmos, MadCap, and many others
Develop online lessons and courses	• CourseBuilder, Dictera, e-learning Course Authoring Tool, Elucidat, Lectora, Luminosity
Develop interactive simulations	• Powersim, Quest, SimQuest, STELLA, Thinking Worlds, Vensim
Develop interactive lessons	• blogs, ClassTools.Net, easygenerator, Lectora, QEDOC, social networking sites, SoftChalk, wikis,
Develop interactive games and stories	• Adrift, Alice, Construct 2, Dark Basic, GameBrix, GameDev.Net, GameMaker, Gamestar, Inform7, Scratch, StoryBricks, Unity3d, and more
Facilitate web meetings	• Connect, DimDim, Elluminate, GoToMeeting, Panopto, WebEx
Assist in implementing and analyzing assessments	• Adit Software, eWebTest, Mettl, Quizlet.Com, Quedoc.Net, Questionmark, Saba, SAS, SPSS, TheGameCreators.Com, and more
Develop evaluation plans for courses and programs	• Logic models (many visualization templates are available); also, PERT and GANTT charting tools (e.g., see www.business.com) and various evaluation tools (www.sharpbrains.com/resources/)
Conduct formative and summative evaluations	• Tools and instruments to support the development, validation, implementation, and analysis of focus groups, interviews, and surveys; also statistical packages and tools such as excel, R, SAS, SPSS for the analysis of quantitative data
Oversee the implementation of an instructional system	• Project management tools such as Microsoft Project, knowledge management systems such as SharePoint or DocuShare and more

Once one or more relevant tools and technologies have been identified as candidates for use and adoption, it is then appropriate to consider the cost of acquisition, implementation, and maintenance of the targeted learning environment or instructional system. This is not a simple task, especially if training developers and users is involved. Determining the scope of an effort, the likely personnel and technologies involved, and the associated resources are standard parts of the planning phase for many medium- and large-scale educational technology projects (see, for example, Tennyson, 1995). The temptation is to focus on short-term costs rather than taking into account life-cycle costs and returns on investments in technologies.

When selecting tools and technologies to support learning and performance, one ought to keep in mind the learning and performance goals and the likely users. It is tempting to use tools one already has even though those might not be optimal for the intended purpose. In addition, one ought to keep in mind the portability and ease of modification with regard to things created using various technologies. Technology changes and upgrades are always a factor. Moreover, the targeted users and subject matter change. Modifications will nearly always be required. *Plan for change.* Finally, with regard to the creation of materials and activities in direct support of learning and performance, one should take into account accessibility issues to comply with legal and ethical requirements to those with disabilities (e.g., hearing and sight impaired students; see www.w3.org/WAI). Universal design is an attempt to do just this (see www. udlcenter.org).

An important distinction pertains to the quotation at the beginning of this chapter. With regard to direct instructional support, a designer or teacher can plan on using a technology to teach—that is to say, to present information and resources to a learner. In such a case, a learner may well learn from using the technology, and such uses are appropriate in many situations (e.g., to supplement classroom activities, for introductory tutorials, and other directed learning activities).

A different use of technology is to have learners engage with the subject matter through the use of a technology, as typically occurs, for example, in an interactive simulation. In this case, it might be said that a person is learning with the technology. Some interactive simulations support hypothesis testing in the sense that a learner has the opportunity to make a decision about the value of one or more variables and then gets to run the simulation to see the effects of that decision (e.g., as in management flight simulators and system dynamics simulations). One interesting use of a simulation environment is to have learners construct missing parts of the simulation or identify what parts have been hidden that would account for observed outputs of the simulation. Learning from technology is not the same as learning with technology. Moreover, it is not inconceivable that the two can be combined in some cases.

Yet another distinction involves learning to use a particular technology. Tutorials are often very effective in developing user competence with a new technology. If the new technology is quite different from previous technologies used, and when many users are involved, it is a good idea to conduct a readiness assessment to determine the ease of adopting the new technology and the extent of training likely to be required.

Test Your Understanding

Which of the following are examples of learning from technology and which are examples of learning with technology?

1. Using the help function in Microsoft Word to learn how to create interactive forms.
2. Interacting with a management flight simulator to determine the approximate delay in advertising impact on sales.
3. Playing spider solitaire on the computer.
4. Using *Flight Simulator* on a computer to become familiar with the fundamentals of flight and aircraft control.
5. Using a minimally interactive simulation of the Towers of Hanoi puzzle to determine the relationship between the number of discs and minimum moves (see www.mazeworks.com/Hanoi for an example).
6. Using mind mapping software to depict the plot of a novel (see http://freemind. sourceforge.net/wiki/index.php/Main_Page).
7. Constructing a concept map to show the relationships among a number of concepts (see http://cmap.ihmc.us for an example).
8. Using a spreadsheet to determine the minimum, maximum, and mean values in a set of numbers.

Support Approaches

Technologies provide different levels of support. Some technologies simply advise the user with regard to a variety of options based on some initial considerations (e.g., a search engine that suggests a number of links based on keywords provided). Other technologies solve a problem presented to the system (e.g., an automated word frequency counter that will find the most frequently used word(s) in text provided by the user).

These two examples correspond roughly with the distinction between strong and weak technology support for instructional designers (Spector, Polson, & Muraida, 1993). A strong technology is one which is intended to completely replace an activity previously accomplished by a human. A weak technology is one which is intended to extend the capability or productivity or quality of performance of the person involved. An example of a strong technology is a system developed at the Air Force Armstrong Laboratory called XAIDA (Experimental Advanced Instructional Design Advisor) that took as input a relatively simple procedural maintenance task, accessed a technical description of the relevant device and its maintenance procedures embedded in existing databases, and then generated in a matter of minutes a refresher or introductory lesson on maintenance for that device (Spector et al., 1993). An example of a weak technology is an advising system for instructional designers called GAIDA (Guided Approach to Instructional Design Advising) that shows a working lesson from either a student's view or the designer's view; in the designer view, a rationale for various design decisions is provided (Spector et al., 1993). In general, there has been more success with weak technologies in the area of technology support for designers and developers (Spector & Anderson, 2000). Perhaps this is because weak technologies are likely to encourage a user to think about the nature of the problem to be solved.

With regard to learning support, one can make a similar distinction. A strong technology would be one that provided the problem and the solution (perhaps also an explanation of the solution) to the student. Worked examples are representative of a strong learning technology in this category (Sweller & Cooper, 1985). Students are shown a complete solution to a problem (sometimes with a solution explanation), and this is expected to improve problem-solving skills. Evidence shows that in many cases it does have that effect, but with more advanced learners this strategy has the opposite effect (Kalyuga, Ayres, & Sweller, 2003), possibly due to boring advanced students with something already well understood and mastered. With more advanced students, the approach, according to cognitive apprenticeship (Brown, Collins, & Duguid, 1989), is to provide less and less support as learners gain competence and understanding. After showing a completely worked example, one could proceed to completion exercises which involve one or more missing parts (such as the last part of the final calculation in an algebra problem). Then one could withdraw even more of the solution. With the most advanced learners, one could ask them to construct an algorithm for solving a particular problem and other problems of the same kind.

Technological, Pedagogical, and Content Knowledge (TPACK)

Shulman (1986) introduced the notion of pedagogical content knowledge. Basically, this is the idea that teachers must not only know the content and understand the fundamentals of pedagogy, they must be able to apply pedagogical principles to a body of knowledge so as to achieve optimal outcomes. The notion of integrating pedagogical knowledge with content knowledge has been expanded to include technological knowledge. It is not sufficient for a teacher or trainer to understand the use of a technology. What is essential for effective learning and instruction is for a teacher or trainer to understand how best to integrate the use of a technology to achieve instructional goals pertaining to a subject area with a group of learners. This notion is called technological, pedagogical, and content knowledge (TPACK; see Mishra & Koehler, 2006). It should be noted that TPACK knowledge and skills might be considered necessary for effective technology integration but those skills alone are not sufficient. The organizational context and culture along with support and system-level issues must also be taken into account.

Test Your Understanding

Which of the following are examples of weak technology support and which are examples of strong technology support, and why?

1. Providing an annotated solution to a quadratic equation explaining each step used to reach the solution.
2. Giving an online objective test that is automatically graded with individual scores sent to students and automatically entered into a grade book.
3. Organizing a role-playing activity with students engaged in a scenario playing different roles, followed by a group debriefing session.
4. Having students submit their essays to and get feedback from Turnitin.com (http://turnitin.com/static/index.php) to be submitted along with their essay as a class assignment.
5. Having students watch a video demonstrating a person performing a complex procedure and talking about each step and particular things to tend to while performing the procedure.

A Representative Educational Technology Challenge

A large international business enterprise has decided to move most of its 250 training courses to be delivered by handheld smartphones which are being purchased for each employee. Many of the targeted users have never taken an online course much less a course delivered on a smartphone. The company has sites in 23 different countries where the primary languages are English, French, German, Japanese, and Spanish. Corporate management wants to know which courses can be delivered this way (the target is 90 percent of the current training courses that cover topics such as Using Microsoft Office and Spreadsheet Management of an Inventory) and what evidence can be collected to show how effective they are.

Learning Activities

1. Identify and describe the key barriers to success involved in achieving the goal stated in the representative problem above.
2. Identify and describe the key factors that are likely to become part of an implementation plan for this problem situation.
3. Indicate and describe the relationships among the key factors that have been identified.
4. Indicate what things are likely to change in the period involved in implementing the plan.
5. Create an annotated concept map that reflects the things indicated in response to the previous four tasks.
6. Reflect on your responses and your concept map, and then describe the assumptions you have made and what resources would be required to implement the solution you have in mind.

Links

W3C Web Accessibility Initiative—www.w3.org/WAI

John Sterman's (MIT Professor) management flight simulators—http://jsterman.scripts.mit.edu/Management_Flight_Simulators_%28MFS%29.html; see also http://web.mit.edu/jsterman/www/BusDyn2.html

Strategy dynamics simulators—www.strategydynamics.com/info/aboutus.aspx#

Towers of Hanoi simulation—www.mazeworks.com/hanoi

Freemind software—http://freemind.sourceforge.net/wiki/index.php/Main_Page

National center on universal design for learning—http://www.udlcenter.org

Turnitin.Com anti-plagiarism site—http://turnitin.com/static/index.php

CMAPS concept mapping software—http://cmap.ihmc.us

The Worked Examples home page—http://workedexamples.org

ClassTools.Net website with templates and tools to create games, quizzes, activities, and tutorials

QEDOC tools for creating lessons and quizzes—www.qedoc.com

Quizlet.com tool for creating assessments—http://quizlet.com

Other Resources

Capterra's directory of courseware authoring tools—www.capterra.com/courseware-software?utm_source=bing&utm_medium=cpc

Directory of authoring tools—http://c4lpt.co.uk/Directory/Tools/instructional.html

Game creation resources—www.ambrosine.com/resource.html

A guide to assessment software on the Web—www.educational-software-directory.net/teacher/assessment

A guide to game development software—www.gamedev.net

Instructional design models—www.instructionaldesign.org/models/index.html

Softpedia authoring support tools—www.softpedia.com/get/Authoring-tools

References

Brown, J. S., Collins, A., & Duguid, P. (1989). Situated cognition and the culture of learning. *Educational Researcher, 18,* 32–42.

Jonassen, D. H., Carr, C., & Yueh, H-P. (1998). Computers as mindtools for engaging learners in critical thinking. *TechTrends, 43,* 24–32.

Kalyuga, S., Ayres, P., Chandler, P., & Sweller, J. (2003). The expertise reversal effect. *Educational Psychologist, 38*(1), 23–31.

Mishra, P., & Koehler, M. J. (2006). Technological pedagogical content knowledge: A framework for teacher knowledge. *Teacher College Record, 108*(6), 1017–1054.

Shulman, L. S. (1986). Those who understand: Knowledge growth in teaching. *Educational Researcher, 15*(2), 4–14.

Spector, J. M., & Anderson, T. M. (Eds.) (2000). *Integrated and holistic perspectives on learning, instruction and technology: Understanding complexity.* Dordrecht: Kluwer Academic Press.

Spector, J. M., Polson, M. C., & Muraida, D. J. (Eds.) (1993). *Automating instructional design: Concepts and issues.* Englewood Cliffs, NJ: Educational Technology Publications.

Sweller, J., & Cooper, G. A. (1985). The use of worked examples as a substitute for problem solving in learning algebra. *Cognition and Instruction, 2*(1), 59–89.

Tennyson, R. D. (1995). Instructional systems development: The fourth generation. In Tennyson, R. D. & Barron, A. (Eds.), *Automating instructional design: Computer-based development and delivery tools,* 33–78.

six

Integrative Approaches to Planning and Implementation

"The procedure of working ... from goals to the requirements of instructional events is one of the most effective and widely employed techniques" (from Robert M. Gagné and M. David Merrill's paper in Educational Technology Research & Development entitled "Integrative Goals for Instructional Design" in 1990)

The Nature of Integration

The concept of integration occurs in many different contexts. In some school settings, it refers to having children of different races or ethnic backgrounds together in the same classrooms; in others, it refers to having boys and girls in the same classroom; in still others, it may involve having students with different abilities together, as in inclusive classrooms in which special needs students participate in general education classrooms. In these cases, the notion of mixing together is involved. According to Merrill's (2002, 2007) *First Principles of Instruction*, however, we ought to take the notion of integration with the context of learning and instruction a bit further. Merrill's (2002) fifth principle is that learning is promoted or enhanced when new knowledge is integrated into the learner's world or everyday life. What does 'integration' mean in this context and how could it be assessed? Clearly, it means more than simply mixing in the new knowledge with what one already knows or can do, or mixing together persons with different backgrounds and abilities.

A demonstration of skill improvement is one measure of effective integration. How much skill improvement? For simple procedural skills, improvement could be considered to be complete mastery or automaticity—that is, the learner could perform the procedure quickly and correctly, even while talking about or doing something else. Another indicator of effective integration of new knowledge would be the ability to modify or adjust that knowledge to satisfy the requirements of a new problem or situation. This kind of indicator (the ability to modify knowledge to solve new problems) would be relevant for more complex procedures and nonrecurrent tasks (van Merriënboer, 1997). Merrill's principle of integration includes both kinds of integration since both kinds of situations (recurrent and novel) are encountered in everyday life.

The point to consider is that integration in either case implies that the knowledge has become transparent in a certain sense. In the first case of automaticity, the knowledge has become a routine part of the person's set of skills and may be performed without much attention or thought. In the second case, the knowledge is so well developed that its limitations are known along with how it can be adjusted to meet the requirements of new situations. A person with this high level of understanding recognizes when a modification is required and makes the appropriate adjustment in performing the task at hand.

Most education and training fails to meet Merrill's integration principle. This is not really all that surprising. If one thinks about the parallel case of integration in schools, the test for effective integration would be that those involved no longer pay any attention to the race, ethnic group, gender, disability, religion, or other individual difference that was the basis for school integration. In a word, something is well integrated when it is no longer the focus of attention. This notion applies to integration of technology into learning and instruction. One did not focus on chalk and the blackboard in traditional school rooms—they were there and effectively integrated. When computers and digital projectors were introduced, these technologies were the focus of attention for some time, but when used in classrooms these days, they are no longer the focus of attention and can be said to be well integrated. This does not mean that the use of an integrated technology actually contributes to improved learning. More is required. What it does mean is that the focus of learners and teachers can shift from the technology (chalk, a blackboard, a computer, an interactive whiteboard, a tablet, a smartphone, etc.) to the content, which is a prerequisite condition for learning in most cases. That is to say, the focus of effective learning is typically on content, activities, problem solving, and so on, rather than on a particular technology, although technology can certainly support and facilitate learning. It is also true that in some cases, the focus is on the technology involved. For example, when using a 3D printer to fabricate an object, it is important to match the print medium/material to be used (plastic, metal, photopolymer, etc.) to the object being created and how it will be used.

A Systems Perspective

It makes some sense to think of the effective integration of technology as an educational goal—more specifically, as an enabling objective that supports more effective learning and instruction, which is assessed in part by satisfying Merrill's fifth integration principle. What, then, serves to facilitate and support effective technology integration that will then enable the kind of knowledge integration that is a strong indicator of effective learning? There is not an easy or short answer to such a complex question. However, developing a systems perspective is very likely to be a critical aspect of any answer.

Researchers have found that people have difficulty in reasoning about complex situations that involve many interacting components, especially with regard to nonlinear relationships and delayed effects (Dörner, 1996; Sterman, 1994). This means that people often do not reason well with regard to systems. A system is a collection of related and interacting components, some concrete and some abstract, which comprise a meaningful whole. A system has boundaries, although these are not always precisely defined. An obvious example is the solar system. The major components are the various planets and their satellites. The orbits of the planets might also be considered system components; this means that the behavior of a component over time is part of the system. The nature of that behavior, in this case the orbit of a planet, is influenced by the sun and other planets and satellites. There are many delayed effects in our solar system. A solar flare may eventually have noticeable effects on planet earth, including the disruption of electrical grids and radio communications. The dynamic relationships of the components of a complex system can be seen in the way that the tides on planet earth are affected by the location and phase of the earth's satellite—the moon.

Consider an educational system as another kind of complex system. There are many interacting components in an educational system, including students, teachers, administrators, support staff, facilities, information and communications infrastructure, district officials, parents, community funding and support, testing, reporting, state and federal requirements, and much more. These components are interconnected in many complex ways. Some of the relationships among these components are nonlinear. For example, as test scores change, there are effects on community, state, and federal support; should scores drop below a certain threshold, state or federal support may disappear altogether rather than increase to aid a struggling school, as one might reasonably expect.

In some cases, the effects of a change in one of these components on other components may be immediate but in other cases the effects may be delayed. If a school develops a history of not making adequate yearly progress, parents may eventually send their kids to alternative schools or families may move to a different school district.

When a new technology is introduced, it is tempting to believe that its effects will be immediate and significant. However, the reality is that the effects of educational technologies on teaching and learning are typically delayed. The reasons include the time required for teachers and students to learn how to make effective use of a new technology—to make a new technology an integral part of their everyday learning and teaching activities. Additionally, many technologies are effectively integrated only when there are substantial support resources. For example, personalized learning requires a library of learning objects and applications in a particular subject domain in use over a period of time and with many students in order to be useful.

A systems perspective is more than simply thinking about all the many interrelated components and aspects of an educational system. A systems perspective is thinking dynamically as well as holistically. The components change over time. The composition of students changes over time. The number and type of special needs students may change in a short period of time requiring many adjustments within the system. Individual learner characteristics such as motivation and prior knowledge change as well.

One aspect of a systems perspective is thinking systematically. For example, when introducing an innovative technology, one is well-advised to consider the acquisition process, the training process, the maintenance and management process, the evaluation of impact, and the implications for other components of the system in order to develop and implement adequate technology plans. Being comprehensive in planning is a hallmark of thinking systematically.

A second aspect of a systems perspective is thinking about the dynamic relationships that exist within the system. When introducing a new technology, some may feel threatened or anxious about their ability to use the technology. The technology may change job roles and tasks for some individuals. There may be an increase or decrease in demands placed on another system component. There will likely be challenges in transitioning to a new technology and disruptions of service when that technology is introduced. Unanticipated changes may also occur when introducing a new technology. Being flexible in planning and foreseeing the dynamic effects of introducing a new technology is a hallmark of thinking systemically.

Test Your Understanding

Suppose your residential institution is considering adopting a flipped classroom approach in which learners are assigned reading and viewing tasks outside the classroom (reading targeted entries in a reputable online encyclopedia, viewing TED talks on relevant subjects, etc.) and then given small group problem-solving activities when in the classroom, with the instructor serving as an on-call adviser. What factors are likely to be relevant to successful integration of this flipped classroom approach and how are those factors related?

A critical reflection question: Many of the learning activities in this book ask the learner to identify and describe key factors and their various relationships involved in a problem situation. Is such an exercise designed to promote systematic and/or systemic thinking? Why and how? Do you think that this technique is effective?

A Representative Educational Technology Challenge

There are many learning and content management systems available to support instruction. Some are commercial systems such as BlackBoard and Saba, and some are open-source systems such as Moodle and Sakai. Your organization has extensive teaching and training activities, primarily with adult learners. You have been using an expensive commercial system. Top management has asked you to develop a plan to transition from the commercial system to an open-source solution. Your plan should address needs, costs, diffusion issues, and how impact might be assessed.

Learning Activities

1. Identify and describe the key barriers to success involved in achieving the goal stated in the representative problem above.
2. Identify and describe the key factors that are likely to become part of an implementation plan for this problem situation.
3. Indicate and describe the relationships among the key factors that have been identified.
4. Indicate what things are likely to change in the period involved in implementing the plan.
5. Create an annotated concept map that reflects the things indicated in response to the previous four tasks.
6. Reflect on your responses and your concept map, and then describe the assumptions you have made and what resources would be required to implement the solution you have in mind.

Links

Gagné & Merrill's "Integrative Goals for Instructional Design"—see www.ibstpi.org/Products/pdf/chapter_5.pdf

Other Resources

Directory of authoring tools—http://c4lpt.co.uk/Directory/Tools/instructional.html

Education Northwest Site for instructional planning and design—see http://educationnorthwest.org/taxonomy/term/204

MIT system dynamics in education guide—see http://ocw.mit.edu/courses/sloan-school-of-management/15-988-system-dynamics-self-study-fall-1998-spring-1999/readings/part8.pdf

References

Dörner, D. (1996). *The logic of failure: Why things go wrong and what we can do to make them right* (R. Kimber & R. Kimber, Translators). New York: Metropolitan Books.

Gagné, R. M., & Merrill, M. D. (1990). Integrative goals for instructional design. *Educational Technology Research & Development, 38*(1), 23–30.

Merrill, M. D. (2002). First principles of instruction. *Educational Technology Research and Development, 50*(3), 43–59.

Merrill, M. D. (2007). The future of instructional design: The proper study of instructional design. In R. A. Reiser & J. V. Dempsey (Eds.), *Trends and issues in instructional design and technology* (2nd ed., pp. 336–341). Upper Saddle River, NJ: Pearson Education.

Sterman, J. D. (1994). Learning in and about complex systems. *System Dynamics Review, 10*(2–3), 291–330.

van Merriënboer, J. J. G. (1997). *Training complex cognitive skills: A four-component instructional design model for technical training.* Englewood Cliffs, NJ: Educational Technology Publications.

part two

THEORETICAL PERSPECTIVES WITH EXAMPLE APPLICATIONS

seven
Theories
of Human
Development

"All that is valuable in human society depends upon the opportunity for the development accorded to the individual" (Albert Einstein on his departure from Germany in 1933)

Just as technologies change, so do humans. However, the changes within a human are quite different from changes in technology. Technologies evolve and new technologies are introduced on account of humans. Humans create and change technologies. Changes within a human are more complex. An individual human naturally changes over time. The physiological changes are perhaps most obvious as the infant becomes a child and matures into an adult. Those physiological changes tend to occur regardless of what other humans do or fail to do. Of course, the result of human growth can be nurtured or impeded by a number of factors such as diet, exercise, exposure to others, and so on.

Humans also develop psychologically and cognitively, in the sense that some things are simply not able to be easily understood at certain stages of development. As Piaget (1929, 1970) noticed, a very young child does not understand that a quantity (for example, water in a container) does not change when its spatial arrangement has changed (e.g., the water is poured into a differently shaped container). Language and experience clearly play important roles in psychological and cognitive development.

Moreover, humans develop socially and culturally, although there is perhaps more variation in social and cultural development than in physiological or psychological development. While various areas of human development have been studied, including those mentioned here, it is reasonable to expect that development in these areas are interrelated and, in many cases, interdependent (Newman & Newman, 2007).

For example, a high level of cognitive development might be indicated by the ability to engage in inquiry activities that reflect a questioning attitude with regard to previously accepted claims along with an openness to alternative explanations. However, in some cultural or social contexts such an inquiring attitude might be considered inappropriate and discouraged early in an individual's development. Likewise, a physiological condition such as color blindness might prevent or inhibit a person from cognitive development in areas pertaining to color theory (I have no idea if this is true. Do you?)

Before taking a short tour of different theories of human development, two additional comments are in order. First, many of the physiological and psychological changes alluded to above might be regarded as macro-changes in the sense that they apply generally to all humans and refer to major aspects of being at a certain stage in life. In addition, these different stages of development are relatively easy to identify. However, humans also undergo many micro-changes that are particular to individuals and not so easily identified. For example, a person may experience a loss of hearing or lose a certain prejudice that had influenced many prior choices. Both macro- and micro-changes in human development have implications for learning and instruction. However, for the sake of brevity, physiological development is omitted from this discussion of human development. It is clear that hormones and other physiological factors affect learning and development, but such a discussion would take us far from the core concept of the foundations of educational technology.

Second, humans have the ability to bring about some changes in themselves. Not all of human development is pre-coded or determined by external circumstances. Humans make choices and decisions, and those choices and decisions can affect human development. For example, Marie Curie noticed unusual electro-magnetic activity associated with pitchblende. She suspected it was related to something similar to uranium and decided to try to find out the cause. She devoted several years of concentrated investigation and discovered two new radioactive elements (polonium and radium) with the help of fellow physicist and husband, Pierre Curie. The point here is that because of her decision to investigate, she developed a much deeper understanding of the substance called pitchblende, a mineral ore found in many parts of the world, now used in processing uranium. Within any field of inquiry or endeavor, one can cite levels of human development that might include absolute beginner, advanced beginner, competent performer, proficient performer, and intuitive expert (Dreyfus & Dreyfus, 1986).

Based on the notions of physiological, psychological, social, and self-directed development, a few prominent theories of human development are briefly reviewed. The point of understanding these perspectives on human development is to make more effective use of technology to improve learning and instruction in various circumstances with different learners. These theories point to differences in learners that are pertinent to proper support for learning. There are additional individual differences (e.g., prior knowledge and experience, learning styles, gender, culture, etc.) that ought to be considered when planning and implementing support for learning.

Cognitive Developmental Theory (Piaget)

Cognitive developmental theory is the notion that, as a person matures, he or she naturally progresses through different stages of cognitive development. The theorist most closely associated with this theory of cognitive development is Jean Piaget, a Swiss genetic epistemologist who studied the cognitive structures of children. Piaget (1929, 1970) proposed four primary stages of cognitive development (see Figure 7.1): (a) a *sensorimotor stage* in which motor control is developed and identifies the self as separate from other objects (roughly birth to 2); (b) a *preoperational stage* in which objects are identified and associated with symbols through the use of language (roughly ages 3 to 7); (c) a *concrete operational stage*, in which the ability to think logically about objects and events, and the notion of conservation is understood (roughly ages 7 to 11); and (d) a *formal operational stage*, which involves the ability to think logically about abstract objects and hypothetical propositions (roughly age 11 and up).

Piaget's basic outlook is that as a person matures, he or she adapts to the world in different ways. The two basic processes of adaptation are assimilation and accommodation. Assimilation involves taking in that which is perceived, creating internal representations and associating them with pre-existing representations; the assimilation process implies that what is experienced is internally represented so as to fit within existing internal knowledge structures. Accommodation occurs when internal structures must change or be created in order to account for new experiences.

While assimilation and accommodation are complementary processes and often occur together, the process of accommodation is related to the notion of *cognitive dissonance* introduced by Festinger (1957). Festinger argued that people in general seek to avoid

Piaget's Cognitive Stages: Genetic Epistemology

Stage of Cognitive Development	Typical Ages Involved	Representative Example
Sensorimotor	Birth to 2	Focusing on and grasping an object
Preoperational	3 to 7	Talking about something directly experienced
Concrete operational	7 to 11	Sorting objects into similar groups
Formal operational	11 and up	Reasoning about something not directly experienced

FIGURE 7.1 Piaget's stages of cognitive development

conflicting beliefs and opinions. When an occasion arises that creates such a conflict, the individual typically rejects or modifies one or both beliefs to eliminate the dissonance.

A related perspective can be found in Quine and Ullian's (1978) *The Web of Belief*, which is a landmark work in the area of naturalistic epistemology—the same field with which Piaget identified. Quine and Ullian (1978) argue that a person naturally strives for coherence among a set or sets of beliefs. When a new experience is encountered which appears to introduce an inconsistency, minor adjustments are made so as to make the internal representation of the new experience as compatible with representations of existing experience. That is to say, we first try to assimilate our understanding of new experiences into our understanding of prior experiences.

When such adjustments become excessive or when assimilation fails in some way, the existing internal structure must be reconstructed, similar to Kuhn's (1962) notion of a paradigm shift and Piaget's notion of accommodation. The related concepts of accommodation, cognitive dissonance, and paradigm shift within the context of naturalistic epistemology are captured in Wittgenstein's (1922) remark in the Tractatus *Logico-Philosophicus* that the world waxes and wanes as a whole (see #6.43 in the *Tractatus*). While Wittgenstein noted in the *Tractatus* that a person creates internal representations in response to experiences (e.g., see "we picture facts to ourselves" at *Tractatus* #2.1), he acknowledged that these internal representations are not separate entities unconnected to or uninfluenced by other internal representations.

A person does not process perceptions and beliefs in a discrete, one-at-a-time manner. On the contrary, a person gradually develops sets of internal mental structures, with the implication that multiple beliefs are nearly always involved in a learning experience. Figuring out how best to leverage existing beliefs and mental structures to make learning effective is an ongoing challenge for teachers and instructional designers, as these beliefs and structures can vary dramatically from one individual to the next.

A final point associated with the cognitive developmental theory is the notion of internal mental structures, which are dealt with in different ways by different cognitive scientists. Johnson-Laird (1983) argued that mental models are fundamental to human reasoning and cognitive development. It is possible to distinguish internal representations created just when needed to explain an unusual phenomenon or puzzling situation from internal structures that are well established and invoked automatically and often without conscious thought in order to deal with a problem or situation. Some psychologists call the former transient structures *mental models* and the latter more established structures *schema*. Mental models can be transformed into schema when created often in similar circumstances. The process of transforming mental models into schema is associated with the notion of developing automaticity in performing recurrent tasks, which is often a targeted outcome in many training programs. The process of transforming or decomposing a schema into easily alterable sets of mental models is akin to the process of unlearning, which presents particular challenges to teachers and trainers. It is often more difficult to help a learner unlearn a procedure or complex set of beliefs that have been automated than it was to help that learner acquire the knowledge in the first place (for example, see www.learninginnovationslab.org/wp-content/uploads/2013/12/LILA-Theme-for-2013–14-finalmembers.pdf).

Cognitive Social Mediated Theory (Vygotsky)

The emphasis in cognitive development theory is primarily on the individual. While cognitive development researchers acknowledge the influence of things outside the individual, the focus is on determining markers of individual progress and identifying different stages of cognitive development. However, it is obvious that children are influenced by their peers, teachers, and parents. Moreover, much learning is mediated by language. This realization has led researchers to enlarge the focus to include the social and cultural context in which individual cognitive development occurs. The general premise of cognitive social mediated theory is that individual development is in large part determined by the social and cultural context in which a person is situated (see www.funderstanding.com/content/vygotsky-and-social-cognition).

With regard to child development, it is clear that parents, teachers, and other children provide the context of many or most experiences associated with learning. A child growing up in a rural community on a farm will have experiences quite different from a child growing up in a large urban environment. I recall my parents taking me on a shopping trip to a large nearby city when I was six or seven. The department store had an escalator. I had no idea that such things existed. I had to ask how it worked and why there would be such a thing. The word 'escalator' was not part of the vocabulary of a small town child in the USA in the 1950s. Likewise, one can imagine that whatever the context in which a child is raised that there will be some things with which that child will be familiar and many with which the child will not be familiar.

Introducing language about things completely alien to someone's prior experience is not likely to be very meaningful unless that language is accompanied with some kind of realistic experience with which the person can relate. This discussion then comes back to the fundamental role that language plays in learning. Language serves to mediate experience.

An early psychologist who realized this was Lev Vygotsky (1896–1934), whose work did not become widely known outside Russia until decades after his death (Vygotsky, 1962, 1978). In addition to emphasizing the important role of social and cultural interaction, Vygotsky contributed two other significant ideas to cognitive development. First, a more knowledgeable other (MKO; such as a parent, teacher, or another child with more experience) plays a critical role in individual development. Before a child internalizes an idea, it is presented in a social context by a more knowledgeable other. Second, the distance between a child's ability to understand a concept or perform a task independently (indicating internalization of the relevant concepts and individual cognitive development) and that child's ability to understand and perform with the assistance of a MKO is called the zone of proximal development (ZPD). The implication

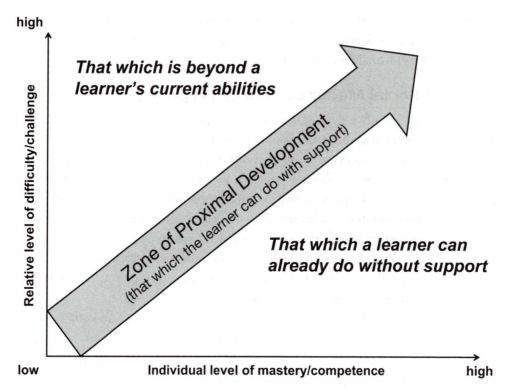

Relative level of difficulty/challenge

That which is beyond a learner's current abilities

Zone of Proximal Development
(that which the learner can do with support)

That which a learner can already do without support

low   Individual level of mastery/competence   high

FIGURE 7.2 Lev Vygotsky's Zone of Proximal Development

for educational technologists and teachers is that they should focus on the ZPD, as that is where learning progress will most often occur. These extensions to individual cognitive development theory are widely accepted, although there are many variants.

Psychosocial Development Theory (Erikson)

Erik Erikson (1902–1994) was a Danish-German-American psychoanalyst who was especially interested in the development of identity. Erikson (1959, 1968) postulated eight stages of development that span the entire life of an individual (see Table 7.1). The basic idea is that within each stage there are representative crises that form one's identity.

Erikson was influenced by Freudian psychology, partly through Sigmund Freud's daughter Anna. The Freudian influence can be seen in the central notion that a person's identity and personality develop in stages. Ego and personal identity play a central role in Erikson's theory of development; the way an individual responds to the inherent conflicts that arise at each stage of development largely determine a person's identity. A lasting aspect of Erikson's contribution is the extension of cognitive development theory beyond adolescence into adulthood, maturity, and old age. Those involved with designing and implementing learning environments, including those for adults, are well advised to consider Erikson's theory. As with all of the development theorists, one conclusion is that not all learners are the same. Many differences are due to different

TABLE 7.1

Development stage	Prototypical psychosocial crisis	Age range/description
Infancy	Hope: trust vs. mistrust	0–1.5 years, birth to walking
Early childhood	Will, autonomy vs. shame/doubt	1–3 years, toilet training, talking
Play age	Purpose: initiative vs. guilt	3–6 years, pre-school, reading
School age	Competence: industry vs. inferiority	5–12 years, early school
Adolescence	Fidelity: identity vs. role confusion	9–18 years, puberty, teens
Young adult	Love: intimacy vs. isolation	18–40 years, dating, parenthood
Adulthood	Care: generativity vs. stagnation	30–65 years, parenting, middle age
Maturity	Wisdom: integrity vs. despair	50+ years, old age

stages of development, whichever development theory guides one's work. In addition to individual differences due to stages of development, there are other individual differences that educational technologists and instructional designers will attend; these will be discussed in Part III of this volume.

Test Your Understanding

Which of the following is/are generally regarded as true statements:

1. Some individual differences are a result of being at a particular state of development.
2. Language and thought develop independently.
3. Certain learning tasks are virtually impossible for individuals at an early stage of cognitive development.
4. Mental models are directly observable markers of development.
5. The concepts of a more knowledgeable other and the zone of proximal development are closely related.
6. Development theorists are engaged in descriptive research—describing how individuals develop rather than how individuals should develop.

A Representative Educational Technology Challenge

A government agency that wants to support foreign workers in the country has asked your organization to develop a second language course for the families of workers being hired by business and industry. These families include spouses, children, and, in some cases, elderly parents. They come from a variety of different countries and speak different languages. The government agency would like the language course(s) to be offered online at no charge to these families. You have been asked to conduct a needs assessment and training requirements analysis and report the critical factors that will then inform the design of the course(s).

Learning Activities

1. Identify and describe the key factors involved in a needs assessment and training requirements analysis for the representative problem above.
2. Identify and describe the key factors that are likely to become part of an implementation plan for this problem situation.
3. Indicate and describe the relationships among the key factors that have been identified.
4. Indicate what things are likely to change in the period involved in implementing the plan.
5. Create an annotated concept map that reflects the things indicated in response to the previous four tasks.
6. Reflect on your responses and your concept map, and then describe the assumptions you have made and what resources would be required to implement the solution you have in mind.

Links

Explorations in Learning & Instruction: The Theory into Practice Database (TIP), created by Greg Kearsley—see http://tip.psychology.org

David Perkins on Unlearning—https://lila.pz.harvard.edu/pdfs/Unlearning_Insightv2010.pdf

Funderstanding.com site on Lev Vygotsky and Social Cognition—see www.funderstanding.com/content/vygotsky-and-social-cognition

Learning Theories site on Vygotsky—www.learning-theories.com/vygotskys-social-learning-theory.html

Other Resources

George Mason University Site with online resources for developmental psychology—http://classweb.gmu.edu/awinsler/ordp/index.html

Lone Star College site with links to anatomy and physiology tutorials—http://nhscience.lonestar.edu/biol/tutoria.html

NCREL (North Central Regional Educational Laboratory) on Theories of Child Development and Learning—www.ncrel.org/sdrs/areas/issues/students/earlycld/ea7lk18.htm

Resources for Human Development—www.rhd.org/Home.aspx

References

Dreyfus, H., & Dreyfus, S. (1986). *Mind over machine: The power of human intuition and expertise in the era of the computer*. New York: Free Press.

Erikson, E. H. (1959). *Identity and the life cycle*. New York: International Universities Press.

Erikson, E. H. (1968). *Identity, youth and crisis*. New York: Norton.

Festinger, L. (1957). *A theory of cognitive dissonance*. New York: Wiley.

Johnson-Laird, P. N. (1983). *Mental models: Towards cognitive science of language, inference and consciousness*. Cambridge: Cambridge University Press.

Kuhn, T. S. (1962). *The structure of scientific revolutions*. Chicago: University of Chicago Press.

Newman, B. M., & Newman, P. B. (2007). *Theories of human development*. Mahwah, NJ: Erlbaum.

Piaget, J. (1929). *The child's conception of the world*. New York: Harcourt Brace Jovanovich.

Piaget, J. (1970). *The science of education and the psychology of the child*. New York: Grossman.

Quine, W. V. O., & Ullian, J. S. (1978). *The web of belief* (2nd ed.). New York: Random House.

Vygotksy, L. S. (1962). *Thought and language*. Cambridge, MA: MIT Press.

Vygotsky, L. S. (1978). *Mind in society*. Cambridge, MA: Harvard University Press.

Wittgenstein, L. (1922). *Tractatus Logico-Philosophicus* (Trans. C. K. Ogden). London: Routledge & Kegan Paul.

eight
Theories of Learning and Performance

"What a child can do today with assistance, she will be able to do by herself tomorrow" (from Lev Vygotsky's Mind in Society *published posthumously in the USA in 1978)*

A theory of learning is intended to describe and explain how people learn, including the mechanisms and processes involved. A theory of learning provides a descriptive account of various aspects of learning, including such things as rates of learning and retention, limitations of memory, impediments to learning, and so on. A theory of learning also provides a basis for explaining whether and to what extent learning occurred in a particular context as well as predicting what might happen if conditions involved in the learning context were changed. There are a number of educational positions related to learning theories, including behaviorism, cognitivism, constructivism, connectivism, humanism, and more (Bransford, Brown, & Cocking, 2000). These perspectives on learning do not themselves constitute a learning theory, as they are at a higher level; however, specific learning theories are associated with these perspectives, and these more specific theories will be discussed in what follows.

First, let's examine what a theory is. What constitutes a theory of learning is subject to much discussion and debate, with the result that theories of learning and performance are categorized quite differently by different authors. In this chapter, a modest attempt is made to briefly describe some of the different perspectives associated with different theories of learning. This is followed by a short description of several prominent theories of learning. The notion of a theory of change is briefly introduced, as that has a bearing on the transition from theories of learning to expected outcomes of various instructional interventions. No attempt is made to be comprehensive or treat the many issues associated with learning theory in any depth. For a more comprehensive treatment of theories of learning, see Driscoll (2005), Richey, Klein, and Tracey (2011), or Schunk (2007).

What Constitutes a Theory?

The word 'theory' has many uses and occurs in many different contexts. With regard to learning theories, the word is typically used in a scientific context rather than in an informal context in which 'theory' might be roughly synonymous with 'supposition.' In science, a theory is developed to explain a set of facts and observations with regard to certain phenomena that are unusual or puzzling in some way. Theories are provisionally accepted as true and used to generate a number of testable hypotheses; in many cases, specific hypotheses become confirmed and are taken together to generate a theory. In either case, theories can be used to generate testable hypotheses, explain past events, and make predictions with regard to future events. It occasionally happens in science that an accepted theory comes into conflict with observations, and the accepted theory then must be refined or discarded.

Figure 8.1 depicts the general relationship of observations, hypotheses, and theories. While the general representation of scientific method includes a cycle of observation, hypothesis formulation and testing, and theory building or refinement, the process is

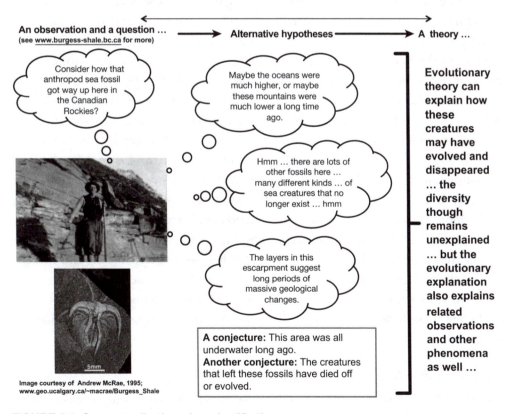

FIGURE 8.1 Conceptualization of a scientific theory

not so linear as depicted in Figure 8.1 or in representations of the scientific method. Scientists often have unstated assumptions and intuitions that lead them to make particular observations, sometimes to question an accepted theory. This latter process is called *abduction* (in contrast with induction and deduction) by Charles Sanders Peirce (1931).

In science, a theory is generally regarded as a set of well-established statements and principles that are used to explain groups of facts or a range of observed phenomena and generate hypotheses. Popular usage might suggest that 'theory' refers to an as yet untested claim, but 'hypothesis' or 'supposition' would be more appropriate in those cases, from a scientific perspective. Scientists use the word 'theory' (as in the phrase 'theory of evolution' or 'theory of relativity') to refer to a set of well-established statements and principles used to explain groups of facts and a range of observed phenomena. However, the use of 'theory' in 'theory of change' is more consistent with the notion of a hypothesis to be tested.

Scientists are interested in explaining many observed facts, such as genetic changes in populations of organisms over successive generations and long periods of time. The case represented in Figure 8.1 refers to evolutionary theory which has two major processes—natural selection and genetic drift or mutation (the latter is indirectly mentioned in Figure 8.1). Evolutionary biologists can explain a large number of observed facts and make predictions with regard to as yet unobserved phenomena.

A further difference between scientific and popular discourse is that scientific claims, including scientific theories, are generally subject to refutation; that is to say, the scientist making a claim or defending a theory is, in principle, willing to be shown that the claim is wrong or the theory wrong-headed. The willingness and readiness to be wrong is what makes scientific progress possible (Popper, 1963, 1972). Kuhn (1962) and others argue that scientific theories are quite resistant to change and scientists are not nearly as willing as Popper suggests to embrace refutation of a long-held or well-established theory. Quine and Ullian (1978) provide an excellent account of how beliefs can be considered as a system, and a change in one can lead to a requirement to change related beliefs (hypotheses or theories). Festinger's (1957) notion of *cognitive dissonance* is related to this issue as is Wittgenstein's remarks in the *Tractatus Logico-Philosophicus* that every proposition alters something in the general (perceived) structure of the world (remark 5.5262) and that the world of the happy person is not the same as that of the unhappy person (remark 6.43). The point here is that beliefs, sets of hypotheses, and theories are intertwined and best considered together rather than as separate, discrete, and disconnected statements. Evidence (in the form of data and observations), hypotheses (including those based on intuitions), and theories are best considered and analyzed together.

Perspectives

Theories arise within the context of something larger and more comprehensive. That something could be a traditional research paradigm or canonical view of the world (e.g.,

Newtonian mechanics), but it might also be comprised of values (e.g., freedom) and perspectives (e.g., epistemology). With regard to learning theories, relevant perspectives include behaviorism, cognitivism, constructivism, critical theory, and humanism. One can find other perspectives that shape particular theories of learning, but these are perhaps the most frequently encountered learning perspectives.

Behaviorism

Behaviorism is a perspective that focuses almost exclusively on directly observable things to explain learning. That which is directly observed and believed most relevant to learning are the immediate things in the learner's environment, and most closely contiguous in time and place to the targeted learning—the stimulus condition for learning. The response of the learner to the stimulus is also directly observable. The stimulus-response sequence is obviously iterative and offers opportunities for a teacher, trainer, coach, or parent to intervene in two quite different ways: (a) by manipulating the stimulus condition, and (b) by post-response reinforcers to encourage desired responses.

Watson (1913) was an early proponent of behaviorism who proposed such a view. There are many who denigrate behaviorism as dehumanizing and believe that behaviorism is no longer a dominant perspective. However, there are several things worth noting about behaviorism. First, it did provide a scientific and systematic basis for the investigation of human behavior. Second, it failed largely because it did not take into account mental activity that was necessary to explain complex human behavior (for example, language learning). Third, a modern variant of behaviorism is emerging in neural science in which one theory to explain some human behaviors includes an account of synaptic reinforcement in the brain's neural network. It is conceivable that synaptic activity can be mapped and predictors of responses developed on the basis of observed synaptic associations. In any case, behaviorism has contributed a great deal to our understanding of human learning, and one can argue that it has been modified and subsumed within other perspectives rather than having been replaced in its entirety.

Cognitivism

Cognitivism arose within psychology as behaviorism proved to be inadequate to explain complex human learning, notably language learning (Chomksy, 1967). In many cases, some observed behaviors appeared impossible to explain in terms of the stimulus conditions and other directly observable things in the learner's environment. In order to explain some human behaviors, psychologists turned to what had been regarded as an unobservable black box by behaviorists—the mind.

As a simple example, consider that which a person reports seeing. An observer can take note of most things in a person's visual field given adequate time. When asked what an individual person sees, not all that is directly observable is mentioned. People report different subsets of what is in principle observable, and some will report incorrectly. Perceptual bias and selectivity are widely recognized in the legal system as a problem with regard to eye-witness accounts. Why do different people report seeing different things in the same situation? A cognitive explanation might involve the notions of expectations and executive processing of visual information. These constructs (expectation and executive processing) are not directly observable; rather, they are hypothetical entities used to explain that which is directly observed (in this case a person's report of what he or she sees). There are far too many variations of cognitivism to discuss here. For an introduction to a cognitive perspective on learning, see Anderson (1996) and the ACT-R website at Carnegie Mellon University (http://act-r.psy.cmu.edu/). A reasonable way to conceive of cognitivism is as a dramatic extension of behaviorism to include things that are only indirectly observable (such as the cognitive architecture of the mind) to account for learning.

Constructivism

Constructivism is a naturalistic epistemological perspective that describes how it is that people come to know and understand the world. It is naturalistic in the sense that the focus is on *describing* what happens in the development of understanding rather than *deducing* what must have happened or *advocating* what should happen based on various a priori assumptions. The basic argument is that individuals actively construct internal representations in order to explain their experiences.

In one sense, constructivism can be viewed as an extension of cognitivism in that things that are only indirectly observable are used to help explain observed learning outcomes and knowledge gains. In this case, the indirectly observables are the internal representations created when needed to interpret a situation, respond to a puzzling situation, explain unusual phenomena, or predict outcomes if a new situation occurs. The constructivist perspective is that people naturally create these internal representations (also known as mental models); learners will actively create internal representations regardless of what a teacher is doing. However, not all internal representations are equally productive in terms of promoting understanding of complex or novel phenomena. Moreover, this process is mediated by language and in large part dependent on prior experience in the sense that the internal representations constructed by a person typically build on prior internal constructions, as knowledge and experience considered together are cumulative. As an epistemological perspective, constructivism is widely accepted. For more information on a mature constructivist perspective, see Johnson-Laird (1983).

Critical Theory

Critical theory arose in Germany in reference to philosophical perspectives that emphasized human freedom and liberty as opposed to perspectives and practices that tended to oppress individuals; unfortunately, there are all too many oppressive perspectives that people fail to recognize due to clever slogans that disguise their implications (Horkheimer & Adorno, 1972). In a broader sense, critical theory refers to any perspective that challenges accepted practices on the grounds that the impact and effects on people are dehumanizing and oppressive. Dewey (1916) and Habermas (1971) are two widely known philosophers who are often associated with critical theory and the implications for education. With regard to Figure 2.1 (a pyramid depicting a hierarchy of sorts with regard to learning and instruction), one might say that critical theory and humanism (discussed next) are focused on the topmost component of that pyramid—namely, values.

Humanism

Humanism is a perspective that focuses on the value of the individual and personal freedom. In a sense, humanism is not incompatible with other perspectives as the proponents are primarily concerned with arguing for the primacy of the individual and the needs of an individual, much like critical theory argues for the primacy of individual freedom from oppression. When individual needs are taken into consideration within the context of learning and instruction, issues pertaining to motivation and volition rise to the forefront (Kim & Keller, 2010). Many humanistically oriented learning theorists and researchers refer to Maslow's (1943) hierarchy of needs that has physiological (e.g., food and water) and safety (e.g., shelter and health) needs at the bottom of the hierarchy that must be satisfied before higher order needs such as belongingness, esteem, and self-actualization can be meaningfully addressed. Self-actualization is different from the lower needs as it is not driven by a particular deficiency as are the others. Rather, self-actualization evolves as a person matures and reconceptualizes him- or herself.

A Theory of Learning[1]

Learning involves stable and persisting changes in what a person (or group of people) knows and can do. Learning occurs all throughout a person's lifetime in both structured and unstructured environments. Learning is often incidental, occurring while a person is engaged in an activity not directed at learning. Learning is sometimes intentional and goal driven. A theory of learning is aimed at explaining how it is that people learn and come to understand the world. The focus, therefore, is on processes that can explain and predict many or most of what is called learning. Learning theories do not prescribe how to design instruction or implement learning environments, but they are certainly helpful in providing a way to conceptualize instruction and design practical frameworks to support learning and instruction. One would also expect a learning theory to account for the many cases in which learning fails to occur. Moreover, learning theories, along with empirical studies of learning, can form the basis for a theory of change to predict or justify a planned instructional intervention or educational reform.

An early example of a learning theory can be extracted from Plato's dialogues. In Plato's middle dialogues (*Meno* and *Phaedo*) Plato argues that the soul is immortal and has existed from eternity. As a result, the soul has come to know everything—knowledge being defined by Plato as involving eternal truths about the unchanging nature of reality. However, being born involves a traumatic process of putting the soul into a new body; this is so traumatic that the soul forgets what it has learned over the ages. The process of coming to know, for Plato, is a process of being reminded of that which the soul knew but forgot. Learning, in this Platonic theory, is a process of remembering. One implication is that teaching then becomes a process of reminding. While Plato's theory is problematic in many ways, it illustrates the nature of a theory of learning. First, it is grounded in a larger perspective—in Plato's case that larger perspective involved immortal souls. Second, a learning theory involves a characterization of what can be learned—in Plato's theory, learning involves eternal truths. Third, it provides an account of the essential process that results in learning—for Plato, that process was remembering. Finally, a theory of learning does have implications for teaching and instruction—for Plato, a teacher is a *reminder*—a person who reminds others (perhaps also him/herself). Five modern learning theories are briefly described next, none of which are at all like Plato's account but more in line with modern perspectives and practice.

Operant Conditioning Theory (Skinner)

Skinner (1954) is credited with operant condition theory, which is a behavioral learning theory. In this theory, learning is defined as a change in overt behavior. The key process involved in such changes is reinforcement; a reinforcer is basically designed to strengthen the connection between a stimulus condition and a desired response. The notion of an operant is that an individual operates on the environment by an action that has consequences. Reinforcers are designed to encourage desired consequences. Operant conditioning still informs some clinical treatments, classroom management techniques, programmed instruction, and animal training. A major principle established in operant conditioning involves the importance of providing timely and informative feedback to learners, which is a cornerstone of most modern instruction.

Social Learning Theory (Bandura)

Bandura's (1977, 1986) social learning theory builds on Vygotsky's work and emphasizes the notion that people learn from each other by such processes as observation, imitation, and modeling. Social learning theory can be viewed as forming a bridge between behaviorism and cognitivism. It is somewhat grounded in behaviorism as it focuses on observable processes such as watching someone else who is modeling or demonstrating that which is to be learned. Modeling as an instructional method requires the attention of the learner, the retention of what has been observed in some internal cognitive form, the ability to reproduce the action observed with some degree of fidelity to be judged by others and oneself, and the motivation to engage in the previous three processes. Because the situation in which the learner is engaged is critical, there are links to situated learning theory, which is discussed next.

Situated Learning Theory (Lave)

Lave's (1988) situated learning theory focuses on the unintentional and situated aspects of learning. While much learning occurs in structured classroom environments focused on concepts and declarative learning, a great deal of learning occurs in everyday activities involving human actions and performance. The relevant process in such learning is legitimate peripheral participation, which involves a learner moving from an observer-only status (e.g., an apprentice) to a practitioner guided by others. This naturalistic description of how people come to know many things in everyday situations has led instructional designers to create similar environments in intentional learning environments. The most robust instructional design theory based on situated learning is *cognitive apprenticeship* (Brown, Collins, & Duguid, 1989) in which early learners are provided a great deal of learning support (scaffolding), whereas more advanced learners are provided a great deal of freedom to explore and devise their own solutions.

Experiential Learning (Kolb)

Experiential learning theory is a four-stage, cyclical theory of learning that is fundamentally a cognitive theory with some behavioral aspects (true of many cognitive theories). The basic notion is that learning is grounded in experience—learning involves the transformation of an experience through internal processes into active knowledge that will inform future actions (Kolb, 1984). Just as the philosophical empiricists maintained that the starting point of a theory of knowledge must be experience, so does Kolb. First comes an experience. Then the learner naturally observes and reflects on that experience. The learner then forms concepts and perhaps rules based on how the experience has been filtered and understood by observation and reflection processes. Finally, a learner tries out this new understanding in novel situations. Each of these four stages occur naturally and without effort as part of a natural learning process, according to Experiential Learning Theory. However, each of these stages can also be more or less well supported by teachers, trainers, and a variety of technologies.

Cognitive Load Theory (Sweller)

Cognitive load theory is well within the cognitive information-processing perspective, although it also builds on behavioral principles (especially those pertaining to perception). The fundamental notion is that the human cognitive architecture has certain characteristics and limitations that account for why learning may or may not occur in some situations (Sweller, 1988). One serious limitation is that of short-term memory (also referred to by some as working memory; some use the term 'short-term memory' to refer to a physiological process whereas the term 'working memory' refers to a cognitive process; no distinction is made in this discussion); a person can only hold about seven things (plus or minus two) in short-term memory at any given time (Miller, 1956). Yet it would seem that experts are able to hold much more in short-term memory. How can we account for the apparent differences between experts and novices? Moreover, how can we account for differences in the usability of interfaces and learning environments among different users? Basically, cognitive load theory is aimed at providing such explanations. First, in addition to short-term memory limitations, different kinds of cognitive load are distinguished. Intrinsic load is that which is inherent in the problem or situation itself and cannot be manipulated to any significant extent. Second, extrinsic cognitive load is that which occurs in the situation context and which might be reduced or minimized. Third, germane cognitive load is that which directs the learner to the essential features of the problem situation and allows some things to be ignored. Experts have developed the ability to ignore nearly all of the extrinsic load factors and focus without assistance on the essential features of the situation. They have the same short-term memory limitations of novices, but they have learned to manage that which enters short-term memory. The implications for instructional design are clear: (a) minimize extrinsic load factors in an instructional situation ("when in doubt, leave it out"), and (b) help new learners focus on that which is essential without generating additional extrinsic load ("when in doubt, point it out").

A Theory of Change

When designing an instructional intervention or educational reform, it is helpful and sometimes required by funding agencies and others to provide a theoretical and

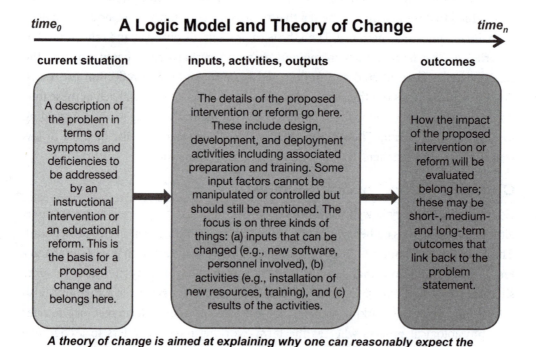

A theory of change is aimed at explaining why one can reasonably expect the proposed intervention or reform (middle column) to transform the problematic situation (first column) into a more desirable situation (last column). Both theory and empirical evidence are part of a theory of change.

FIGURE 8.2 A representation of a theory of change in a logic model

empirical justification for the change. That justification is often developed in association with a logic model that describes the current problem or situation, the things that influence the situation, aspects of the intervention or reform, interim results of the development and deployment of the intervention, and the short-, medium-, and long-term outcomes anticipated to result from the intervention. Since intervention is essentially a change, a theory of change is intended to explain why one would expect the proposed intervention to result in the anticipated outcomes. Such a theory is typically built on the basis of existing theories and related studies implemented that suggest the applicability of the theory and proposed change to the current situation (see Figure 8.2).

Test Your Understanding

Match the things in Column A with the things most closely associated in Column B (each Column A entry has 0 to 4 pointers to entries in Column B).

Column A	Column B
Behaviorism	a. is a learning theory
Cognitivism	b. is a philosophical perspective
Constructivism	c. is a debating theory
Operant conditioning	d. involves mental stress
Cognitive load	e. argues that learners create internal representations
Social learning	f. maintains that humans are not animals
Experiential learning	g. is a cyclical theory of learning
Situated learning	h. posits that what is observable is paramount
Critical theory	i. presumes that internal representations exist
Humanism	j. is associated with cognitive apprenticeship
	k. emphasizes timely and informative feedback
	l. involves reinforcement processes
	m. is in the behaviorist perspective
	n. involves abductive logic

A Representative Educational Technology Challenge

As an educational technology expert, you have been invited to a meeting of a parents' association at a school that has recently introduced many innovative technologies for students. A great deal of taxpayers' money was used to completely renovate the school's technology infrastructure, and then acquire and deploy many new technology-based learning materials and instructional systems. Among the new materials are a series of simulation-based game environments known popularly as the SIMs. These games are highly interactive and allow students to manipulate about a half dozen variables in order to achieve a desired outcome such as maximizing the number of adults who vote in an election. The new learning technologies have been in the school for two years but there have been no noticeable changes in graduate rates, dropout rates, attendance, or scores on state and national tests. The parents are concerned that their investment has been wasted. You have been asked to testify as to whether or not that is the case, and why or why not.

Learning Activities

1. Identify and describe the key factors that you would consider in framing your response to the problem situation stated above.
2. Identify and describe the key factors that are likely to be in contention between parents, teachers, administrators, and designers.
3. Indicate and describe the relationships among all of the key factors that have been identified.
4. Indicate what things should be targets of change in order to make the best of this problematic situation.
5. Create an annotated concept map that reflects the things indicated in response to the previous four tasks.
6. Reflect on your responses and your concept map, and then describe the assumptions you have made and what resources would be required to implement the solution you have in mind; present this response in the form of a logic model that includes a theory of change.

Links

The ACT-R website at Carnegie Mellon University—http://act-r.psy.cmu.edu

Learning Theories site on Bandura's Social Learning Theory—see www.learning-theories.com/social-learning-theory-bandura.html

Other Resources

The Burgess Shale Geoscience Foundation site—see www.burgess-shale.bc.ca

John Dewey's *Democracy and Education* (now in the public domain)—see http://en.wikisource.org/wiki/Democracy_and_Education

Learning Theories site—www.learning-theories.com

The Mental Models & Reasoning Lab at Princeton University—see http://mentalmodels.princeton.edu

Nova Southeastern University's Collection of Learning Theory Resources—see www.nova.edu/~burmeist/learning_theory.html

Stanford Encyclopedia of Philosophy on Critical Theory—see http/plat:/o.stanford.edu/entries/critical-theory

Note

1. The emphasis here is on human learning. A general theory of learning would apply to all sentient creatures, but that issue is not taken up in this book.

References

Anderson, J. R. (1996). A simple theory of complex cognition. *American Psychologist, 51*, 355–365.

Bandura, A. (1977). *Social learning theory*. New York: General Learning Press.

Bandura, A. (1986). *Social foundations of thought and action*. Englewood Cliffs, NJ: Prentice-Hall.

Bransford, J. D., Brown, A. L., & Cocking, R. R. (2000). *How people learn: Brain, mind, experience and school*. Washington, DC: National Academy Press.

Brown, J. S., Collins, A., & Duguid, S. (1989). Situated cognition and the culture of learning. *Educational Researcher, 18*(1), 32–42.

Chomsky, N. (1967). A review of B. F. Skinner's *Verbal Behavior*. In L. A. Jakobits & S. M. Murray (Eds.), *Readings in the psychology of language* (pp. 142–143). Englewood Cliffs, NJ: Prentice-Hall.

Dewey, J. (1916). Democracy and education: An introduction to the philosophy of education. New York: Macmillan.

Driscoll, M. P. (2005). Psychology of learning for instruction (3rd ed.). New York: Allyn & Bacon.

Festinger, L. (1957). *A theory of cognitive dissonance*. Stanford, CA: Stanford University Press.

Habermas, J. (1971). *Knowledge and human interest*. Boston, MA: Beacon Press.

Horkheimer, H., & Adorno, T. W. (1972). *Dialectic of enlightenment*. New York: Seabury.

Johnson-Laird, P. N. (1983). *Mental models: Towards a cognitive science of language, inference, and consciousness*. Cambridge: Cambridge University Press.

Kim, C., & Keller, J. M. (2010). Motivation, volition and belief change strategies to improve mathematics learning. *Journal of Computer Assisted Learning, 26*, 407–420.

Kolb, D. A. (1984). *Experiential learning: Experience as the source of learning and development*. Englewood Cliffs, NJ: Prentice-Hall.

Kuhn, T. S. (1962). *The structure of scientific revolutions*. Chicago: University of Chicago Press.

Lave, J. (1988). *Cognition in practice: Mind, mathematics and culture in everyday life*. Cambridge: Cambridge University Press.

Maslow, A. H. (1943). A theory of human motivation. *Psychological Review*, 370–396.

Miller, G. A. (1956). The magic number seven, plus or minus two: Some limits on our capacity for processing information. *Psychological Review, 63*(2), 81–97.

Peirce, C. S. (1931). *The collected papers of Charles Sanders Peirce Volume 5: Pragmatism and pragmatism*. Cambridge, MA: Harvard University Press. Retrieved from www.textlog.de/peirce_pragmatism.html

Popper, K. (1963). Conjectures and refutations: The growth of scientific knowledge. London: Routledge.

Popper, K. (1972). *Objective knowledge: An evolutionary approach*. Oxford: Clarendon Press.

Quine, W. V. O., & Ullian, J. S. (1978). *The web of belief* (2nd ed.). New York: McGraw-Hill.

Richey, R. C., Klein, J. D., & Tracey, M. W. (2011). *The instructional design knowledge base: Theory, research and practice*. New York: Routledge.

Schunk, D. H. (2007). *Learning theories: An educational perspective* (5th ed.). New York: Prentice Hall.

Skinner, B. F. (1954). The science of learning and the art of teaching. *Harvard Educational Review, 24*(2), 86–97.

Sweller, J. (1988). Cognitive load during problem solving: Effects on learning. *Cognitive Science, 12,* 257–285.

Watson, J. (1913). Psychology as a behaviorist views it. *Psychological Review, 20,* 158–177.

Wittgenstein, L. (1922). *Tractatus logico-philosophicus* (Trans. C. K. Ogden). London: Kegan Paul, Trench, Trubner & Co. Retrieved from www.gutenberg.org/files/5740/5740-pdf.pdf?session_id=bb209e50f65d 3ca148f096fe9bbb569e1024044b

nine

Theories of Information and Communications

"'When I use a word,' Humpty Dumpty said in rather a scornful tone, 'it means just what I choose it to mean—neither more nor less'" (from Lewis Carroll's Alice in Wonderland*)*

It is not uncommon to find the phrase 'information and communications technology' (ICT) in many papers and presentations pertaining to educational technology. It is interesting to find 'information' and 'communication' used together in this way, particularly because they have somewhat different theoretical foundations. Clearly, the two are related in the sense that when we communicate, which occurs often in educational settings, we generally intend to communicate something and that something is often information. In what follows, the two are discussed individually prior to providing remarks about the implications of the two considered together for purposes of educational technology implementations and instructional design, development, and deployment.

Information and Information Theories

What Is Information?

Figure 9.1 depicts a familiar hierarchical view of the relationship between data, information, knowledge, and wisdom. If one thinks about the generations of computers, the first generation of programmable computing machines created during and just after World War II was aimed at data processing. These early computers were essentially very large calculators, able to perform calculations faster and with more accuracy than was previously possible. Machine language was used to code programs that could collect, analyze, and generate reports of large data sets. Many early applications for computers were for the military; this was the case with ENIAC (Electronic Numerical Integrator and Computer), which was designed to compute ballistic firing tables during WWII. One can then imagine a representative bit of data in ENIAC as a set of coordinates locating a target encoded as a series of zeroes and ones. The sequence of zeroes and ones could be considered unstructured data. Only when a sequence was translated into coordinates did those data become information.

The 1950s saw the introduction of commercial applications and transistors that replaced the vacuum tubes used previously. Higher level languages such as COBOL and FORTRAN were also introduced, and commercial applications began to proliferate. This marked a transition from computers as data processors to computers as information processors; the latter flourished in a third generation of computers that made use of even smaller integrated circuits and the introduction of mini-computers. These developments made it possible for businesses to use third-generation computers to process information—structured data—that could manage inventories, payrolls, and many other daily business applications. From the perspective of information-processing computers, a bit of information might be something like the ratio of sales revenue to salary expenditures—that is to say, the data were structured and provided support for interpretation.

To carry the story forward, a fourth generation of computers is typically associated with even smaller and more powerful microprocessors (large-scale integrated circuits) introduced in the 1970s and the subsequent introduction of personal computers in the 1980s. These machines brought information processing into the hands of millions of users who became linked together in ever larger and more powerful computer networks.

A fifth generation of computers is in the works that is aimed at making a transition to knowledge processing through a group of technologies collectively referred to as artificial intelligence. While there have been advances in knowledge processing, the challenges of processing open-ended, natural language sequences (such as occur in every-day conversation) remain a serious challenge. Progress will certainly continue, as shown by how smartphones are now integrating natural language feedback to their users based on the current situation and information stored from prior activities. In short, the age of knowledge processing is arriving.

One can only wonder if there will ever be a transition to machine processors of wisdom (since humans only sporadically demonstrate wisdom, this may be out of reach for machines). With regard to the top part of the hierarchy in Figure 9.1, there can only be speculation at this point in human history.

What can be taken away from this discussion? Hopefully, the quick review of computer generations will provide historical context and an improved understanding of what might become possible in future generations of computers and so-called smart technologies (those that adapt automatically and appropriately to situations and users). Douglas

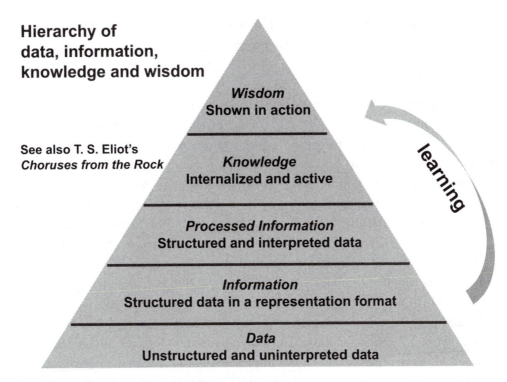

Hierarchy of data, information, knowledge and wisdom

Wisdom
Shown in action

See also T. S. Eliot's
Choruses from the Rock

Knowledge
Internalized and active

Processed Information
Structured and interpreted data

Information
Structured data in a representation format

Data
Unstructured and uninterpreted data

learning

FIGURE 9.1 Data, information, knowledge, and wisdom

Engelbart, the inventor of the computer mouse and timesharing, among other computer innovations, speculated in the early 1960s that computer circuits would continue to get smaller and more powerful at a rapid rate. Engelbart's hypothesis was put into a formula in 1965 by Gordon Moore, the cofounder of Intel; the formula predicted that the number of transistors on an integrated circuit would double about every two years. This formula is known today as Moore's Law and has been extended from the number of transistors on a circuit to reflect the general trend of computing devices to become smaller, faster, and more powerful every few years (Meindl, 2003). There is ample evidence to support that general trend to smaller and more powerful devices—smart watches and interactive glasses bring wearable computing power to humans, and nano-computing devices embedded in the human body will most likely follow.

Figure 9.1 makes a distinction between information and processed or interpreted information. There is a parallel distinction to make with regard to people. Information may exist as structured data to be used by people, but people must still find and interpret that information. Cognitive scientists create models of the human mind that are inspired by models of computer processors, but there is a significant difference in that different people may interpret the same set of information quite differently. Interpretation and use of information is quite important for human information processors. Understanding how humans perceive, interpret, and use information is important to those designing systems and technologies to support learning and performance. While knowledge of how to make and use smart technologies is progressing at a very rapid rate, our knowledge of how to help people become smarter is progressing much more slowly.

Information Theory

The classical treatment of information theory is within the context of applied mathematics as a way of explaining and predicting the limits of signal processing. In other words, there is an historical connection between information theory and communication theory. Claude Shannon (1948) is generally regarded as the founder of information theory with his mathematical treatment of communication. Key concepts in the model of communication developed by Shannon and Weaver (1949) include: (a) information, (b) uncertainty, (c) entropy, (d) redundancy, and (e) noise. For Shannon and Weaver, who were concerned with the transmission of messages through electronic signals, 'information' is a measure of the freedom of choice in selecting a message. As the message is designed to remove uncertainty in the situation, the message generally becomes more detailed and requires more information to be transmitted. Entropy refers to the lack of order or randomness in a given situation; as entropy increases so do uncertainty and the need for more detailed and specific messages. Redundancy in a message adds no new information but is important in dealing with the issue of noise or disturbance of signals. In other words, in addition to information, the intent and the interpretation play a significant role in communication. Shannon and Weaver focused on the message and the means of transmission rather than on the human interpreter, although many of their findings have strong implications for supporting human interpretation and predicting the occurrence of misinterpretations.

The Shannon and Weaver model assumes an initiator of a message, an encoder, a means of transmission, and a decoder and receiver. Noise intervenes primarily during the transmission process, but noise can interfere with both encoding and decoding processes as well. The aim of Shannon and Weaver's model was to make efficient use of information by reducing uncertainty and improving the quality of communication. The theory was developed to support the goal of getting the required information to the destination with minimal distortion using the most efficient means possible. That goal is of keen interest to instructional designers and teachers who want to provide information to a variety of students who are likely to process the received information quite differently. In short, efficiency of representation is a major concern for message designers with broad application well beyond the domain of signal processing.

Communication and Communication Theories

What Is Communication?

In a familiar albeit informal sense, communicating is simply the sharing of information. However, given that people are creators of internal representations of their experiences (the central tenet of a constructivist epistemology), it is important to take into account communication as far more than a process of moving information from one place to another. If one considers the nuances of meaning between the noun 'communication' and the verb 'communicating,' one might detect a significant difference in emphasis. A communication—the noun—typically refers to a static representation of information, such as a message, a letter, or perhaps a record or memory of a telephone conversation. On the other hand, communicating—the verb—typically refers to a dynamic process in which one or more persons (the source) attempt to provide another person or group with an understanding of something. In the latter case, the ways in which different people interpret messages are relevant and important for successful communication. A communication can be regarded as successful when the information intended to be conveyed has been interpreted as it was intended (more or less, as this is sometimes difficult to determine due to the inherent fuzziness of many intentions and interpretations).

Communication Theory

Communicating is a fundamental aspect of being a person, and different forms of communication are pervasive in human society today as well as in the distant past. The 3,000 or more pictographs and petroglyphs left behind by the Jornado Mogollon people and others at Hueco Tanks in Texas represent a very old form of pictographic communication, probably associated with religious rituals. Ancient written or carved texts date back several thousand years; the *Iliad* was written down around 800 BCE, ancient Hebrew texts around 1000 BCE, the Hindu Vedas around 1500 BCE, and Egyptian Pyramid texts as far back as 3100 BCE. Storytelling and human language presumably go back much further in time. In short, the use of language is part and parcel of human history and everyday existence.

As with learning theories, there are multiple perspectives to consider with regard to communication theory. These include a mechanistic perspective (e.g., a simple sender–receiver model), a psychological perspective (e.g., a focus on interpretation and feelings), a social constructivist perspective (e.g., a focus on the creation of internal representations and interpretations along with subsequent external representations and sharing with others), a systemic perspective (e.g., a focus on throughput and efficiency as suggested by Shannon and Weaver), and a critical perspective (e.g., somewhat similar to the critical theory perspective discussed in the previous chapter).

Given such a variety of perspectives and many different contexts for communications, it is difficult to treat communication theory as a unified discipline (for a comprehensive list of communication theories and models, see Em Griffin's website at www.afirstlook.com/main.cfm/book). There is, however, one general principle that appears to be accepted by most theorists—namely Scudder's (1980) *Universal Communication Law*, which states that all living things communicate through sounds, reactions, physical exchanges, movements, gestures, languages or other means. All living things communicate. Do we always communicate effectively? Hardly. An interesting classroom activity would be to relate stories (an ancient form of communicating) about communication gone awry. These stories are likely to be both entertaining and insightful.

What are called theories of communication are really models of communication, which is what Shannon and Weaver called their theory of information. Shannon and Weaver (1949) did, however, have a theory in the traditional scientific sense as their theory identified relevant components, relationships, and processes with operational measures and, as a consequence, supported the ability to predict or explain various cases of effective as well as ineffective communication. What follows are more properly considered models that have many components, relationships, and processes identified but that fall short of being able to systematically generate testable hypotheses. Still, these models of communication are relevant to educational technologists and instructional designers as they involve key aspects of media and representations that are vital to effective learning and instruction (see, for example, http://pegasus.cc.ucf.edu/~rbrokaw/commtheory.html).

Communication Models

Journalistic Models

Lasswell's (1948) model is a standard point of departure for journalists who want to understand communication. Lasswell argues that the relevant components are expressed in the following phrase: "**who** says **what** to **whom** in what **channel** with what **effect**." In other words, the relevant components are the source, the message itself, the destination, the medium or media, and the desired outcome(s) (see also, Berlo, 1960). Many studies have been conducted using these components to determine what impact they have on each other and the desired outcome within the context of learning and instruction.

Such a model can inform much of the message design aspect of instructional development. Message designers take into account the content, the audience, the means used to convey the message, the intended purpose or outcome, and associated development and implementation costs (Fleming & Levie, 1993). None of these are trivial concerns for an instructional designer; message design is a micro-level activity (focusing on specific parts of a unit of instruction) that is closely intertwined with more macro-level (e.g., course level) decisions involving multimedia and related matters such as visual literacy, alternate forms of representation, and support for those with special needs (e.g., the hearing and vision impaired, second language learners, etc.) (Lohr, 2007).

Constructionist Models

A constructionist model of communication builds on the source–message–channel–receiver behaviorist model (Berlo, 1960) and subsequent cognitive extensions to that model. A constructionist model emphasizes (a) the close and dynamic interconnections between the source, message, channel, and receiver, and (b) the pragmatic reality that the four components (source, message, channel, and receiver) are not entirely separable given the nature of people as creators of meaning (via internal representations). In other words, a constructionist model of communication tends to treat communication as a holistic process influenced by language and culture as well as by individual components. Emphasis is placed on the active role of senders in creating an external representation of a message to be sent to a receiver who will actively construct an internal representation as part of the interpretation process. Figure 9.2 is one example of a constructionist model of communication adapted from Foulger's (2004) ecological model. The constructive role that individuals play as creators and as interpreters of messages is what makes this a constructionist model of communication.

The resources section at the end of this chapter provides links to many models and theories of communication. Those discussed here are a very small but hopefully suggestive representation of the richness of this domain of inquiry.

Perspectives on and Criteria for Communication Models and Theories

One can cluster communication models and theories in a number of ways (see www.academia.edu/2910766/Theories_and_Models_of_Communication_Information_ Theories_2013_e). Table 9.1 shows representative relationships between several types of communication models and the perspectives behind and uses of those models. It is clear that aspects of more than one communication model might be pertinent in any given situation.

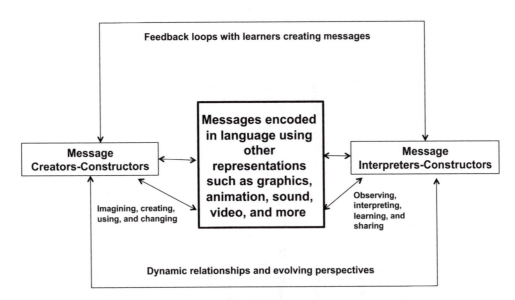

FIGURE 9.2 A constructionist model of communication

TABLE 9.1 Communication models, perspectives, and uses

	Practical–journalist	Scientific–behaviorist	Scientific–cognitive	Humanistic–constructionist
Purpose	Guide practice	Establish universal laws	Establish reliable information	Guide interpretation
Example area of application	Reporting facts; making presentations	Determining efficient communication means	Designing effective messages	Designing learning environments
Epistemology	Common sense	Objective truths	Accepted truths	Meaning making
Research	Best practices	Experimental studies	Mixed methods	Ethnographic studies
Evaluation	Community of practice agreement	Explanatory and predictive power	Understanding effective communication	Understanding of complex phenomena
Example	Lasswell (1948)	Berlo (1960)	Cushman & Whiting (1972)	Foulger (2004)

Implications for Educational Technology

On the practical side, it is worth noting that the International Board of Standards for Training, Performance and Instruction (ibstpi; see www.ibstpi.org) found that professional practitioners in the fields of instructional design and training management ranked communication skills as the most critical skills required in the performance of their jobs and everyday tasks. When one looks at what educational technologists do in any context (K-12, higher education, business, government, etc.), one can see that communication is involved in multiple ways and that effective communication is critical for success in a great variety of contexts.

As an example, an instructional designer will typically need to communicate with project sponsors and management; this requires a business-oriented style and tone of communication. They will also need to communicate with content specialists as a learning environment or training system is being developed; this requires a general understanding of a particular knowledge domain and the vocabulary used by professionals in that domain. An instructional designer might also need to communicate with technical specialists about various aspects of a learning environment or training system, and that requires the ability to speak in terms familiar to those specialists. There are also aspects of message design for which an instructional designer might be responsible; this requires an understanding of the affordances of various media and human factors considerations in many cases. Given the prevalence of multimedia and the Internet, the ability to integrate visual explanations into a communication are increasingly important (see, for example, Tufte, 1997).

Similar comments could be made about the communication requirements of teachers and professors. They, like other professionals, communicate with a variety of people with different backgrounds and knowledge, and the effectiveness of communication will very likely be directly connected with the quality and success of their work.

Table 9.2 is a matrix relating the context of the communication (one-to-one, one-to-many, etc.) with the format (electronic or nonelectronic), timing (synchronous or asynchronous), examples, and instructional uses. Clearly, other dimensions and aspects of communication tools and techniques could be added to this matrix. As many cases involve just one or a very small number of persons on one side of the communication, 'one' and 'a few' are grouped together. One-to-self is also possible, as is one-to-no-one, but these are omitted. Other dimensions are clearly possible, such as whether or not the communication is two-way, whether or not multimedia are involved, using multiple contexts, formats, and timing models together, and so on; such dimensions are clearly important in many contexts. Some examples could appear in other categories. Only a few instructional uses are suggested—others are clearly possible. Specific tools and technologies are not mentioned in the examples column as new tools continually emerge. Students and instructors are invited to fill in blanks in the table and to suggest additional instructional uses and specific tools—there are many.

TABLE 9.2 Communications matrix

Context	Format	Timing	Examples	Instructional uses
One/few → One/few	Electronic	Synchronous	Telephone, online chat, smartphone	Directed dialogue with a student
		Asynchronous	Email, text message, tweet	Reporting outcomes
	Nonelectronic	Synchronous	Conversation over coffee	Individual tutoring session
		Asynchronous	Letter, postcard	Homework with a feedback session
One/few → many	Electronic	Synchronous	Webinar, blog, video-conference	Introductory tutorial
		Asynchronous	Online Q&A page, web-/podcast, forum	Supporting resource or information
	Nonelectronic	Synchronous	Classroom lecture	[P]review basic information
		Asynchronous		
Many → one/few	Electronic	Synchronous	Electronic voting	Determine student readiness
		Asynchronous	Online survey, wiki	Determine student preferences
	Nonelectronic	Synchronous	Focus group discussion	Develop consensus view
		Asynchronous		
Many → many	Electronic	Synchronous	Online polling, group conferencing	Brainstorming session to generate and critique new ideas
		Asynchronous	Online discussion forum, group conferencing	Collaborative development of an artifact
	Nonelectronic	Synchronous	Town hall meeting, protest march	[Sub-]group learning activity
		Asynchronous		

Web 2.0 introduced many tools and technologies to support social networking, and these have found their way into learning and instruction. Blogs, forums, wikis, social networking sites, and many more are now available to students and teachers who wish to create communication-rich learning environments in collaboration and communication with others.

Test Your Understanding

Answer the following short answer questions:

1. What do the individual letters in Berlo's S-M-C-R model stand for?
2. Indicate four of the general questions that Lasswell believes should be asked when gathering facts about a situation.
3. Cite one reason that one might want to treat a communication as a holistic entity rather than a collection of discrete parts.
4. Cite one reason that a communication might be treated as a dynamic activity rather than a static sequence of events.
5. Describe two activities that require an understanding of communication in your everyday work.

A Representative Educational Technology Challenge

As an experienced message designer, you have been asked to provide support for a meeting of the parents' association at a school that has recently introduced many innovative technologies for students. A great deal of taxpayers' money was used to completely renovate the school's technology infrastructure, and then acquire and deploy many new technology-based learning materials and instructional systems. Among the new materials are a series of simulation-based game environments known popularly as the SIMs. These games are highly interactive and allow students to manipulate about a half-dozen variables in order to achieve a desired outcome such as maximizing the number of adults who vote in an election. The new learning technologies have been in the school for two years but there have been no noticeable changes in graduate rates, dropout rates, attendance, or scores on state and national tests. The parents are concerned that their investment has been wasted. You have been asked to create a brief white paper with visuals to support the school principal who will be providing a defense of the investment in educational technology.

Learning Activities

1. Identify and describe the key factors that you would consider in framing your response to the problem situation stated above.
2. Identify and describe the key factors that are likely to be effective in communicating with parents.
3. Indicate and describe the relationships among all of the key factors that have been identified.

4. Indicate what kinds of visual support should be considered in order to make the best argument in this problematic situation.

5. Create an annotated concept map that reflects the things indicated in response to the previous four tasks.

Links

Em Griffin's First Look at Communication Theory website—see www.afirstlook.com/main.cfm/book

Robert Gwynne's website on communication models—see http://pegasus.cc.ucf.edu/~rbrokaw/commtheory.html

Other Resources

The Center for the Study of Complex Systems at the University of Michigan—see http://cscs.umich.edu

Communication Theory Blogsite—see http://communicationtheory.org

Hueco Tanks State Park in Texas—see www.desertusa.com/mag00/may/stories/hueco.html

S. H. Kaminski's website on Communications Models—see www.shkaminski.com/Classes/Handouts/Communication%20Models.htm

McGraw-Hill website with a Glossary of Communications Theory Terms—see www.mhhe.com/mayfieldpub/westturner/student_resources/theories.htm

Theories and Models of Communication (2013 Handbook)—see www.academia.edu/2910766/Theories_and_Models_of_Communication_Information_Theories_2013

University of Colorado website on Communication Theory—see http://carbon.ucdenver.edu/~mryder/itc/comm_theory.html

University of Twente website on Theory Clusters—see www.utwente.nl/cw/theorieenoverzicht/Theory%20clusters

Wikibook on Communication Theory—see http://en.wikibooks.org/wiki/Communication_Theory

References

Berlo, D. K. (1960). The process of communication: An introduction to the theory and practice. New York: Holt, Rinehart & Winston.

Cushman, D., & Whiting, G. C. (1972). An approach to communication theory: Toward consensus on rules. *Journal of Communication, 22*, 217–238.

Fleming, M., & Levie, W. H. (Eds.) (1993). *Instructional message design: Principles from the behavioral and cognitive sciences* (2nd ed.). Englewood Cliffs, NJ: Educational Technology Publications.

Foulger, D. (2004). An ecological model of the communication process. Retrieved on February 25, 2011 from http://davis.foulger.info/papers/ecologicalModelOfCommunication.htm

Lasswell, H. (1948). The structure and function of communication in society. In L. Bryson (Ed.), *The communication of ideas* (pp. 203–243). New York: Harper & Row.

Lohr, L. (2007). *Creating visuals for learning and performance: Lessons in visual literacy* (2nd ed.). Cleveland, OH: Prentice-Hall.

Meindl, J. D. (2003). Beyond Moore's Law: The interconnect era. *Computing in Science and Engineering, 5*(1), 20–24.

Scudder, S. F. (1980). As cited in Wikipedia, Environmental communication. Retrieved from http://digplanet.com/wiki/Environmental_communication

Shannon, C. E. (1948). A mathematical theory of communication. *Bell System Technical Journal, 27*, 379–423 and 623–656.

Shannon, C. E., & Weaver, W. (1949). *The mathematical theory of communication.* Urbana, IL: The University of Illinois Press.

Tufte, E. R. (1997). *Visual explanations: Images and quantities, evidence and narrative.* Cheshire, CN: Graphics Press.

ten
Instructional Theories and Instructional Design Theories

"People may learn facts, but what for? They may learn new concepts, but how are these to function in the context of the larger task that they as human individuals do? Learners can acquire procedures, but in the context of what larger scale activity? Performances may be described, not simply as steps in a sequence but also in terms of their function and purpose in meeting the goal of an activity as a whole" (from Gagné and Merrill, 1990)

What is instruction? The easy but vague answer is that instruction is that which facilitates and supports learning. So, if I am learning how to find cube roots using a slide rule, then a set of directions on how to do that is one example of instruction. Perhaps so, but then suppose that I am trying to find out how to cross a mountain stream with dangerously fast rushing water that is too wide to simply jump across and too dangerous to swim across. I can find a recently fallen tree and place it across the stream and then walk across. In that case, is the dead tree an example of instruction? It supported my finding out how to cross the stream, but perhaps it should not count as instruction. We need to make the definition of instruction somewhat more precise.

Not everything that facilitates and supports learning should count as instruction. The caffeine used to keep someone awake through a long lecture class is not instruction, but it may facilitate learning. Moreover, something intended to support learning may accidentally interfere with learning, but, given the intent to support learning, it might still count as instruction, albeit ineffective instruction in that case. An interesting classroom activity would be to discuss some examples of things intended to serve as instruction and support learning that sometimes fail to help or perhaps even interfere with learning. An initial example to consider might be a short and humorous video clip that is loosely related to the learning topic. Suppose the learning topic is the human brain in a college course on human physiology. The video clip used to start the lesson is a

humorous talk by Mark Gungor found on YouTube (see www.youtube.com/watch?v=
0BxckAMaTDc). Would that support or inhibit learning? How might one determine to
what extent it helped or hindered?

Education and educational theory is, or should be considered to be, overtly and
explicitly value-centered. Values advocated by different educational theorists may differ,
but it is clear that values are at the core. For example, according to Dewey (1907), the
purpose of education is ensure that children become adults who are able to make
informed, pertinent, and effective judgments with regard to the problems they encounter
in their lives and in society. The notion of education being directed toward citizenship
is widespread and certainly not limited to Western democracies. The Marxist view of
education also emphasizes developing informed citizens through activity, collaboration,
and critique (see, for example, Vygotsky, 1978). Ironically, societies that seem far apart
in political terms are quite similar in educational outlook.

Instruction and instructional design are also value-centered but in a much different
way. Whereas educational theorists create arguments to support a position they
advocate, instructional theorists accept a goal as given and then adopt a value proposition
such as achieving the indicated goal for as many learners as possible in the least amount
of time using available resources. For example, according to Bruner (1966), instruction
is concerned with optimal sequences that will help someone master particular goals and
become a self-sufficient problem solver in a targeted area.

At this point in the discussion, it might be worthwhile to pause and critique the
following claims: (a) educational values are widely shared across societies with very
different political, cultural, and religious perspectives, (b) a primary goal of instruction
is to enable students to become self-sufficient problem solvers in a given domain, and
(c) a primary value of instruction is efficiency. One can and should discuss, critique,
and challenge such claims.

Before continuing with a discussion of instructional theories and instructional design
theories, two things are in order—one is an observation and the other is an advance
organizer (Ausubel, 1963) for the next two sections. First, a volume frequently cited in
this book is *The Instructional Design Knowledge Base* by Richey, Klein, and Tracey (2011),
which provides an excellent treatment of instructional and instructional design theories,
as well as many related areas. However, it is noteworthy that 'education' and 'instruction'
are not included in the glossary of that volume. Moreover, there are no references to
John Dewey, although there is a reference to Vygotsky. I suppose this means that
'education' and 'instruction' are either so well understood that they require no precise
definition or extended discussion as that given to 'knowledge' in that volume, or, possibly,
that these terms are indirectly defined throughout the volume.

Second, we should proceed with some sense of the meanings associated with
'instruction,' 'instructional theory,' and 'instructional design theory.' The proposition
recommended herein is to adopt Bruner's definition of 'instruction' indicated above:
instruction is that which is concerned with optimal sequences that will help a learner

master particular goals and become a self-sufficient problem solver in a targeted area. This definition then allows one to think of instructional theories as focused on what is required to master different goals and to conceptualize instructional design theories as focused on optimal sequences. Of course there is much more to be said about all three concepts. In addition, there are other definitions of instruction that might be discussed in class, especially with regard to implications for instructional design, development, and research.

Instructional Theories

A theory is typically composed of various principles. Prior to considering instructional theory per se, it might be useful to discuss a representative instructional principle. One such principle that is supported by substantial empirical research and that occurs in many instructional contexts pertains to teaching concepts. The word 'concept' is used informally to refer to a general idea or notion that pertains to a number of things or situations, such as the concept of education or the concept of efficiency. Concepts are different from facts, which refer to specific instances and situations, such as 'Columbus sailed the ocean blue in 1492.' That fact contains several concepts including 'ocean' and 'blue.' The focus for the moment is on concepts.

For this discussion, a concept can be considered to refer to a kind of thing; the thing can be concrete or abstract and will typically share common features allowing it to be grouped with other things for a purpose. For example, a Boeing 777 (the thing in this case) is an airplane (the kind of thing in this case); it has fixed wings (common to airplanes and not common to other aircraft such as helicopters that have rotating wings). For a student to have mastered a particular concept and become self-sufficient in applying the concept, it would seem necessary to indicate what those common features are—in other words, a rule to guide proper categorization is appropriate for concept learning. To determine mastery of the concepts, both examples (e.g., other airplanes such as the Airbus 330) and nonexamples (e.g., the Apache helicopter) must be included (this also applies to the instructional presentation and not just the assessment of learning), and students would have to determine if the item belonged in the category or not. In effect, this requires two kinds of knowledge on the part of students—declarative knowledge (knowing that something is the case) and procedural knowledge (knowing how to do something, such as identify distinguishing features and then categorize things appropriately; see, for example, Tennyson & Cocchiarella, 1986).

If one analyzes the components involved in a typical concept learning activity, one can identify (a) the name of the concept and possibly its relationship to other concepts, (b) the essential features or typical characteristics used to identify examples, (c) examples of the concept, and (d) nonexamples of the concept. An instructional principle applying to concept learning might then indicate that all four components should be present to ensure concept learning; of course, there ought to be opportunities for practice with timely feedback.

Concepts are clearly important in organizing information and solving problems (Anderson, 1983; Gagné, 1985). Moreover, knowledge is generally cumulative and builds on things previously learned (Gagné, 1985; Gagné & Merrill, 1990; Seel, 2004). For these reasons, it is often helpful to include a representation of where a concept is in relation to other concepts. In short, a concept map in the form of a semantic hierarchy is often useful in focusing attention on a particular concept, and providing such a map can help learners organize information internally to facilitate storage and retrieval of the information—in this case, the information is the definition of a concept. Figure 10.1 provides an example of a concept map (in this case, a semantic network) that might be used to initiate teaching the concept 'tsunami.'

The instructional principle associated with concept learning would then suggest that a rule to guide the application of the term should be provided along with examples and nonexamples of the application of the rule. In this case, the rule is somewhat fuzzy as exactly how large the wave needs to be to qualify is not precisely defined. In such instances of a fuzzy definition, one can conceive of a corollary to the concept learning principle that adds additional features to the definition (e.g., incidental as well as essential or

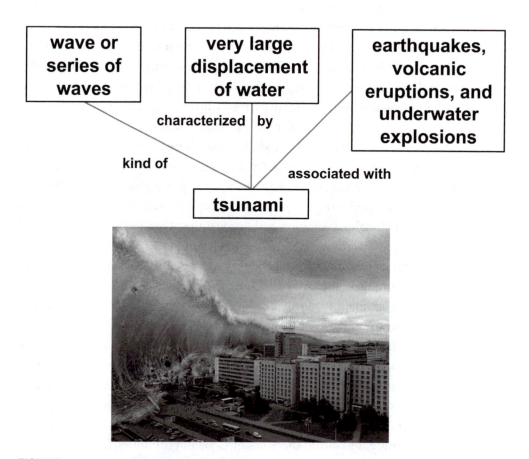

FIGURE 10.1 A sample concept map for 'tsunami'

relevant features) along with both simple and challenging cases to the instruction (see, for example, Taba, 1962). Figure 10.2 illustrates a Taba-inspired concept map for 'fish.'

If the instructional context is appropriate, it might be useful to consider an in-class activity to develop a concept map for 'instruction.' This could be a two-part activity with the first part aimed at a high-level semantic network to indicate what kind of thing instruction is, concepts related to instruction, and the nature of those relationships. The second part would be to provide essential and related but incidental features along with examples and nonexamples.

It is worth noting at this point that instructional designers typically divide concepts into two major kinds: concrete and abstract. Concrete concepts refer to categories that can be learned by pointing to objects—for example, by pointing to an elm tree and telling a child that "that is a tree" and pointing to a cactus plant and saying "that is not a tree." The child might even be able to induce a rule or guide for identifying trees, such as this: a tree is a large, woody perennial plant. Would a child really come up with such a definition? Not likely. What kind of rule might a child be more likely to develop? Of course, the definition or rule might also be taught explicitly, but the definition may introduce other concepts that might not have been learned (e.g., 'perennial plant').

On the other hand, there exist concepts without any specific physical objects to which one could point as examples. Examples of abstract concepts include freedom,

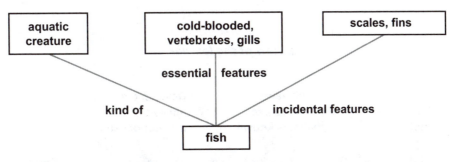

	Essential Features	Incidental Features	Examples
Clear example	cold-blooded, vertebrate, gills	aquatic life-form, scales, fins	bass, cod, salmon, tuna
Clear non-example	invertebrate	aquatic	jellyfish, cuttlefish
Challenging example	cold-blooded, vertebrate, gills	aquatic but lacks scales	catfish, lamprey eel
Challenging non-example	vertebrate	aquatic, fins	dolphins, whales

FIGURE 10.2 A representative concept map for 'fish'

happiness, and wisdom. In such cases, a somewhat fuzzy definition is usually provided along with illustrative cases that serve as examples and nonexamples. In one sense, all concepts are defined concepts because language is a critical part of concept learning, although the definitions might not be used when teaching some concrete concepts. Because language is critical in concept learning, and concept learning is critical for the development of knowledge and expertise, one can rightfully conclude that language plays a central role in learning and instruction.

Having provided an extended example of an instructional principle for teaching concepts, it is now reasonable to move to the larger view of instructional theory, which is the basis for such instructional principles. At a high level consistent with Bruner's (1962) definition of instruction, it is possible to think of instructional theory in terms of a flow from a learner's state of not knowing or not being to do something to a state of knowing or being to do that thing (see Figure 10.3).

Given a model such as that depicted in Figure 10.3, one can take either an instructor-centered or a student-centered approach—in fact, both are relevant to and required in an instructional theory. An instructional theory takes the best knowledge available from cognitive science and learning psychology, and uses that to devise instructional strategies (stated in the form of prescriptive instructional principles) intended to support the general flow indicated in Figure 10.3 (Richey, Klein, & Tracey, 2011; Reigeluth, 1983; Spector & Anderson, 2000).

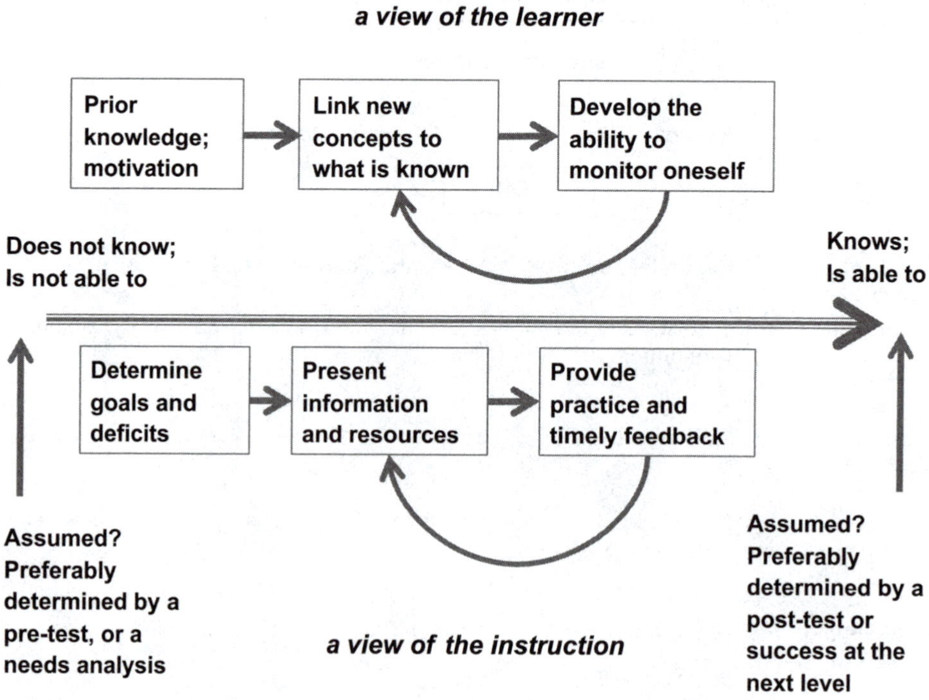

a view of the learner

FIGURE 10.3 A representation of instructional flow

Examples of such prescriptive instructional principles and strategies closely linked to cognitive science and learning psychology include the following:

1. Take into account the limitations of short-term memory and chunk information into manageable units appropriate for a learner's level of understanding.
2. When teaching concepts, be sure to include a definition, examples, nonexamples, and opportunities for practice with feedback; the order may not make much difference but all should be included explicitly.
3. Provide timely and meaningful feedback—what counts as timely and meaningful will depend on the learner's level of understanding.
4. Help the learner focus on the purpose and content of activities and resources.
5. Provide the learner with a basis for becoming motivated to learn and engaged with learning activities.
6. Provide the learner with a basis for becoming self-sufficient in the indicated activity or with the targeted type of task.
7. Align assessments with learning goals, objectives, and activities.

Merrill (2002, 2013) offers five very general principles of instruction: (1) learners should be engaged in solving meaningful problems; (2) existing learner knowledge pertinent to the task should be activated; (3) new knowledge and skills should be demonstrated in an appropriate context; (4) learners should have ample opportunity to apply new knowledge and skills with feedback; (5) learners should be encouraged to make the knowledge and skill a part of their everyday lives to the extent possible. Merrill (2002) called these the first principles of instruction, and they are extensively elaborated in the Merrill's 2013 volume.

Spector (2001) offers a somewhat different set of instructional principles: (a) learning is fundamentally about change, so instruction should be designed to promote desired changes; (b) experience is the starting point for understanding, so experience should be a critical component of instruction; (c) context determines meaning, so instruction should take place in meaningful contexts; (d) relevant contexts are often complex and multifaceted, so instruction should gradually introduce the complexities a learner is likely to encounter outside the learning situation; and (e) people know less than they are generally inclined to believe, so instruction should address what is not known as well as what is known. Spector's principles have two parts—one indicates the reason and the other indicates the action. Many instructional principles are presented in terms of if or when something is the case, then do this or that.

It should be noted that it is sometimes a challenge to get someone to admit that they do not know something that they have believed or assumed to be true for many years. However, the point of ignition for a learning endeavor is admitting that one does not know; the fuel that drives the learning endeavor forward is the desire to find an explanation or understand what is not known; what can help one reach the destination (understanding) is a willingness to explore alternative explanations and hypotheses.

As already noted, other instructional principles can be found in the literature. These examples are not intended to be comprehensive, nor are they meant to be sufficiently detailed to support direct application in an instructional situation. Rather they are intended to be representative of various principles that apply to instruction. These sample principles are generally stated in the form of prescriptions. A meaningful class activity would be to develop a matrix showing alternative instructional strategies that might be associated with each principle. An instructional strategy is a description of an approach to a particular instructional or learning activity. For example, instructional strategies associated with the fourth principle in the first set indicated above (help the learner focus) could be *expository* (e.g., state the purpose of the instructional unit) or *inquisitory* (e.g., ask the learner what useful things might be learned with regard to the subject at hand) or a combination of both.

Instructional strategies are closely linked with the type of thing to be learned. For example, if the thing to be learned is how to remove the radar from an airplane, then it would not be appropriate to only use expository or inquisitory instruction. This is a procedural task that is best learned by doing—of course, some information is necessary such as where the radar unit is located and what safety precautions must be taken. A strategy for learning such a task could be a combination of demonstrating and modeling the task, and then having learners perform the task. A variation could be breaking the task down into major subtasks and using a part-task approach. For example, the first preparatory steps might be treated as one chunk and practice until mastered.

There are many instructional strategies that instructional theorists have developed over the years in addition to the general expository and inquisitory strategies mentioned earlier. Examples include the following (these are only meant to be suggestive, as alternative strategies might be appropriate for the instances cited and this list is far from exhaustive):

a. Drill and practice—appropriate for learning verbal information that for whatever reason must be committed to memory.
b. Tutorial instruction—appropriate for learning simple procedures or how to navigate within a particular software system.
c. Exploratory instruction—appropriate for promoting understanding about phenomena new to the learner.
d. Interactive simulation—appropriate for promoting critical reasoning about dynamic, complex systems.
e. Socratic questioning—appropriate for helping a learner link something new and seemingly unfamiliar to something already understood.
f. Lecture—appropriate for introducing a new topic and creating some motivation and an appropriate foundation for that topic.

Of course, there are many more strategies, and they can be divided in many ways. At a course level, the general approach might be an experiential strategy, but at the unit level a lecture might be effective within that course, and at the activity level, a case-based collaborative discourse might be effective. What is important is to align the strategy with the type of thing to be learned. Determining the appropriate strategy for a particular task is an important aspect of instructional design, as already mentioned multiple times. The designer takes into account various strategies suggested by an instructional theory, along with the type of thing to be learned and the learners involved, and then describes how to deploy those strategies in order to achieve optimal learning outcomes.

Instructional Design Theories

Given the description of instructional theory as the development of principles and strategies to help learners move from states of not knowing and not being able to do certain things to states of knowing and being able to perform, one can characterize instructional design theory as focused on how best to deploy those principles and strategies in various circumstances. According to Reigeluth (1983, 1999), instructional design theory is prescriptive in nature; that is to say, the theory suggests with some degree of probability how to sequence material and activities using various strategies in order to achieve desired or targeted outcomes with a particular group of learners. Instructional design theory is different from instructional theory as previously described because it is both design- and goal-oriented. Learning theory is primarily descriptive, as is constructivist epistemology. Instructional theory provides a bridge between descriptive theories and instructional design by including a goal or targeted outcome. Instructional design theory goes one step further by including the notion of a design that links methods of instruction based on instructional theory with targeted outcomes in an efficient manner. This may seem like a fine distinction to some, but adding the aspect of design creates an entirely new set of considerations and challenges for both researchers and practitioners. Figure 10.4 depicts a concept map representing instructional design theory and its components (adapted from Reigeluth, 1999).

For the sake of illustration, consider the task of learning to tie knots. Based on a behavioral task analysis, the skill involved might be characterized as a psychomotor skill, but that would probably be overly simplistic as the truly critical aspect of knot tying is determining which kind of knot to tie for a particular purpose, and that involves an intellectual skill, as a cognitive task analysis would probably reveal (see Gagné, 1985). Who the learners are might make a huge difference in determining appropriate methods of instruction. If the learners are rescue personnel who might be required to piece together ropes and other materials in a rescue effort, then the desired outcome is the ability to identify the kind of knot required for a particular rescue situation given the resources available along with the ability to tie that kind of knot. With other learners, such as boy scouts, the desired outcome might be much more relaxed. The desired outcome then affects the appropriate methods. In the case involving training rescue personnel, the training must be to the point of automatic recognition and performance with repeated practice sessions until mastery of a large set of cases is complete.

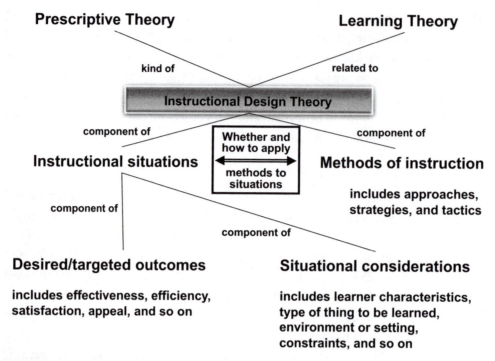

FIGURE 10.4 Components of instructional design theory

The point is that instructional design is far from a formulaic and static enterprise. The components are tightly interconnected. Deciding how best to select materials, develop effective learning activities, and sequence these is far from a simple task. Moreover, the materials, activities, and sequences can change dramatically based on a change in only one of the components to be considered when designing instruction.

All of the things represented in Figure 10.4 are subject to interpretation by different theorists, and that representation of instructional design is itself the subject of much debate (see Richey, Klein, & Tracey, 2011). To conclude this discussion of instructional design theories, representative examples of some of the critical components of instructional are elaborated next.

Types of Learning

It is possible to characterize the kinds of knowledge, skills, and attitudes in a number of ways, and several will be mentioned below. A traditional assumption in instructional design theory is that the type of thing to be learned significantly influences how best to design optimal instruction (support for achieving the desired outcome). What has been challenged in recent years is not the connection between the type of learning and the instructional methods, but rather how significant that connection is given other factors such as learners' characteristics and interests. The traditional chain of design factors is from the desired outcomes to learning needs (based on gaps between what learners know and can do, and what they are targeted to know and be able to do; this can and often does involve significant attention to learner differences) to assessment items, and on to design of appropriate support and activities, and finally to evaluation of outcomes. Some have referred to that generic chain as the ADDIE model—Analysis, Design, Development, Implementation, and Evaluation (see, for example, Dick, Carey, & Carey, 2009).

In the analysis phase of planning instruction, it is reasonable for a designer to consider the kinds of things to be learned (Anderson & Krathwohl, 2001). According to Gagné (1985), there are five different kinds of things that can be learned: (a) verbal information (e.g., facts), (b) intellectual skills (e.g., using rules to solve a problem), (c) cognitive strategies (e.g., selecting a process to address a problem situation), (d) motor skills (e.g., riding a bicycle), and (e) attitudes (e.g., dislike of mathematics). Figure 10.5 shows how Gagné's types of learning to common instructional strategies.

A quite different approach consistent with Merrill's (2002) principles of instruction (that places solving problems at the center of instruction) is to distinguish types of problems and use the type of problem to be solved as a guide to planning and implementing instruction (see, for example, Jonassen, 2000, 2004, 2007), as shown in Figure 10.6.

Problems can be characterized along a continuum from well structured (i.e., clearly and completely specified initial situation and desired outcome situation along with appropriate and recognizable means to transform the initial situation into the desired

Learning Type | Possible Strategies

Learning Type	Possible Strategies
Motor skills	drill and practice, games
Attitudes	role-playing, simulations
Verbal information	drill and practice, tutorial, games, lecture
Cognitive strategies	exploratory learning, simulations, socratic questioning
Intellectual skills – discrimination, concepts	drill and practice, tutorial, case study, lecture
Intellectual skills - principles	tutorial, exploratory learning, simulations, case study, games, lecture
Intellectual skills – problem-solving	exploratory learning, simulations, socratic questioning, case study, games, lecture

FIGURE 10.5 Linking types of learning to instructional strategies

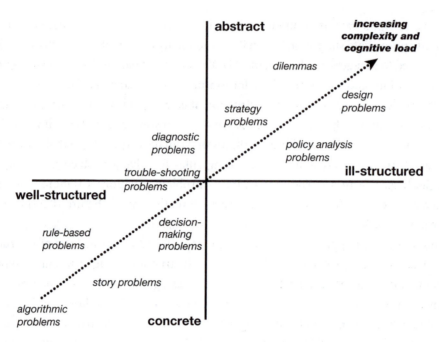

FIGURE 10.6 A taxonomy of problems and their characteristics (adapted from Jonassen, 2000, 2004, 2007)

outcome situation) to ill structured (i.e., missing some of the aspects of a well-structured problem). Problems can also be characterized in terms of the concepts and principles relevant to the problem situation, again along a continuum from concrete to abstract. Problems involving abstract concepts and principles that are also ill structured are generally complex and more challenging for learners to master. Design problems that occur in so many different domains (e.g., economics, education, engineering, management, manufacturing, technology) are among the most challenging to support with effective instruction (see Figure 10.6)

The purpose here is not to argue that one of these or another method of classifying types of learning is best. Rather, the main point is to suggest that the type of thing to be learned is an important aspect of instructional planning as it can help one identify a likely instructional method and strategy that might be appropriate. There are, of course, other aspects to be taken into account, including the learners and the setting in which learning will take place (see, for example, Eckel, 1993; Spector, Johnson & Young, 2014).

Types of Learners

Who are the learners? Are they children, adolescents, college students, working adults? How homogeneous are they in terms of prior knowledge and skills, motivation to learn, culture, language, gender, and so on? Why are they enrolled—is this instruction required, optional, voluntary? Did they pay for the instruction? Are they likely to receive compensation in some form for passing? These and many other questions need to be considered in order to plan activities that are meaningful for the learners as well as relevant to the instructional goals. The outlook suggested here is one of service orientation. Instructors and instructional designers serve those who enroll for instruction— students. We are here to serve and support learners. In order to fulfill that function, we need to know who the learners are and what kinds of support are most likely to be relevant and useful.

Just as there are multiple ways to characterize types of learning, there are multiple ways to characterize types of learners. One way to differentiate learners that has implications for the design of instruction is according to learning styles. Again, there are multiple approaches to describing learning styles, two of which are discussed next.

Kolb (1984) argued that learners pass through four stages of development: (a) concrete experience, (b) observation and reflection, (c) abstract concept formation, and (d) transference to new situations. With that four-stage model of learning and development in mind, Kolb then distinguished four types of learning styles (or learners) and the conditions which are most appropriate for each (see also www.businessballs.com/kolblearningstyles.htm):

a. *Assimilators*—prefer presentations based on a logical progression of concepts and theories.
b. *Convergers*—prefer to have (see and practice) practical applications of concepts and theories.
c. *Accommodators*—prefer to have hands-on experience and directly apply knowledge and skills.
d. *Divergers*—prefer to collect data and information and observe a range of different situations and circumstances.

It should be noted that Kolb's model of the learner has many critics as well as many advocates. There is a learning styles inventory based on Kolb that you can take and which may be available in your library. Several learning styles are available online should you wish to test yourself or your students (www.qcc.cuny.edu/cetl/pedagogy_learningStyles.html).

It is not clear how an instructional designer could plan a course for all the possible permutations of Kolb's learning preferences or any of the other possibilities, but one can suggest to students that it is generally advisable to become aware of one's own preferences, strengths, and limitations; such an awareness is an essential aspect of self-regulated learning. Fleming (1995) characterized learning styles somewhat differently (see www.vark-learn.com/english/index.asp) with four categories: (a) visual learners, (b) auditory learners, (c) kinesthetic learners, and (d) read/write learners. Visual learners prefer to see charts and graphics, and are able to gather information from such visual sources than from written or spoken text. Auditory learners have a preference for speaking as found in lecture and small group discussion settings. Kinesthetic learners have a preference to manipulate objects and see effects. Read/write learners prefer to learn from written texts. One advantage of Fleming's VARK system over Kolb's is that designers can more easily accommodate a variety of these styles in a design. Providing multiple representations of information is one way to accommodate multiple learning styles.

It is also possible to test yourself and your students at the VARK site located at www.vark-learn.com/english/index.asp. You can construct a matrix of likely strategies for each of these styles, and this would make a reasonable small group classroom activity.

Learning styles generally refer to learner preferences according to one or more dimensions. Learners are flexible and can adjust quite a bit. However, learners have other characteristics that are not quite as flexible. One group of such characteristics is called cognitive traits (Graf et al., 2009). Cognitive traits take into account such things as a learner's typical working memory capacity, which depends to a great extent on the learner's relative level of expertise in a particular domain. More advanced learners are able to chunk larger amounts of information into a single memory chunk and thus bring to bear more relevant information more quickly than inexperienced learners. Again, this has implications for the design of instruction. If you know that learners are typically very inexperienced in a particular domain, then much more support is likely to be appropriate for such learners.

Types of Learning Settings

Where will learning take place? Is the setting in a classroom? How is the room arranged? Will learners have computers or mobile devices and access to the Internet? Will they all be together at the same time in the same place? Will they have the ability to listen to audio files without disturbing others? Will they be in their workplace setting while engaged in learning? At home? Who else will be nearby and what will they be doing? Such questions are of obvious relevance to the design of learning materials and activities. Moreover, the setting may well change during an instructional sequence, even within the context of a single lesson. In some situations, the designer may decide that it is desirable to change the setting during an instructional unit or across multiple units of instruction. It is not uncommon to have a hybrid course environment in which some instruction occurs face-to-face (same time, same place for all learners and the instructor) in a traditional classroom and some occurs asynchronously in an online course management system (different time, different place for learners, and the instructor).

Materials developed for presentation in a lecture setting are not likely to work well in an online setting without substantial rework. Learning activities that can be deployed in a classroom typically require substantial reconceptualization to be used in an online setting. As mobile devices become more available to everyone and access to the Internet more affordable for all, taking into account the setting associated with learning becomes a significant challenge. There is no simple answer to such design challenges, but some guidelines are emerging, typically at the operational rather than the pedagogical level. For example, with regard to mobile learning, it is generally a good idea to provide dynamic support in terms of keeping track of what learners have done and providing reminders after a period of noninteraction. While it might not be an example of optimal learning, it is not at all far-fetched to image in a student learning a foreign language with a smartphone while at the beach on holiday, especially if the beach is in a foreign country where a different language is spoken.

Types of Learning Methods/Models

In concluding this discussion of instructional design theories, there are three quite general instructional frameworks that seem to hold a great deal of promise for instructional designers. These frameworks embody a number of instructional principles and methods, and might be considered models of instruction that have wide applicability. The three that are discussed next are by no means the only such frameworks available. Rather, the notion is to suggest that principles of instruction and instructional design principles can inform a general approach or framework for designing, developing, and deploying instruction.

Nine Events of Instruction

Gagné (1985) proposed nine events of instruction that should be included in the design of any instructional unit and that are associated with representative cognitive aspects of learning (see Table 10.1).

Cognitive Apprenticeship

The notion of cognitive apprenticeship arose in the 1980s in association with situated cognition (see Collins, Brown, & Newman, 1990). The basic notion is that as a learner progresses less explicit support is required and the learner should be expected to gradually

TABLE 10.1 Gagné's (1985) events of instruction and learning processes

Instructional event	Learning process
1. Gain attention	Focusing senses and the mind
2. Inform learner of the objective	Establishing expectations
3. Stimulate recall of relevant prior learning	Retrieving information from long-term memory
4. Present the content	Encoding and storing information
5. Provide learning guidance	Recognizing cues for performance, storage, and retrieval
6. Elicit performance	Activating mental models and developing automaticity
7. Provide feedback	Developing competence, confidence, and satisfaction
8. Assess performance	Recognizing problem areas and developing self-monitoring abilities
9. Enhance retention and transfer	Developing more robust mental models and more elaborate cues for retention and retrieval

become self-sufficient in managing progress and negotiating goals. This approach to instruction requires flexibility and skill on the part of the instructor to adjust support and feedback to meet individual student needs. There are six general instructional methods associated with cognitive apprenticeship and the notion of gradually fading scaffolding:

1. *Modeling*—the teacher or expert models or demonstrates the desired knowledge and skill for the learner; this is typically necessary with new learners in a domain and can be repeated at various learning stages.
2. *Coaching*—the teacher or expert observes a learner's performance, and provides feedback aimed at helping the learning improve and become aware of specific aspects requiring improvement.
3. *Scaffolding*—the designer or instructor deploys various support mechanisms for learners; these typically become less explicit and less supportive as learners gain competence and confidence.
4. *Articulation*—the teacher encourages a student to talk about what he or she is doing or knows with regard to a particular task; this can occur at many points in an instructional sequence.
5. *Reflection*—a teacher encourages a student to compare his or her response to a problem situation with that of an expert or possibly with that of another student as a way to draw attention to differences for purposes of developing understanding and insight.
6. *Exploration*—a teacher provides students with opportunities to explore new problems and perhaps different types of problems requiring alternative problem-solving strategies.

It should be obvious that cognitive apprenticeship is compatible with many of the instructional models and principles already discussed. Merrill's (2002) principles of problem-centered instruction have been characterized in a simple form as including these activities: (a) tell, (b) ask, (c) show, and (d) do. Telling can occur with modeling, coaching, and articulation depending on who is telling—the teacher or the student. Asking is more directly associated with articulation, and showing is closely associated with modeling. Doing is associated most closely with exploration. One can and should find correlates of cognitive apprenticeship in other methods and models.

Whereas Merrill (2002, 2013) has argued that too much instruction is focused on telling and asking, it is interesting that many cognitive apprenticeship approaches place little emphasis on the early stages and focus a great deal on reflection and exploration. As Seel (2004) notes, learning is best viewed as a progression, which suggests that all of Gagné's (1985) events of learning are important, as are all of Merrill's (2002, 2013) first principles and all stages of cognitive apprenticeship. Learning is not a magical event that happens all at once. Rather, learning is cumulative and develops over time with experience and guidance. Moreover, learning often happens with missteps and misunder-standing, which is why formative feedback is so important.

The Four-Component Instructional Design Model

The four-component instructional design model (4C/ID) developed by van Merriënboer (1997) distinguished types of things to be learned into recurrent and nonrecurrent task categories. As previously mentioned, recurrent tasks are those that are performed basically the same way regardless of variations in the surrounding context. Nonrecurrent tasks are those that are performed differently depending on specific variations in the surrounding context. Often, recurrent tasks that involve long procedural sequences can be broken down into subtasks and trained to automaticity, as in part-task training in which procedural information is provided when and as needed. A simple example might be removing and replacing the memory chips in a computer. This task might be divided into subtasks such as (a) preparing the computer, (b) removing and replacing the memory, and (c) testing the new memory.

More complex tasks, however, are typically not supported as well with part-task training and procedural information. Rather, such tasks should be presented and practiced in their entirety, according to 4C/ID, gradually introducing complexities as students master simpler whole tasks. An example could be training an air-traffic controller to communicate with pilots and land planes entering the air space for a particular airport. A simple whole task to begin with might be one airplane in the flight pattern and no active planes on the runway (this can be considered a task class in 4C/ID). The entire task of communicating with the pilot from time of entry into the airspace to parking at the terminal gate can be practiced. Once that whole task is mastered, a more complex whole task can be introduced such as two planes entering the traffic pattern and then some planes on the runway and so on. These various sets of tasks can be grouped together in task classes that involve similar levels of complexity. To help learners distinguish factors creating complexity and key decision points with regard to a complex cognitive task, heuristics are introduced. A heuristic is a general guide rather than a step-by-step procedural mandate for what to consider when deciding what to do next in solving a complex problem. Table 10.2 shows the relationship of the four basic components to the associated steps involved in complex learning.

Instructional Objects

Given the prior discussion of instruction and support for learners, it is worth making a distinction between the various kinds of objects that comprise instruction. Figure 10.7 depicts a hierarchy of these objects.

The reason for making the distinctions reflected in Figure 10.7 is that much that is called instruction lacks the critical attributes of instruction. Some training sessions are basically sessions for the dissemination of information. In many training sessions, that information is reliable, in which case it could be called a knowledge dissemination session.

TABLE 10.2 Components of 4C/ID (van Merriënboer & Kirschner, 2007)

Components	Steps to complex learning
Learning tasks	1. Design learning tasks
	2. Sequence task classes
	3. Set performance objectives
Supportive information	4. Design supportive information
	5. Analyze cognitive strategies
	6. Analyze mental models
Procedural information	7. Design procedural information
	8. Analyze cognitive rules
	9. Analyze prerequisite knowledge
Part-task practice	10. Design part-task practice

A Hierarchy of Components to Support Learning and Instruction

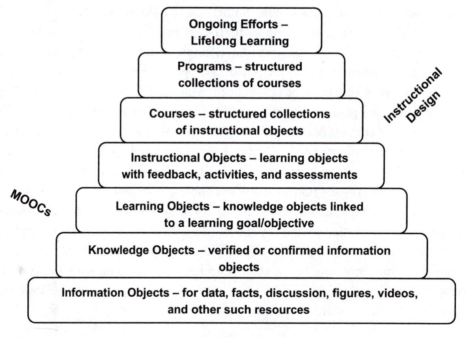

FIGURE 10.7 A hierarchy of educational objects (adapted from Spector, 2004a)

If there is an associated goal, then the objects can be used to support learning. However, without learning activities, feedback, and assessments, there is no way to determine if learning did occur, so it would be wrongheaded to consider a knowledge dissemination session as instruction, although it could become part of an instructional sequence.

Many of the early massive open online courses (MOOCs) lack feedback and assessments, and are more properly considered collections of learning objects. For that reason, the 'C' in 'MOOC' might more appropriately refer to 'community' rather than 'course'; in fact, the first MOOCs were intended to establish communities of inquiry and practice (Spector, 2014b, 2015). It is also worth emphasizing that as one proceeds up the hierarchy of educational components, instructional design becomes increasingly significant. How to select and sequence objects and activities in order to optimize outcomes requires the knowledge and skills that one often associates with instructional design and that are trained in nearly every instructional design program.

Smart Learning Environments and Technologies

Given the hierarchy of educational components presented in Figure 10.7, one might go on to say that a learning environment or technology that is likely to help a learner reach the top of that hierarchy in terms of ongoing and productive lifelong learning is a smart learning environment or a smart technology. Spector (2014b) argues that to be considered a smart learning environment an environment needs to be demonstrated to be engaging, effective, and efficient.

As it happens, smart technologies and smart learning environments are among what many consider to be emerging educational technologies. The New Media Consortium (NMC; see www.nmc.org) publishes the *Horizon Report* each year identifying those technologies in a sector that are likely to have a positive impact on education. MOOCs (previously discussed) and smart learning environments appear in recent *Horizon Reports*, among other technologies such as gamification, social media, and wearable devices.

Smart learning environments are those which make use of adaptive technologies and other innovations to be able to respond to the specific interests and needs of a particular learning (Sleeman & Brown, 1982; Spector, 2014a). A smart technology is one that supports the creation of smart learning environments. The intelligent tutoring systems developed in the 1980s and 1990s are an early example of smart learning environments (Spector, 2014a).

Test Your Understanding

Answer the following short answer questions:

1. Describe a typical instructional flow for a small unit of instruction such as a single lesson, including the knowledge and learning objects involved along with an activity, sample feedback, and an assessment.
2. Describe a flow for learning that might be associated with that instructional flow; in this case, the perspective will be how the learner might be constructing an understanding based as he or she proceeds through the instructional sequence.
3. Indicate the difference between a descriptive theory or model (such as constructivist epistemology) and a prescriptive theory of model (such as cognitive apprenticeship).

4. In terms of developing empirical support, which kind of theory (descriptive or prescriptive) is typically more difficult to support and why?

5. Using Jonassen's taxonomy of problems, locate where instructional design might fall and explain why.

6. Which of Gagné's nine events of instruction might be associated with the scaffolding method in cognitive apprenticeship and how so?

7. Identify a smart learning environment and list four characteristics that one is likely to find in that environment.

A Representative Educational Technology Challenge

An institution of higher learning that has traditionally focused on aeronautical engineering has discovered that while the overwhelming majority of incoming first-year students select aeronautical engineering as their major, by the time these students have completed the required two-semester sequence of aeronautical engineering they have changed their majors to something else. When asked why, students typically indicated that they simply found some other subject area more interesting. A preliminary analysis of the aeronautical sequence of instruction indicates that it has changed little in the last 20 years. It is taught as a lecture class with an associated laboratory section in which students work in small teams solving mathematical aspects of particular problems. The course uses a standard set of final exams that reflect little change in student performance in the last 20 years. Students who do complete the required sequence with good grades and manage to remain aeronautical engineering majors and graduate perform well in their after-college experiences, as demonstrated by follow-up interviews with alumni and their employers. However, the goal of having 75 percent of graduating seniors majoring in aeronautical engineering is not close to being met, as only about 15 percent of graduating seniors retain that major. As an expert instructional designer, you have been hired to diagnose this problematic situation and recommend what might be done to correct it.

Learning Activities

1. Identify and describe the key factors that you would consider in framing your response to the problem situation stated above.

2. Identify and describe the key factors that are likely to be effective in communicating with parents.

3. Indicate and describe the relationships among all of the key factors that have been identified.

4. Indicate what kinds of additional support should be considered in order to make the best case for your solution approach.

5. Create an annotated concept map that reflects the things indicated in response to the previous four tasks.

Links

Indiana University site for instructional design theories and other resources—see www.indiana.edu/~idtheory/home.html

Indiana University site for instructional strategies and technology use—see www.indiana.edu/~tltc/from_tltl/projects/strategies.html

BusinessBalls.Com site on Kolb's learning styles and experiential theory of learning—see www.businessballs.com/kolblearningstyles.htm

Penn State University site for instructional theories and other resources—see http://ide.ed.psu.edu/idde/theories.htm

Greg Kearsley's Theory into Practice database for theories related to learning and instruction—see http://tip.psychology.org

University of Colorado at Denver website on instructional design models—see http://carbon.ucdenver.edu/~mryder/itc/idmodels.html

VARK website for Learning Styles Developed by Neil Fleming—see www.vark-learn.com/english/index.asp

Other Resources

Don Clark's website on Kolb's learning styles and experiential learning theory—see www.nwlink.com/~donclark/hrd/styles/kolb.html

Idaho State University Site on ADDIE—see http://ed.isu.edu/addie/Research/Research.html

Instructional strategies based on research by Marzano, Pickering and Pollack—see www.tltguide.ccsd.k12.co.us/instructional_tools/Strategies/Strategies.html

Kathy Schrock's guide and resources for educators at Discovery Education—see http://school.discoveryeducation.com/schrockguide/index.html

Leslie Owen Wilson's Curriculum Pages and Cognitive Taxonomy—see www.uwsp.edu/education/lwilson/curric/newtaxonomy.htm

Nadia Dabbagh's Instructional Design Knowledge Base with Instructional Strategies—see http://classweb.gmu.edu/ndabbagh/Resources/IDKB/strategies_tactics.htm

Saskatoon Public Schools website for Instructional Strategies—see http://olc.spsd.sk.ca/de/pd/instr/index.html

References

Anderson, J. R. (1983). *The architecture of cognition*. Cambridge, MA: Harvard University Press.

Anderson, L. W., & Krathwohl, D. R. (Eds.) (2001). *A taxonomy for learning, teaching and assessing: A revision of Bloom's taxonomy of educational objectives*. New York: Longman.

Ausubel, D. P. (1963). *The psychology of meaningful verbal learning*. New York: Grune & Stratton.

Bruner, J. S. (1966). *Toward a theory of instruction*. Cambridge, MA: Harvard University Press.

Collins, A., Brown, J. S., & Newman, S. E. (1990). Cognitive apprenticeship: Teaching the crafts of reading, writing, and mathematics. In L. B. Resnick (Ed.*), Knowing, learning, and instruction: Essays in honor or Robert Glaser* (pp. 453–494). Hillsdale, NJ: Lawrence Erlbaum.

Dewey, J. (1907). *The school and society*. Chicago: University of Chicago Press.

Dick, S., Carey, L., & Carey, J. O. (2009). The systematic design of instruction (7th ed.). Boston, MA: Allyn & Bacon.

Eckel, K. (1993). *Instruction language: Foundations of a strict science of instruction*. Englewood Cliffs, NJ: Educational Technology Publications.

Fleming, N. D. (1995). I'm different, not dumb: Modes of presentation (VARK) in the tertiary classroom. In A. Zelmer (Ed.), Research and development in higher education. *Proceedings of the 1995 Annual Conference of the Higher Education and Research Development Society of Australasia (HERDSA), 18*, 308–313.

Gagné, R. M. (1985). *The conditions of learning* (4th ed.). New York: Holt, Rinehart & Winston.

Gagné, R. M., & Merrill, M. D. (1990). Integrative goals for instructional design. *Educational Technology Research & Development, 38*(1), 23–30.

Graf, S., Liu, T-C., Kinshuk, Chen, N-S., & Yang, S. J. H. (2009). Learning styles and cognitive traits: Their relationships and its benefits in web-based educational systems. *Computers in Human Behavior, 25*(6), 1280–1289.

Jonassen, D. H. (2000). Toward a design theory of problem solving. *ETR&D, 48*(4), 63–85.

Jonassen, D. H. (2004). *Learning to solve problems: An instructional design guide.* San Francisco, CA: Pfeiffer/Jossey-Bass.

Jonassen, D. H. (2007). Toward a taxonomy of meaningful learning. *Educational Technology, 47*(5), 30–35.

Kolb, D. A. (1984). *Experiential learning: Experience as the source of learning and development.* Englewood Cliffs, NJ: Prentice-Hall.

Merrill, M. D. (2002). First principles of instruction. *Educational Technology Research & Development, 50*(3), 43–59.

Merrill, M. D. (2013). *First principles of instruction: Identifying and designing effective, efficient, and engaging instruction.* San Francisco, CA: Wiley & Sons.

Reigeluth, C. M. (Ed.) (1983). *Instructional-design theories and models: An overview of their current status.* Hillsdale, NJ: Erlbaum.

Reigeluth, C. M. (Ed.) (1999). *Instructional-design theories and models: A new paradigm of instructional theory* (Volume II). Mahwah, NJ: Erlbaum.

Richey, R. C., Klein, J. D., & Tracey, M. W. (2011). *The instructional design knowledge base: Theory, research and practice.* New York: Routledge.

Seel, N. M. (2004). Model-centered learning environments: Theory, instructional design and effects. In N. M. Seel & S. Dijkstra (Eds.), *Curriculum, plans and processes in instructional design* (pp. 49–74). Mahwah, NJ: Erlbaum.

Sleeman, D. H., & Brown, J. S. (Eds.) (1982). *Intelligent tutoring systems.* New York: Academic Press.

Spector, J. M. (2001). A philosophy of instructional design for the 21st century? *Journal of Structural Learning and Intelligent Systems, 14*(4), 307–318.

Spector, J. M. (2014a). Conceptualizing the emerging field of smart learning environments. *Smart Learning Environment, 1.*

Spector, J. M. (2014b). Remarks on MOOCs and mini-MOOCs. *Educational Technology Research & Development, 62*(3), 385–392.

Spector, J. M. (Ed.) (2015). *The encyclopedia of educational technology.* Thousand Oaks, CA: Sage.

Spector, J. M., & Anderson, T. M. (Eds.) (2000). *Integrated and holistic perspectives on learning, instruction and technology: Understanding complexity.* Dordrecht: Kluwer Academic Press.

Spector, J. M., Johnson, T. E., & Young, P. A. (2014). An editorial on research and development in and with educational technology. *Educational Technology Research & Development, 62*(1), 1–12.

Taba, H. (1962). *Curriculum development: Theory and practice.* New York: Harcourt, Brace & World.

Tennyson, R. D. & Cocchiarella, M. J. (1986). An empirically based instructional design theory for teaching concepts. *Review of Educational Research, 56*(1), 40–71.

van Merriënboer, J. J. G. (1997). *Training complex cognitive skills: A four-component instructional design model for technical training.* Englewood Cliffs, NJ: Educational Technology Publications.

van Merriënboer, J. J. G, & Kirschner, P. A. (2007). *Ten steps to complex learning: A systematic approach to four-component instructional design.* Mahwah, NJ: Educational Tehcnology Publications.

Vygotsky, L. (1978). *Mind and society: The development of higher mental processes.* Cambridge, MA: Harvard University Press.

part three

PRACTICAL PERSPECTIVES WITH EXAMPLE APPLICATIONS

eleven

Introducing Innovative Technologies and Managing Change

"Everyone thinks of changing the world, but no one thinks of changing himself" (Leo Tolstoy, Pamphlets, *1900)*

In the famous Turing award lecture entitled "The Humble Programmer" delivered at the annual ACM (Association of Computing Machinery) Conference, Edgars Dijkstra (1972) made the deeply insightful observation that computers had yet to solve a single problem—they had only introduced the new problem of learning to use them effectively. In the essay published with the same title (see http://portal.acm.org/citation.cfm?id=361591), Dijkstra cited a number of factors contributing to the problem. One factor, of course, is the rapidly increasing size and complexity of programs. Another factor that had gone largely unnoticed was the fact that the use of tools and technologies to a large extent determined how programmers were thinking, but those who would become end-users of those programs were not necessarily thinking the way programmers were thinking. What might seem obvious to a programmer with regard to an interaction might not be so obvious to a nonprogrammer.

Tools and technologies strongly influence our habits of thinking, and that should be recognized in the world of educational technology (Jonassen, Carr, & Yueh, 1998; Norman, 2002; Papert, 1980). Seymour Papert (1980) believed that children's experience in programming a turtle (initially a remotely controlled physical turtle and then a computer turtle) could accelerate passage through Piaget's stages of cognitive development. David Jonassen and colleagues (1998) took this argument further and made the more general claim that technologies could be conceived of as cognitive problem-solving tools (i.e., *mindtools*) and designed accordingly. Don Norman (2002) went on to observe that the design of tools and technologies determined how they would and could be used; as it happens, people often make use of a tool or technology in ways that were not specifically intended by designers. Tools and technologies can influence learning and how learning can be effectively supported.

However, the situation with regard to educational technologies can be characterized in much the same way as Dijkstra characterized the situation with computers in 1972. There are at our disposal amazing and powerful tools and technologies to support learning and instruction, and new ones are emerging at a rapid rate (see the last chapter in this volume). Moreover, the resources available for little or no cost on the Internet that can be used to support learning and instruction are increasing at an even more rapid rate. In short, designers and teachers have to confront the sheer magnitude of the resources available to use in support of learning and performance. In the spirit of Dijkstra's remarks, one might say that educational technologies have yet to solve a single problem—they have only introduced the new problem of learning to use those tools and technologies effectively in support of educational goals and learning objectives.

What has gone awry in the past, and how might educational technology professionals improve in the future to introduce innovative technologies and manage their use to support learning and instruction? These questions suggest that it is appropriate to adopt a systemic approach to change (see, for example, Ellsworth, 2000; Reigeluth & Duffy, 2008). Training and preparation of instructional designers and educational technologists is specifically addressed in a subsequent chapter in this volume.

Technology Needs

As with any intervention process, it is wise to begin by determining what problems exist and are likely to occur with regard to technology use and support, and then use that information to determine specific needs. To determine existing and likely problem areas, one can and should involve all relevant stakeholders. In a school or school district, the relevant stakeholder group includes teachers, students, parents, administrators, and support staff. In a business context, the stakeholder group might include staff, managers, clients, and stockholders.

It often happens that what appear to be problems are actually symptoms. For example, suppose students drop out of a required course at a high rate. One might conclude that the high drop-out rate is a problem. However, upon closer analysis, it might be the case that the course was designed poorly or that the instructor was not properly prepared. The point here is to look beyond surface symptoms to underlying causes of those symptoms prior to committing to a course of action.

Once problems have been identified and prioritized, they can be restated in terms of needs. For example, a problem in a high school context might be that a significant number of students are dropping out prior to graduation. The reason this could be a problem is that high school dropouts are not likely to be properly prepared to succeed as adults.

The school's mission might involve preparing students to be productive members of society, so the link to the school's mission is clear. The need, then, is to increase the graduation rate and reduce the drop-out rate. A further step would be to state the need in terms that can be measured, which in this case is not hard to do. A possible technology intervention in this case might be to develop, validate, and use an instrument that would identify students likely to drop out as early as possible, and then target those students for an appropriate intervention, such as interaction with a human mentor or a virtual pedagogical change agent to address motivational and volitional issues on a personal but nonthreatening level. Of course, many other possibilities exist, which makes instructional design and technology a very challenging discipline. In this sense, the vast array of educational technologies has significantly increased the complexity of instructional design.

An example from a military training context could be that most apprentice aircraft maintenance technicians who have completed the initial sequence of aircraft maintenance courses are arriving in the field unable to perform simple maintenance tasks on existing aircraft. The reason this is a problem is that experienced technicians are then required to provide extensive one-on-one training resulting in a loss of their productivity and a slow-down in repairing aircraft. The unit's mission might involve maintaining 100 percent readiness of all aircraft, so the problem is clearly linked to a priority of the unit and the unit's mission. The need might then be stated as preparing aircraft maintenance technicians to be competent in performing routine maintenance tasks on existing equipment when they arrive at their field units. A possible technology intervention in this case might be to introduce aircraft maintenance simulators based on existing aircraft into the training curriculum rather than using actual but outdated aircraft.

Different individuals and groups are likely to focus on different problems and problem areas, so it is often useful to consider the mission and goals, prioritize identified problems in terms of the mission and goals, and state the related needs in measurable terms. Such an exercise might create a need to revisit and revise the organization's vision, mission, goals, and values statements, but that is beyond the scope of this discussion. The point here is that prior to committing to adopting a new technology, one should be clear about the problem and associated need that the technology is intended to address. Ideally, one should also have a good sense of how to evaluate the degree to which the technology addressed the underlying problem and need. How much did drop-out rates drop? Were most apprentice aircraft maintenance technicians now able to perform routine maintenance on existing aircraft? Creating a formative evaluation plan to determine that what was implemented was aligned with the problem and subsequent solution specification (i.e., a fidelity of implementation study) then becomes an important skill for the design team. Likewise, creating a summative evaluation plan to determine and explain to what extent the intended goal was met is an additional challenge. Are educational technologists and instructional designers being properly prepared to create and implement formative and summative evaluations? This question is probably worth discussing in class or in an online discussion forum as a precursor to discussions in a subsequent chapter.

In addition to being skilled in developing and deploying effective educational technology solutions, and being competent in creating and implementing formative and summative evaluation, educational technologists and instructional designers need to be able to create cost-effectiveness estimates. For example, in the previous example about aircraft maintenance technicians, an interactive aircraft maintenance simulator would be quite expensive to build, especially were it designed to be easily modified to accommodate changes and upgrades in the actual aircraft. Can the cost be justified in terms of improved aircraft readiness and long-term productivity? Is there a more affordable option that is likely to be equally effective and more easily maintained and sustained? Cost-benefit analysis for educational technologies is more complex than ever before (Levin, 2001).

Technology Readiness

Let us suppose that a problem area has been thoroughly explored, a need with measurable aspects properly stated, and a promising new technology identified that is expected to perform well in this situation. The next question one might ask is how prepared the relevant users are for such a technology. This, of course, will change from situation to situation, and from user to user. Relevant factors include previous experience with similar technologies, willingness to consider changes due to new technologies, the involvement of users in identifying problems and proposing solutions, perceptions with regard to how a new technology will meet individual needs, and much more (Wejnert, 2002).

Rogers' (2003) diffusion of innovation model identifies five groups of users:

- Innovators, who will drive the change process and may or not may not be members of the community but who will be effective in communicating the significance of the innovation.
- Early adopters, who are nearly always willing to try out new things and who are generally influential within the specific community of users;
- Early majority, who are generally thoughtful and willing to change once the advantages of change have been clearly demonstrated.
- Late majority, who are generally skeptical of change and new ideas and only adopt an innovation when the vast majority are already regular users;
- Laggards or traditional resistors, who are generally critical of anything new and reluctant to adopt any innovation, and who may resist long after the vast majority are supportive users.

Figure 11. 1 depicts how Rogers (2003) believes that people are distributed in a typical organization (based on the assumption of a normal distribution). The percentages may change for particular organizations, so the normal distribution depicted in Figure 11.1 is only suggestive. However, there are likely to be two key groups to consider in facilitating

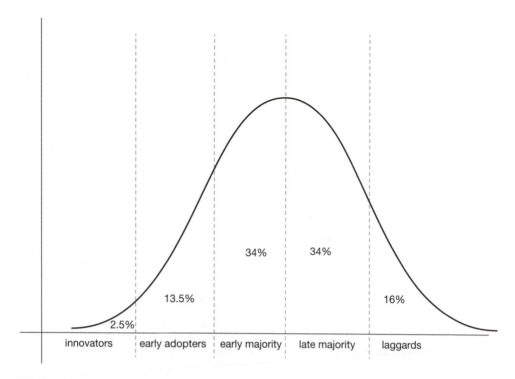

FIGURE 11.1 Roger's (2003) innovation adoption curve

a change process: early adopters and traditional resistors (labelled 'laggards' in the figure using Rogers' language).

The reason that early adopters and the traditional resistors are important for managing the diffusion of innovation is that each of these groups can either help accelerate or become obstacles to successful change. It is important to identify the key people in each of these groups. One way to accomplish this is to use a simple survey instrument based on Rogers' (2003) characterization of the different groups that is appropriately modified for the context of use.

Early adopters can be used in several ways early in a diffusion of innovation process. They can become the in-house advocates and speak to other users in terms of recurring tasks or problems that new technology is intended to assist or alleviate. Early adopters can also become the trainers of others in the organization as the technology spreads. Using early adopters in this way can be rewarding for those willing to be on the leading/bleeding edge of technology innovation, and it can provide the early majority with needed encouragement from their peers rather than from those higher up in the organizational hierarchy.

It is also important to know who the likely resistors will be. It would not be productive to try to include a serious resistor in the group of early adopters, and it can also be counter-productive to include resistors in the group to be targeted after early adopters—the early majority. Resistors can influence those who otherwise might be willing to try

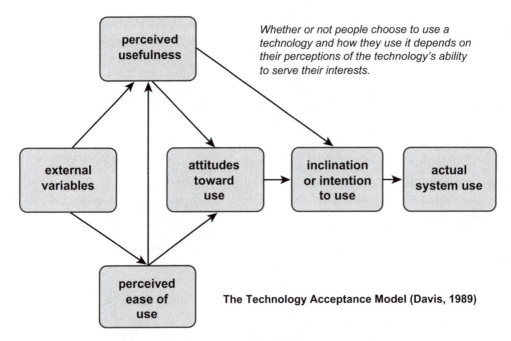

FIGURE 11.2 The Davis technology acceptance model

out something new to retreat into the background. When planning the introduction of a new technology, it may be wise to leave those most likely to resist until the end of the process so that it will be clear to them that the technology has gained traction within and throughout the organization.

In a private discussion with Rob Foshay, it was suggested that it may make sense to target the typical user in the middle of Rogers' curve—namely, representative users who later might be majority adopters poised to become early adopters. If others in the organization see that a more or less ordinary person can be successful with a new technology, others may be likely to follow, and the adoption of a new technology might spread more quickly. This could be a good item for a classroom or forum discussion, and it is certainly worthy of investigating to see when and to what extent it might be true in various situations.

In determining how likely people are to embrace or resist a new information system or computer technology, Davis' (1989) technology acceptance model suggests that perceived usefulness and perceived ease-of-use are primary considerations. With regard to educational technologies, this can be extended to include perceived enhancement of learning and instructional tasks and activities. Figure 11.2 depicts Davis' technology acceptance model.

Technology Deployment

Technology deployment has been partially addressed in that the general guideline is to identify and initially involve early (or possibly middle) adopters in the deployment process. Deployment considerations are somewhat different from but do overlap adoption considerations. Adoption basically refers to actual use of a technology whereas deployment refers to making the technology widely available. Deployment includes infrastructure and training requirements. One question to ask is whether early (or middle) adopters are likely to be effective in training others, if such a role is planned as part of the deployment. The larger the system to be deployed the wiser it may be to stage the deployment and emphasize training throughout the process. Beginning with a pilot group may be useful so that unforeseen problems can be detected and accommodated without a negative impact on everyone else who will eventually be involved. In some cases, not all of the technical requirements become obvious until the first implementation occurs, which is one reason to start with a small trail-blazing group of early adopters.

When deploying a new technology, new terminology may be involved. Making sure that users are familiar with new concepts and terminology is a part of the deployment process and can serve as a significant stepping stone to the adoption process. As Dijkstra (1972) implied in "The humble programmer," a technology has certain affordances that impact how we think and talk about particular tasks. The language of deployment can support the adoption process and both are critical from the point of view of TPACK (technological, pedagogical, and content knowledge). Rather than treat planning, deployment, adoption, and eventual use as separate and distinct processes, it is generally wise to adopt a systems perspective and think of these as tightly interconnected and mutually influential processes (Spector & Anderson, 2000; Spector, 2015a).

Management of Change

Effective management of change involves continually assessing to what degree the measurable targets associated with the driving need are being met and ensuring that benefits continue to justify the costs of change. There are many indicators that one can examine along the way to determine the efficacy of a technology innovation. For example, if the technology involves what teachers do in their classrooms, as would be the case when introducing personalized learning at the school level, for example, then one might consider looking at changes in teacher retention rates, changes in teacher absenteeism, or changes in complaints of teachers to administrators. Finding early and accurate indicators of success, or lack thereof, is needed in order to make appropriate adjustments during the deployment and adoption phases of diffusion of innovation. Documenting expenditures as well as cost savings as the effort matures is also quite important. Periodic attitude surveys among users can be useful in identifying trouble spots, and they can also serve to indicate when it might be appropriate to move forward, for example from use with the early majority group to the use with the late majority group.

It is not generally wise to try to change everything all at once, although there are occasions when such a strategy has worked well. More typically, it is safer to adopt a graceful evolution approach to change. Remaking the entire world of education in one fell swoop has been the fool's folly of too many educational researchers and reformers.

However, it is perhaps worthwhile to take note of a particular case where a change-everything strategy did work.

This case was presented in the previous chapter as a representative educational technology challenge. It is presented here as an actual problem that was resolved using educational technology. The case is based on the memory of the author and of those involved in the case as it has not been fully documented anywhere. The United States Air Force Academy (USAFA) is an undergraduate military academy focused on aeronautical engineering and the mission of preparing career officers for the Air Force. It was discovered in the 1980s that while the overwhelming majority of incoming first-year cadets did select aeronautical engineering as their major, by the time these students had completed the required aeronautical engineering courses they had changed their majors to something else. When asked why, students typically indicated that they simply found some other subject area more interesting. Aeronautical engineering instruction at USAFA had changed little in the previous 20 years. It was taught as a lecture class with an associated laboratory section in which students worked in small teams solving mathematical aspects of particular aeronautical engineering problems. The course used a standard set of final exam questions; final exams reflected little change in student performance in the last 20 years. Students who do complete the required sequence with good grades and manage to remain aeronautical engineering majors and graduate did perform well in their after-college experiences as demonstrated by follow-up interviews with alumni and their employers. However, the goal of having the overwhelming majority of graduating seniors major in aeronautical engineering was not close to being met.

The problem was that cadets were not retaining their major in aeronautical engineering. The reason this was a problem is that it meant that USAFA was not completely fulfilling its mission to prepare career officers for the Air Force. The need then was to significantly increase the number of students who retained aeronautical engineering as their major. The solution approach was to completely change the course into one that made use of a series of interactive simulations. The same final exam was retained as a way to benchmark learning, and the targeted goals were to increase retention in aeronautical engineering and improve learning as measured by the standard final exam. This way of teaching the course completely changed what the instructors and the students did. As it happens, USAFA was an ideal place for such a radical change as most students and instructors could be regarded as early adopters of technology and change, possibly as a natural consequence of the selection processes for cadets and instructors. In any case, this innovation proved to be successful. While performance on the test did not change significantly, the retention of aeronautical engineering majors improved dramatically. One might argue that the reason that test scores did not improve was that the test was designed for the traditional version of the course and did not measure deep understanding of aeronautical engineering problem solving.

The point to be made here is that change management is a complex and challenging task. There are no ready-made formulas that fit all circumstances. One has to be willing to try something new and perhaps to change oneself along the way.

Test Your Understanding

With regard to each of the following problem statements, indicate why it is a problem, what goal or mission might be involved, transform it into a needs statement, and indicate how change might be measured:

1. The problem is that too many teachers abandon their teaching careers in the first five years.
2. The problem is that students are graduating from high school who cannot read at a fifth grade level.
3. The problem is that physicians who treat diabetes are not keeping up with the most recent research findings and recommended patient interventions based on those findings.
4. The problem is that automobile technicians graduating from that company's training program only know how to troubleshoot one kind of vehicle, and training them on multiple vehicles takes our most advanced technicians away from their own work.
5. The problem is that when that older operating system was used, people knew how to update their own systems, but now that a new system is in place they have to call on our very limited technical personnel to perform frequent and routine system updates.

A Representative Educational Technology Challenge

A large suburban school district that is generally performing well on most measures (e.g., high graduation rates, low drop-out rates, above-average test scores, etc.) has decided to implement a radically new approach to instruction called personalized learning. In personalized learning, a dynamic profile of each student is kept that keeps track of previous performance on instructional units associated with mandated state standards along with student characteristics (e.g., shy personality) and learning styles (e.g., prefers visually oriented materials and demonstrated with auditory explanations rather than text). The system creates and manages an individual learning plan for each student. Students are scheduled into clusters for each of their courses every three or four weeks with a group that is working on the same mandated standards. Students proceed at their own pace and do not move to a new cluster until they have successfully mastered all the instructional units in the assigned cluster for that course. The system has access to a huge repository of learning objects and activities that can be assigned to particular students based on the individual's profile. The role of teachers is to help individual students as they encounter problems. You are the Associate Superintendent for Curriculum and

Instruction for the district. Your task is to develop a diffusion of innovation plan for this effort throughout all the district's elementary, middle, and high schools.

Learning Activities

1. Identify and describe the key factors that you would consider in framing your response to the problem situation stated above.
2. Identify and describe the key factors that are likely to be obstacles in implementing the effort.
3. Indicate and describe the relationships among all of the key factors that have been identified.
4. Indicate what kinds of additional support should be considered in order to make the best case for your solution approach.
5. Create an annotated concept map that reflects the things indicated in response to the previous four tasks.

Links

Edgars Dijkstra's Turing Award Lecture entitled "The Humble Programmer"—see http://portal.acm.org/citation.cfm?id=361591

Other Resources

The Change Management site located at ChangingMinds.Org—see http://changingminds.org/disciplines/change_management/change_management.htm

Journal of Educational Change published by Springer—see www.springer.com/education+%26+language/journal/10833

The Learning Development Institute—www.learndev.org

Learning Innovations Laboratory at the Harvard Graduate College of Education—see http://lila.pz.harvard.edu

North Central Regional Educational Laboratory on leading and managing change and improvement—see www.ncrel.org/sdrs/areas/issues/educatrs/leadrshp/le500.htm

Rosalyn McKeown's education for sustainable development toolkit—see www.esdtoolkit.org/discussion/default.htm

References

Davis, F. D. (1989). Perceived usefulness, perceived ease of use, and user acceptance of information technology. *Management Information Systems Quarterly, 13*(3), 319–340.

Dijkstra, E. W. (1972). The humble programmer. *Communications of the ACM, 15*(10), 859–866.

Ellsworth, J. B. (2000). *Surviving change: A study of educational change models.* Syracuse, NY: ERIC Clearinghouse on Information and Technology.

Jonassen, D. H., Carr, C., & Yueh, H-P. (1998). Computers as mindtools for engaging learners in critical thinking. *TechTrends, 43*(2), 24–32.

Levin, H. M. (2001). Waiting for Godot: Cost-effectiveness analysis in education. *New Directions for Evaluation, 90*, 55–68.

Norman, D. A. (2002). *The design of everyday things.* New York: Basic Books.

Papert, S. (1980). Mindstorms: Children, computers and powerful ideas. New York: Basic Books.

Reigeluth, C. M., & Duffy, F. M. (2008). The AECT Future Minds initiative: Transforming America's school systems. *Educational Technology, 48*(3), 45–49.

Rogers, E. M. (2003). *Diffusion of innovations* (5th ed.). New York: Free Press.

Spector, J. M. (Ed.). (2015). *The encyclopedia of educational technology.* Thousand Oaks, CA: Sage.

Spector, J. M., & Anderson, T. M. (Eds.) (2000). *Integrated and holistic perspectives on learning, instruction and technology: Understanding complexity.* Dordrecht: Kluwer Academic Press.

Wejnert, B. (2002). Integrating models of diffusion of innovations: A conceptual framework. *Annual Review of Sociology, 28,* 297–326.

twelve
Teaching with Technology

"If we teach today as we taught yesterday, we rob our children of tomorrow" (John Dewey, 1916)

Due to rapid changes in technologies, one might wonder what can be said with confidence about teaching with technology that will apply today and in the next five years? The short version of an answer that might be gathered from previous chapters in this volume is that (a) there will surely be new technologies and new teaching methods associated with those technologies; (b) these technologies will come with particular affordances that will shape how we think and talk about using them to support learning and instruction; and (c) making effective use of new technologies will be more challenging than ever. We will probably need to facilitate changes in educational settings, in learners, and in ourselves. It is difficult to specify what those changes will be without considering specific new and emerging educational technologies (see the last chapter in this volume). So, in a concrete sense this is a disappointing response to an important question. This somewhat disappointing answer could be paraphrased as follows: "Be thoughtful and flexible and you will be fine." This is just the sort of advice that can cause you to take 40 years to cross a desert that should be easily traversed in 40 days or less. However, just as those ancient people wandering in the desert had a sense of what the promised land would be like, we can develop a sense for what we would like to see with regard to the future of technology-infused education. Speculation about such a future can be the basis for an interesting discussion topic, especially when participants are asked to provide some rationale for their responses.

So, what can we expect? Probably (these statements are made with great hesitation as they are not founded on either theory or evidence), we can expect to see Moore's (1965) Law about the doubling of the computer power of integrated circuits about every two years reaching a limit and declining rapidly. Moore's Law is not a law of nature on an equal footing with the law of gravity. We can quite reasonably expect to see in the future that a massive object will continue to attract other objects in direct proportion to the product of their masses and inversely proportion to the square of the distance between them. Now, consider a version of Moore's Law that is stated in terms of computation costs and in longer periods of time. Roughly, this means that computing costs decrease by an order of magnitude (factor of 10) every five years (Hellman, 2003; Kleinman & Moore, 2014). Assuming a direct correlation between computing costs and computers, we might then imagine that a personal computer costing $1,000 in 2012 will only cost $100 in 2017 and then $10 in 2022 (this does not seem very likely). It is quite possible that we will no longer be talking about personal computers in 2017 or 2022. In short, we should be wary of such projections with regard to the future.

Why, then, bring up the example of Moore's Law? The reason is to make an important distinction between principles that apply to the natural world and are based on observation and principles that apply to things that are manufactured and which are subject to many complicating assumptions and confounding factors, such as the context of use, human characteristics, differences, and so on. A second reason for mentioning Moore's Law is to highlight an optimism with regard to technology that may be unfounded. While we have seen dramatic and sustained improvements in computing power over the last 50 years, there is no reason to expect to see those improvements continue at the same pace in the next 50 years, especially when applied to educational technology. While we have seen computing power doubling every two years, we have not seen any such doubling in learning outcomes or teaching productivity. Indeed, many of the promises of educational technologists have not been attained (Spector, 2000, 2015). Let's take a quick look at some of these promises before discussing more practical issues.

Some thought that the Internet would result in the disappearance of schools, and that widely available online learning resources would result in the disappearance of teachers and instructional designers. Others have wondered if the appearance of personal tablet devices and digital books would result in the disappearance of paper-based books. Schools have not disappeared, nor have teachers, instructional designers, and books. Schools are changing, albeit slowly, as are teachers, instructional designers, books, and learners. While many have talked about a revolution in learning and instruction brought about by the Internet and mobile devices, what is actually happening is a rather gradual transformation of books, schools, approaches to teaching, and learner expectations. What is happening is an evolution and not a revolution. Let's be honest. Being an evolution, it does seem possible to see trends and directions.

The underlying promise that has been made over the years by many educational technology advocates is that simply adopting a particular technology and integrating its use into instruction will lead to dramatic improvements (e.g., one or more standard deviations) in terms of learning outcomes. This simply has not happened except in very isolated cases that have not been replicated on a large scale. Consider the case of intelligent tutoring systems (ITSs) that were first introduced in the 1970s with many implementations and applications in the 1980s and 1990s. An intelligent tutoring system has (a) a model of the knowledge domain (requires a well-structured knowledge domain such as LISP programming, or elementary mathematics, or the operation of a physical device), (b) a model of each student's knowledge of the subject domain, (c) an instructional model (or a model of a tutor), and (d) a two-way communication system (Corbett et al., 1997). A common promise was that an ITS would produce a one-sigma (standard deviation) improvement in learning compared with the two-sigma improvement observed by Bloom (1984) for one-on-one human tutoring. The evidence has not supported that promise. Nonetheless, many ITSs have been constructed and some improvements in learning have been recorded in well-structured domains and well-supported situations (Corbett et al., 1997).

A great deal has been written about the potential gains of using technology to support learning and instruction in the form of intelligent tutoring systems. Still, it is important to realize that ITSs did not make human teachers or tutors obsolete, nor did they revolutionize education as promised. One prominent educational researcher went so far as to name his tutoring systems as nonintelligent tutoring systems to make this point clear at a meeting on advanced learning technologies hosted at the Defense Advanced Research Projects Agency in the 1980s in the USA. The impact of the research and development in the area of intelligent tutoring systems is still evident today in the form of adaptive systems, personalized learning environments, and virtual worlds. While most promises were not met or kept, much that is of value in educational technology did emerge from the intelligent tutoring system community. For example, the attention now paid to personalized tutoring and formative assessment can in large part be credited to the intelligent tutoring movement. In other words, what can be said based on the available evidence is that such innovations as ITSs have led to gradual changes and gains in how technology is used to support learning and instruction.

Practical Applications

In spite of their significant potential, new technologies have yet to be fully implemented in classrooms and training environments (Stewart et al., 2010). In exploring the implications of teaching with technology, it is worthwhile to revisit the basic processes involved in planning and implementing instructional systems and learning environments, and to more carefully consider the affordances of various technologies and how they might be leveraged to improve learning and instruction given existing educational goals and learning objectives. Consistent with the notion of user-centered and participatory design, Tennyson's model of instructional design (Figure 12.1) is again worthy of particular attention.

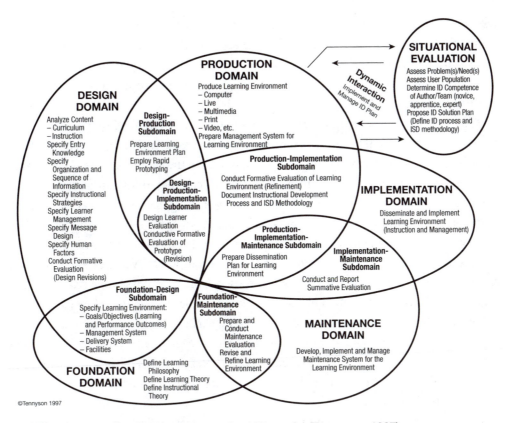

FIGURE 12.1 Tennyson's fourth-generation ISD model (Tennyson, 1997)

There are many models and representations of instructional design and development, which are often referred to collectively as ADDIE (Analysis, Design, Development, Implementation, and Evaluation) models (see, for example, Andrews & Goodson, 1980; Gustafson & Branch, 2002). One rather unique model is Tennyson's fourth-generation ISD model (see Figure 12.1) as it focuses on what people do rather than on high-level, idealized processes. A situational evaluation informs this model and includes considerations with regard to the problems, needs, users, development team, resources available, and so on.

Unlike the design and development models often presented in programs preparing educational technologists and instructional designers, Tennyson's model depicts many interactions and overlapping concerns among the various clusters of activities. Such a model reflects real world activities and can be considered a precursor of recent layered models (Gibbons, 2015). In the foundation cluster of activities, Tennyson notes the significance of a learning philosophy, learning theories, and instructional strategies, which have all been mentioned previously in this volume. Formative evaluation shows up in a central intersection in Tennyson's model. Because formative evaluation (determining how well the development is progressing and what issues need to be addressed in order to achieve success) is ongoing as the learning environment or training system is refined and matures, this is necessarily an iterative activity that informs many other aspects of the implementation. Keeping in mind many of the activities in Tennyson's model, particularly a situational evaluation, foundation issues, and formative evaluation, will certainly help instructional designers, teachers, and trainers make more effective use of technology.

What are the affordances offered by new educational technologies and what issues arise with regard to their use? As previously discussed in this volume, the term 'affordance' was introduced by Gibson (1977) to refer to the actions that an object makes possible. This term has migrated from cognitive psychology to human factors and has found its way into instructional design and development, where it more generally refers to the perceived utility or function of something. It is worth noting that people often find a use for something that was not originally intended by the designer. For example, email was not designed to support the corruption of computers by a virus, but computer viruses are an unintended and undesirable affordance of email—best to be wary and keep anti-virus software up to date. On the other hand, some unintended affordances have proven worthwhile. For example, Microsoft's PowerPoint software was designed for business presentations, but it has found its way into elementary classrooms where children are using many features to create visual representations of their ideas, often in ways that reflect more creative uses than the common usage in higher education criticized by Tufte (2003) and others.

There is no exhaustive taxonomy and account of educational technology affordances, and it is difficult to imagine such an account being made due to the frequent and dramatic changes in technology. However, in an effort to create a framework for thinking about technology affordances in education, there are some considerations to examine that can be linked to instructional design activities as well as to instructional goals and objectives (see Table 12.1). Again, it is useful to think of activities and what people will do rather than focus on idealized processes or functions. Linking the technology to the purpose and associated user activity is one way to identify how to evaluate alternative technologies and their affordances. In addition, tracing the links between users, goals, activities, and a particular technology can help identify potential issues that may arise with regard to various technologies. The assumption herein is that no one technology is likely to serve any particular goal for all those involved. There are nearly always alternatives and issues to be considered when planning to integrate technology in learning and instruction.

An interesting group activity would be to add items to Table 12.1 discussing the affordances of particular technologies, especially new and emerging technologies, and how they align with educational goals and learning objectives. As mentioned elsewhere in this volume, including specific technologies has been kept to a minimum due to the rapid evolution of existing technologies and the fact that new technologies emerge so frequently.

Given the complexities of designing effective instruction, the rich array of technologies, and the amazing variety of instructional resources now available, the task of teaching

TABLE 12.1 A notional framework for educational technology affordances

Role/goal	Activity/affordance	Possible technology	Potential issue
Designer			
Determine learning needs	Conduct cognitive task analysis	ACTA (Applied Cognitive Task Analysis; Militello & Hutton, 1998)	Difficult to generalize cognitive demand levels across users
Evaluate the quality of resources	Rate learning objects	LORI (Learning Object Review Instrument; Leacock & Nesbit, 2007).	Difficult to reconcile perceived quality differences of teachers and learners
Teacher			
Increase learner engagement	Encourage collaborative writing	HyLighter (Lebow, 2009)	Requires group facilitation skills and a common shared platform
Provide meaningful formative feedback	Assess learner progress	HIMATT (Highly Integrated Model-based Assessment Tools and Technologies; Pirnay-Dummer et al., 2010)	Useful for complex cognitive tasks; requires expert models and training of teachers
Student			
Understand long-term planning processes	Interact with a simulation to support decision making	BLEND (Bergen Learning Environment for National Development; Kopainsky et al., 2009)	Students need to believe that the underlying simulation model reflects real-world dynamics
Develop meta-cognitive skills	Improve self-regulation in solving complex problems	ePEARL (Web-based, student-centered, electronic portfolios; Abrami et al., 2008).	Requires meaningful feedback from peers and teachers; focuses on cognitive aspects of tasks with little support for affective aspects

effectively with appropriate technologies is a challenge for all involved. There simply is no secret to success in teaching with technology. Being flexible and open to alternatives is important, as is a careful analysis of the situation and the involvement of students and instructors in selecting and integrating technologies in teaching and learning. A few of the implications and challenges are discussed next (for more on these and related topics, see http://aect-president-2009–2010.blogspot.com).

Student Implications

There are many who write about the so-called digital natives who were born after the advent of the digital age in the late 1970s (Prensky, 2001). The argument is that those born into a digital society and who grew up using all sorts of digital devices think about and use technology differently than those born prior to the advent of the digital age (digital immigrants). Digital natives may be more likely to be early adopters of new technology and are more likely to adapt to new technologies more quickly than digital immigrants. Perhaps digital natives, especially those who grew up with personal digital devices in their hands since early childhood, think, learn, and behave somewhat differently than their elders. There is likely some truth in this distinction and mega-generalization, in which case their interests and expectations need to be taken into consideration.

There is also some tension in the notion that individual learner characteristics need to be taken into consideration, and the generalization that digital natives expect to have digitally supported learning tools and technologies in their education and training. Not everyone born in the last 20 or so years can be considered a digital native. There is also a reality called the digital divide that distinguishes those with ready and affordable access to digital information and communications technologies from those with limited or no access at all (Compaine, 2001). Moreover, while digital natives may have ready access to new tools and technologies, they may not be adept in using them to support their own learning and development. The caution here is to avoid over-generalizing, especially with regard to learners. It is important to know a great deal about the learners in order to address issues pertaining to motivation and access to resources as well as to select, sequence, and structure appropriate and meaningful learning activities.

Teacher Implications

Many of the same considerations with regard to students apply to teachers. Not all teachers are equally ready and willing to integrate technology into instruction, as suggested in the discussion about the diffusion of innovation and early adopters. Moreover, while some technologies simply replace an existing task or activity with an automated version, others require teachers to change how they interact with students, how they select and use resources, and occasionally to reconceptualize their roles and obligations as teachers. For example, consider a technology to create objective tests from an online database, generate different versions of equal difficulty, and then deliver, monitor, and score those tests automatically. The teacher can create the questions and perhaps even rank questions of similar difficulty. The system then automates things the teacher might have been doing without automated support. One can easily imagine teachers viewing such a system as a productivity enhancer and would, in many cases, embrace such a system, assuming they were already committed to objective testing in that situation. The impact on teaching in this case might be minimal and training teachers would probably go quite smoothly.

Consider the popular notion of flipping the classroom so that students read assignments and view resources outside school and work on problems in class, either individually or in small groups. While teachers may see the benefit of flipping the classroom, doing so dramatically changes what they do in the classroom, and some may not be well prepared for such a dramatic change. In other cases, a teacher may feel threatened by a new technology and worry that it might eventually replace the teacher completely. Discussing such a possibility in class or online might be a worthwhile activity.

On the other hand, consider a case where the training of nurses was going to be changed by introducing simulated patients. Some nurse training programs make use of humans playing the role of patients and most programs introduce nurses into actual medical situations in the course of the training. Patient simulators offer many new affordances; while they introduce an initial capital investment, the advantages may justify the investment. A patient simulator can be programmed to have and to react realistically to many different ailments in the context of a wide variety of training scenarios. As a result, nurse trainees can be provided with a wide variety of realistic training scenarios. Such a dramatic change in nurse training, however, has a significant impact on those training the nurses. First, the didactic aspect of teaching will probably change so as to allow knowledge-based materials to be introduced in the context of specific interactions with a patient simulator; in other words, the context of didactic teaching is likely to change, and there may be less didactic instruction and much more hands-on instruction. Because the new training environment will be highly experiential, the role of the teacher-trainer is likely to become more like that of a coach and facilitator. Using the simulator effectively and adjusting teaching techniques accordingly are new skills that need to be supported with substantial training programs.

When the visual, turtle-based Logo programming language was introduced in the 1970s, many thought it would revolutionize teaching and learning in schools (Papert, 1980). That did not happen. While there are many remarkable cases of innovative learning using Logo to support many instructional activities, Logo and its successor Lego-Logo have had only a minor and marginal impact on teaching and learning. The answer is that in part Logo never became part of the teaching repertoire of most teachers and it did not fit the educational culture of most schools very well (see the next section). In addition, there was inadequate training and professional development available for teachers. Typically, teachers either learned it on their own and in their spare time, or they left Logo as entertainment for kids. Logo was not integrated into very many teaching and learning activities. Are there other promising technologies that had little impact on teaching and learning? This is another topic worth discussing in class or in an online forum.

In summary, when introducing a new educational technology, it is important to take into consideration those who will be supporting its use, especially the teachers, trainers, or tutors. A user-centered technology innovation approach will involve these key persons in the decision and planning processes leading up to the use of a new technology. To ensure success of the technology innovation, proper training of teachers and support staff must be a high priority consideration. Making such training an added task to a full load of existing responsibilities is probably not a good path to pursue, as it can create resentment and result in the development of negative attitudes. Rather, treating the teaching and training staff as professionals being introduced to a new technology is likely to result in better integration of the new technology. Providing adequate time and support for training and professional development is a high priority issue for successful diffusion of educational technology innovations.

Educational Culture Implications

Bruner (1996) identifies nine tenets or principles with regard to culture and education, which are briefly characterized here:

1. Meaning making is relative to and dependent on context and perspective.
2. There are two major kinds of constraints on meaning making: human mental functioning and symbol systems.
3. Individuals construct a sense of reality (recall the discussion about mental models and Wittgenstein's remark that we picture facts to ourselves).
4. Education is interactional in the sense that teachers and learners interact dynamically with teachers providing scaffolding to engage students who are enactive in learning.
5. What is learned can be externalized in the form of works that support discussion, debate, and further learning.
6. Education is instrumental in the social and economic lives of learners.
7. Learning is situated and institutionalized.
8. Education shapes identity and self-esteem.
9. Narrative creates cohesiveness and a sense of belonging.

As with any of the many topics introduced in this introductory text, this topic of educational culture could be treated at length in one or more dedicated and focused volumes. Bruner's (1996) *The Culture of Education* is certainly a good point of departure for such an endeavor. The interaction of language and culture is well developed in the literature and is worth pursuing, especially by those interested in distance learning involving learners from around the world (see, for example, http://anthro.palomar.edu/

language/default.htm). In the introductory chapter of *The Culture of Education*, Bruner (1996) includes a discussion of the philosophy of mind and culture. He contrasts a purely cognitive, information processing perspective of the mind with a cultural perspective. The former focuses on individuals and discrete knowledge items, whereas the latter focuses on communities and interacting groups of individuals sharing and using knowledge for various purposes. Bruner and many modern educational professions adopt the latter view, recognizing that learning and education are nearly always situated in a cultural context. Such a view makes analysis and design tasks more complex and challenging. However, a cultural perspective, especially when mixed with a cognitive perspective, is well aligned with that of naturalistic epistemology—a descriptive account of how people come to know and understand the world rather than a deductive treatment of knowledge (Spector, 2012).

Test Your Understanding

Provide brief definitions or explanations for each of the following:

1. affordance;
2. early majority;
3. Bloom's two-sigma effect;
4. laggards/resistors;
5. Moore's Law;
6. situational evaluation;
7. participatory design.

A Representative Educational Technology Challenge

You are the Dean of a college of education in a prominent university that has programs to prepare teachers among others. The teacher preparation program has been relatively stable for the last 20 years: the curriculum has remained about the same, most of the instruction occurs in traditional classroom settings, there is an active internship program in the fourth year of the program that places pre-service teachers in nearby schools under the tutelage of experienced public school teachers, and there is a standardized state-wide exam that graduating teachers must pass in order to complete the teacher certification process. The State Board of Education recently convened a meeting with all of the provosts and education deans in the various state colleges and universities to pass along disappointing data with regard to retention of new teachers, performance of students on state-mandated standardized tests, and misuse/disuse of new educational technologies purchased at significant expense in the last two years. The Board of Education has been tasked by the governor to propose changes to improve the situation, and the Board is now asking the various provosts and deans for specific recommendations about what can be done to improve this situation in college and university teacher preparation programs.

Learning Activities

1. Identify and describe the key factors that you would consider in framing your response to the problem situation stated above.
2. Identify and describe the key factors that are likely to be obstacles in implementing the effort.
3. Indicate and describe the relationships among all the key factors that have been identified.
4. Indicate what kinds of additional support should be considered in order to make the best case for your solution approach.
5. Create an annotated concept map that reflects the things indicated in response to the previous four tasks.

Links

Mike Spector's blog discusses a number of issues related to learning and instruction—http://aect-president-2009–2010.blogspot.com

Palomar College site on language and culture—see http://anthro.palomar.edu/language/default.htm

Tennyson's Fourth Generation ISD Model—see http://onlinelibrary.wiley.com/doi/10.1002/pfi.4140380607/pdf

Other Resources

Andrew Gibbons' model-centered instruction and design layers—www.instructionaldesign.org/theories/design-layers.html

The Concord Consortium website—realizing the promise of educational technology—see http://www.concord.org

The New Media Consortium's 2014 Horizon Report on new and emerging educational technologies—see www.nmc.org/publications/2014-horizon-report-higher-ed

A roadmap for education technology (NSF Study edited by Beverly Woolf, 2010)—see www.cra.org/ccc/files/docs/groe/GROE%20Roadmap%20for%20Education%20Technology%20Final%20Report.pdf

References

Abrami, P. C., Wade, A., Pillay, V., Aslan, O., Bures, E. M., & Bentley, C. (2008). Encouraging self-regulated learning electronic portfolios. *Canadian Journal of Learning and Technology, 34*(3). Retrieved from www.cjlt.ca/index.php/cjlt/article/view/507/238

Andrews, D. H., & Goodson, L. A. (1980). A comparative analysis of models of instructional design. *Journal of Instructional Development, 3*(4), 2–16.

Bloom, B. (1984). The 2 sigma problem: The search for methods of group instruction as effective as one-on-one tutoring. *Educational Researcher, 13*(6), 4–16.

Bruner, J. S. (1996). *The culture of education.* Cambridge, MA: Harvard University Press.

Compaine, B. M. (Ed.) (2001). *The digital divide? Facing a crisis or creating myth?* Cambridge, MA: MIT Press.

Corbett, T., Koedinger, K. R., & Anderson, J. R. (1997). Intelligent tutoring systems. In M. Helander, T. K. Landauer, & P. Prabhu (Eds.), *Handbook of human-computer interaction* (2nd ed.) (pp. 849–874). Amsterdam: Elsevier.

Dewey, J. (1916). *Democracy and education: An introduction to the philosophy of education.* New York: Macmillan.

Gibbons, A. S. (2015). Instructional design models. In J. M. Spector (Ed.), *The encyclopedia of educational technology*. Thousand Oaks, CA: Sage.

Gibson, J. J. (1977). The theory of affordances. In R. Shaw & J. D. Bransford (Eds.), *Acting and knowing* (pp. 67–82). Hillsdale, NJ: Erlbaum.

Gustafson, K. L., & Branch, R. M. (2002). *Survey of instructional development models*. Syracuse, NY: The ERIC Clearinghouse on Information Technology.

Hellman, M. E. (2003). Moore's Law and communications. Retrieved from www-ee.stanford.edu/~hellman/opinion/moore.html

Kleinman, D. L., & Moore, K. (Eds.) (2014). *Routledge handbook of science, technology and society*. New York: Routledge.

Kopainsky, B., Pedercini, M., Davidsen, P. I., & Alessi, S. M. (2009). A blend of planning and learning: Simplifying a simulation model of national development. *Simulation & Gaming, 41*(5), 641–662.

Leacock, T. L., & Nesbit, J. D. (2007). A framework for evaluating the quality of multimedia learning resources. *Educational Technology & Society, 10*(2), 44–59.

Lebow, D. G. (2009). Document review meets social software and the learning sciences. *Journal of e-Learning and Knowledge Society, 5*(1), 171–180.

Militello, L. G., & Hutton, R. J. (1998). Applied cognitive task analysis (ACTA): A practitioner's toolkit for understanding cognitive task demands. *Ergonomics, 41*(11), 1618–1641.

Moore, G. E. (1965). Cramming more components onto integrated circuits. *Electronics, 38*(8), 114–117.

Papert, S. (1980). *Mindstorms: Children, computers and powerful ideas*. New York: Basic Books.

Pirnay-Dummer, P., Ifenthaler, D., & Spector, J. M. (2010). Highly integrated model assessment technology and tools. *Educational Technology Research & Development, 58*(1), 3–18.

Prensky, M. (2001). Digital natives, digital immigrants. *On the Horizon, 9*(5). Retrieved March 15, 2011 from www.marcprensky.com/writing/Prensky%20-%20Digital%20Natives,%20Digital%20Immigrants%20-%20Part1.pdf

Spector, J. M. (2000). Trends and issues in educational technology: How far we have not come. *Update Semiannual Bulletin 21*(2). Syracuse, NY: The ERIC Clearinghouse on Information Technology. Retrieved on March 15, 2011 from http://supadoc.syr.edu/docushare/dsweb/Get/Document-12994/trends-tech-educ-eric.pdf

Spector, J. M. (2012). Naturalistic epistemology. In N. M. Seel (Ed.), *The encyclopedia of the sciences of learning*. New York: Springer.

Spector, J. M. (2015). *The encyclopedia of educational technology*. Thousand Oaks, CA: Sage.

Stewart. C. M., Schifter, C. C., & Selverian, M. E. M. (Eds.) (2010). *Teaching and learning with technology: Beyond constructivism*. New York: Routledge.

Tennyson, R. D. (1997). Instructional development and ISD[4] methodology. *Performance Improvement Quarterly, 38*(6), 19–27.

Tufte, E. R. (2003). *The cognitive style of PowerPoint*. Cheshire, CN: Graphics Press.

thirteen
Educational Technologies in the Workplace

"And is it not by means of lessons and practice—that is by means of change—that the mind acquires and information and its healthy condition improved? But inactivity—lack of practice and learning—leads the mind not only to learn nothing, but even to forget what it has learned" (Socrates, from Plato's Theaetetus)

In recent history, there has been a strong separation between learning in school settings and pursuing a career after completing one's education. Of course there has been additional job-related learning after school, including apprenticeships, on-the-job training, and professional development. In spite of the fact that learning continues throughout a person's lifetime, education in modern times has been associated with formal programs in schools and colleges, and work has been associated with what one does after completing an education (see, for example, Jarvis & Watts, 2012; Zepeda, 2014).

Technology and the globalization made possible by new technologies are changing this distinction (Spector & Wang, 2002a, 2002b). According to data available at the National Center for Education Statistics, in 1970 there were about 2,765,000 part-time college students in the USA; that number grew to about 6,978,000 by 2007; the percentages of part-time students in that period grew from 32 percent to 38 percent (see http://nces.ed.gov/fastfacts/display.asp?id=98). In addition to more students working while advancing their education, the average age of college students in the USA has been increasing. The United States Census Bureau reported that in 1970, the percentage of college students 35 years and over was about 8 percent; by 2009, the percentage of college students 35 years of age and over in the USA had doubled to 16 percent (see www.census.gov/hhes/school/=index.html). Such data suggest that the traditional boundary between working and studying is eroding.

It is worth noting that such indicators as those cited here can be misleading. For example, increasing education costs could be driving more students to work while in college, and opportunities to take online courses may account for more working adults pursuing further education. Additionally, workers are moving to new positions and new jobs more frequently, and such movement often requires preparatory training. Nevertheless, the indicators do suggest a fuzzier boundary between studying and working, which may or may not be a good thing. This is another good topic for classroom discussion.

On the positive side of the evaporating boundary between working and studying is the recognition of the importance of and social support for lifelong learning. Adults are continuing their education in support of their personal interests and professional goals more than ever before. Technology is helping to make this possible through widely accessible online courses and personalized instruction. The ability to further one's education while working may be regarded as a highly desirable social end in and of itself. Education is generally regarded as something good, and this remains true regardless of the age of the person involved. A 2006 Norwegian law encapsulates the concept of further education as a social good quite well. In that law, Norwegians who have worked for three years for any enterprise have the right to be on leave either part-time or full-time for a period up to three years. Other European countries and many Asian countries systematically provide support for continuing education (see www.eurofound.europa. eu/ewco).

For example, Universitas Terbuka in Indonesia provided support for a senior administrator in a critical position to earn a Ph.D. at Florida State University because Universitas Terbuka wanted all senior administrators to have a relevant doctoral degree. The trade-off was the short-term (three years) loss of her productivity and expertise for potential future gains in terms of quality and reputation that are hard to quantify. The willingness to make such trade-offs and invest in the future may be more common in innovative enterprises than in higher education and elsewhere. Discussing specific examples of such trade-offs could be an insightful activity in class or in a discussion forum.

Employers can make use of distance-learning technologies and workplace-based training to maintain a highly skilled and adaptive workforce. This might also be regarded as a desirable social benefit. A society with a highly trained and educated workforce is likely to be a productive society with a high standard of living. However, the benefits to a particular employer that accrue due to highly skilled workers might result in some workers being let go and others being coerced to pursue training and development that may not be all that well aligned with their own interests. Still, from the perspective of the global marketplace, society places a high value on innovative and productive organizations.

On a slightly darker side of the fuzzy boundary between studying and working, there is the issue of a liberal arts education and its value and place in an industrialized and globalized economy. At one time, a person who had read the classical great books (e.g., Homer's *Odyssey*, Herodotus' *Histories*, Plato's *Republic*, Aristotle's *Physics*, Euclid's *Elements*, Dante's *Divine Comedy*, Chaucer's *Canterbury Tales*, Descartes' *Discourse on Method*, Newton's *Principia Mathematica*, and Heisenberg's *The Physical Principles of the Quantum Theory*, to name just a few) might have been regarded as a well-educated person ready to be a leader in modern society. The Great Books Program was initiated at Columbia University in 1919 by John Erskine and continued at the University of Chicago when Erskine moved there in the 1920s. There are still a few college curricula structured around the great books, notably at St. John's College in Annapolis, MD and Santa Fe, NM. Currently, enrollments in great books and liberal arts programs are declining. One conclusion might be that the markers of a well-educated person are changing. These days, indicators of being well-educated might include an awareness of international affairs, a scientifically oriented perspective with regard to a variety of social problems, and familiarity with the latest digital technologies. Discussing such changes could make for a lively discussion.

While it is well beyond the scope of this book to pursue a definition and discussion of being well educated, it is worth noting that technologies associated with the modern digital era are changing society and that which society values. What is highly valued is not the ability to recite a set of facts, because anyone can easily find and confirm/refute those facts somewhere in cyberspace. What is highly valued is the ability to reason critically and think clearly with regard to complex problem-solving situations. People are problem solvers—this has been true since recorded history. While historically people have confronted puzzling and complex problems, such problems seem to permeate the modern digital era. The biblical Abraham had to resolve several challenging problems. For example, Abraham reportedly heard a voice that said something like this: "Get up and go to a faraway place." Surely he wondered why he should and what he would find there. Later that same ominous voice told Abraham to take his only son up to Mount Moriah along with a knife and the makings for a burnt offering. Surely that created a tough problem for Abraham to resolve.

While such dilemmas as those with which Abraham was confronted have been around since ancient times, in modern times there are many more technically oriented but equally challenging and complex problem situations to resolve. For example, patents and copyrights typically protected intellectual property and rewarded innovation and creativity. However, they also limited access and use of new ideas and information. In the digital era, things happen very fast and an increasing number of innovators are willing to share ideas and information without the full benefits and protection of patents and copyrights. Information and communications technologies have introduced new challenges while providing the affordances of rapid dissemination. Among these challenges are the verification of information found on the Web and the proper recognition of the intellectual property of others. Creative Commons represents a community attempting to resolve part of this problem (see http://creativecommons.org). The open source software movement (see http://opensource.org) is another example of this trend of making more digital things available to more people at little or no cost.

Twenty-First-Century Skills

Next we turn to the issue mentioned earlier about jobs and productivity driving what is valued in an education. There is a certain tension between the goal of developing independent critical thinkers and the goal of developing a highly skilled workforce. In former times, and especially in Europe, there were two tracks in higher education— one aimed at vocational and technical training, and one aimed at scholarship in the arts and sciences. There are still many institutions of higher education around the world that emphasize one or the other of these two types of education, and such institutions are likely to continue to exist for some time. However, there is an increasing emphasis in developed and developing countries on preparing students for jobs in the twenty-first century, especially those jobs that are likely to result in a productive and prosperous society.

What skills are associated with those jobs? What comes to mind first might be skills that are technical and oriented to specific information and communication technologies, such as the ability to use the Internet to find, verify, and synthesize information on a particular topic or the ability to quickly create an easily modified, widely accessible, and highly portable visual representation of something. An interesting class exercise at this point would be to present or request a problem situation, and then elicit all the relevant knowledge and skills that a professional organization would require in order to achieve a satisfactory resolution of that problem situation. Next, one can imagine a discussion about whether or not colleges and universities are preparing students to have the requisite knowledge and skills. The likely outcome is partly yes and partly no—the details are well worth considering in a group of diverse people.

Initially, one might argue that critical twenty-first-century jobs include communication engineers, economists, engineering designers, environmental planners, medical specialists, network technicians, therapists (technology can drive anyone crazy), and so on. While each of these highly valued jobs requires domain-specific knowledge, skills and training, there are an identifiable set of skills that cut across these and other jobs that are particularly pertinent to advancement and career success in the industrialized and globalized world of the twenty-first century. It is this latter set of more generic knowledge and skills that are generally called twenty-first-century skills.

The global knowledge economy is a widely recognized development and has been characterized in a number of ways (see, for example, Rooney, Hearn, & Ninan, 2005). A rough and ready summary of the global knowledge economy is that it is a result of the confluence and synergy of a number of factors, including powerful information and communications technologies, knowledge engineering methods, database- and evidence-based planning and decision making, and emerging global markets. In the resulting economic environment, enterprises must be flexible and continuously innovating to remain competitive. This creates a demand for workers who can adjust to changing job requirements and quickly learn new skills. Successful knowledge workers will have multiple literacies, including digital literacy, information literacy, visual literacy, and technology literacy (these are treated separately in Spector, 2015b). In addition, successful knowledge workers will need to be creative and critical thinkers, and have good communication and self-regulation skills.

Somewhat surprisingly, these twenty-first-century skills place a premium on independent higher order reasoning skills, which educators and scholars have long argued should be emphasized in school-based curricula. The partnership for twenty-first-century skills (see www.p21.org) summarizes such thinking in terms of three different sets of skills as depicted in Table 13.1.

To develop these skills in students and in workers is a significant challenge for twenty-first-century educators and managers (National Center on Education and the Economy, 2007). Engaging students in real-world problem-solving activities is one step in this direction. Developing a scientific attitude (i.e., an attitude that values evidence, accepts risk taking, and places a premium on questioning accepted wisdom and challenging what some regard as obvious) toward problem solving and decision making is another important step.

The development of the global knowledge economy, of course, has strong implications for the preparation of those working in the area of advanced learning technology (ALT). Hartley and colleagues (2010) conducted a three-year study to explore those implications and developed the framework depicted in Figure 13.1.

This committee (Hartley et al., 2010) adopted a competence perspective with the definition of a competence as a related set of knowledge, skills, and attitudes required

TABLE 13.1 Overview of twenty-first-century skills

Learning and innovation skills	Creativity and innovation
	Critical thinking and problem solving
	Communication and collaboration
Information, media, and technology skills	Information literacy
	Media literacy
	ICT literacy
Life and career skills	Flexibility and adaptability
	Initiative and self-direction
	Social and cross-cultural skills
	Productivity and accountability
	Leadership and responsibility

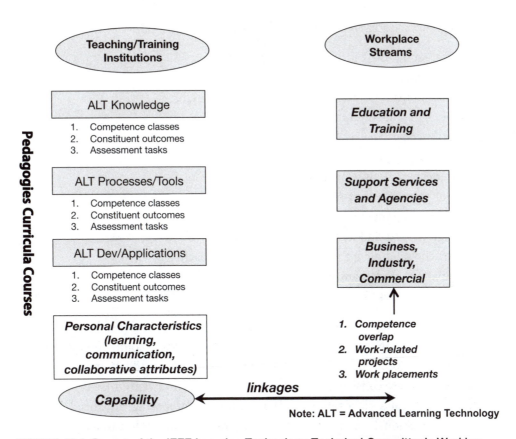

FIGURE 13.1 Report of the IEEE Learning Technology Technical Committee's Working committee on new curricula for advanced learning technologies

to successfully perform a task or job function. The work was conducted by a team of five experts over a period of three years. After a series of focus group discussions, interviews with experts from industry and education, and multiple global surveys, the committee identified 13 topics to be addressed in an ALT curriculum that fit into five domains for education and training ALT professionals (see Table 13.2).

TABLE 13.2 Five domains of ALT competence domains

Knowledge competence	E.g., learning theory, pedagogy, experimental design, societal concerns, etc.
Process competence	E.g., operational skills in using ICT for education and training
Application competence	E.g., skills in applying ALT skills (e.g, instructional design) in education and training
Personal/social competence	E.g., self-regulation skills, communication skills, collaboration skills, etc.
Innovative/creative competence	E.g., using new technologies in innovative ways to solve education and training problems.

The thirteen topic areas recommended by the committee for an ALT curriculum were:

1. Introduction to ALT.
2. Introduction to human learning.
3. Foundations, evolution, and developments in ALT.
4. Typologies and key approaches to ALT.
5. Users' perspectives of ALT.
6. Learners' perspectives of ALT.
7. Systems perspectives of ALT.
8. Social perspectives of ALT.
9. Design requirements.
10. Design process and development life cycles.
11. Instructional design: the learning objects approach.
12. Evaluation: models and practices.
13. Emerging issues in ALT.

It remains to be seen to what extent educational technology and instructional design education and training programs will adopt part or all of the recommendations of the IEEE Technical Committee on Learning Technology. Basically, that committee's recommendations are consistent with the various reports on twenty-first-century skills and demonstrate one elaboration in the context of preparing advanced learning technology professionals for work in the twenty-first century. Educational technology and instructional design preparation programs are discussed in more detail in a subsequent chapter.

Education and Training in the Workplace

With the introduction of new technology applications in workplace settings on a regular basis, it is now commonplace to find training conducted in work settings. In addition, progressive enterprises encourage their workers to take distance courses during working hours. There are a variety of ways that various enterprises accomplish workplace-based training and education. Some enterprises make use of Internet-based video conferencing when one-to-many or many-to-many communication methods are appropriate. Some of these technologies allow screen sharing and support collaboration in a variety of ways.

When the situation involves a new computer-based or cloud-based technology, the training is often in the form of an individual tutorial or a Webinar in which workers can participate at their individual workstations. Sometimes, a new procedure for operating equipment or solving complex problems is introduced, and an interactive simulation may be provided to help workers gain competence; such simulations are somewhat costly to develop, so this typically only happens when there are many people and/or costly equipment involved. With the introduction of personal tablet computers (e.g., the iPAD), training can occur in almost any setting with Internet or cell/mobile phone access.

One concern that arises with workplace training and education involves time. Workers who are involved in workplace training are not performing their daily tasks. Unfortunately, some employers do not reduce the expected workload when workers are occupied with required workplace training and education. Notwithstanding that concern, workplace training and education is likely to expand and evolve in many innovative ways as enterprises seek to develop the skills of their workers and training at work often has the advantage of being properly situated.

Test Your Understanding

Briefly define, elaborate, or illustrate each of the following terms:

1. Competency
2. Twenty-first-century skill.
3. Technology literacy.
4. Workplace-based training.
5. Well-educated person.
6. Lifelong learning.
7. The traditional boundary between studying and working.

A Representative Educational Technology Challenge

A small pharmaceutical company has hired you, an educational technology expert, to help the company make a transition from developing a product in which it had specialized for the last 20 years to delivering medical information to professionals and the general public. The historical product was a tablet used to treat adult onset diabetes, but the patent has expired and generic alternatives now dominate that market. However, the corporation has a great deal of knowledge and experience about diabetes and especially with regard to marketing to medical providers. The corporate leadership has decided to refocus on developing medical information, initially pertaining to diabetes, and then marketing that information to the medical community as well as to the public. The business case shows that sufficient revenue might be developed from pharmaceutical advertisers and the medical community; much of the information can be provided to the public at no charge as a way to ensure a large number of hits on the corporate website, which will attract advertisers. Your task is to develop a corporate retraining plan to minimize layoffs and lost personnel in this small, family-owned enterprise. The training will first focus on the sales and public relations personnel (to market a different product), and the chemists who had been producing the pill but who will be producing medical information about diabetes if they manage to stay with the company.

Learning Activities

1. Identify and describe the key factors that you would consider in framing your response to the problem situation stated above.

2. Identify and describe the key factors that are likely to be obstacles in implementing the effort.

3. Indicate and describe the relationships among all the key factors that have been identified.

4. Indicate what kinds of additional support should be considered in order to make the proposed solution feasible and affordable.

5. Create an annotated concept map that reflects the things indicated in response to the previous four tasks.

Links

LIFE—a National Science Foundation Science of Learning Center focused on informal and formal environments—see http://life-slc.org

NCES (National Center for Education Statistics) Fast Facts—see http://nces.ed.gov/fastfacts/display.asp?id=98

OECD (Organisation for Economic Co-operation and Development) site on nonformal and informal learning—www.oecd.org/edu/skills-beyond-school/recognitionofnon-formalandinformallearning-home.htm

United States Census Bureau School Enrollment Data—see www.census.gov/population/www/socdemo/school.html

Creative Commons—see http://creativecommons.org

Other Resources

Center for Public Education—see www.centerforpubliceducation.org/Learn-About/21st-Century/The-21st-century-job.html

European Working Conditions Observatory: Quality of Work and Employment in Norway—see www.eurofound.europa.eu/ewco/studies/tn0612036s/no0612039q.htm

Partnership for 21st Century Skills—see www.p21.org

Open source software movement—http://opensource.org

References

Hartley, R., Kinshuk, Kooper, R., Okamoto, T., & Spector, J. M. (2010). The education and training of learning technologists: A competences approach. *Educational Technology & Society, 13*(2): 206–216.

Jarvis, P., & Watts, M. (Eds.) (2012). *The Routledge international handbook of learning.* New York: Routledge.

National Center on Education and the Economy. (2007). Tough choices for tough times: The report of the new commission on the skills of the American workforce. San Francisco, CA: Jossey-Bass.

Plato (1987). *Theaetetus* (Trans. R. A. H. Waterfield). London: Penguin Books.

Rooney, D., Hearn, G., & Ninan, A. (Eds.) (2005). *Handbook on the knowledge economy.* Cheltenham: Edward Elgar.

Spector, J. M. (Ed.) (2015). *The encyclopedia of educational technology.* Thousand Oaks, CA: Sage.

Spector, J. M., & Wang, X. (2002a). Integrating technology into learning and working: Introduction. *Education, Technology and Society, 5*(1). Retrieved from www.ifets.info/journals/5_1/editorial.pdf

Spector, J. M., & Wang, X. (2002b). Integrating technology into learning and working: Introduction. *Education, Technology and Society, 5*(2). Retrieved from www.ifets.info/journals/5_2/editorial.pdf

Zepeda, S. J. (2014). *Job-embedded professional development: Support, collaboration, and learning in schools.* New York: Routledge.

fourteen
Designing Technology-Supported Learning Environments

"Good design, at least part of the time, includes the criterion of being direct in relation to the problem at hand—not obscure, trendy or stylish. A new language, visual or verbal, must be couched in language that is already understood" (Ivan Chermayeff)

Design is fundamentally about specifying how something should be implemented in order to best fulfill its intended purpose. Many of the things we use everyday are designed so as to make the performance of a particular task possible, easier, more pleasant, and, in some cases, more affordable (see, for example, Norman, 1988). In short, design permeates our experience of the world in the form of various artifacts and technologies. As a consequence, the literature on design is vast and far beyond a fair review or summary in this volume. This is still true if we limit our concern to instructional design, although instructional design has much to learn and has borrowed extensively from the general field of design (see Gibbons & Brewer, 2005 and Gibbons, Boling, & Smith, 2014 for fundamental instructional design issues). In this chapter, the focus will be first on some general principles of design and then on principles to consider when designing systems and environments to support learning, instruction, and performance.

Design is a goal-oriented enterprise. Things are designed so as to make the use of those things easy and pleasant. This overarching principle applies to handles on refrigerators as well as to the interface in a computer-based system. Human use, therefore, is a primary consideration in design. Design is a human-centered activity (see, for example, www.jnd. org). While this seems obvious, the fact that design is human-centered has significant implications. First, it is seldom clear at the outset how people will use something; it often happens that people will use something in ways that were not imagined by the designer.

For example, a web-based learning management system designed to host course materials and learning activities may be used for noninstructional purposes to support project teams; this has, in fact, happened with mainstream web-based learning management systems, which have been redesigned to support such use. An interesting class discussion activity might be to identify other things designed for one purpose and then used by some users for a different purpose that result in a redesign of those things. In any case, the point here is that human-centered activities inherently involve some degree of uncertainty, especially with regard to use. While this uncertainty might be minimized by conducting extensive needs assessments and involving users in the design, there will always be some degree of uncertainty. This means that in many cases design should be considered an iterative activity—there are likely to be redesigns and modifications as use of the designed entity spreads to more users. This is one reason that design-based research and development have become prominent in the educational literature (see DBRC, 2003; McKenney & Reeves, 2014; Richey & Klein, 2014).

To set the stage for the design principles to follow, a brief discussion about context and culture is in order. The following discussion is centered around the concept of a normal distribution of users—students or workers—and it obviously involves a degree of overgeneralization. Figure 14.1 depicts a normal distribution curve. Normal distributions occur naturally and are useful in statistical analysis. When dealing with a large number of users (students or workers), one can consider that they will be more or less distributed as depicted in Figure 14.1 with regard to many characteristics. Two key measures of a distribution are the mean (average) and the variance (width of the distribution). When one assumes a normal distribution, sigma (σ) is used to signify a standard deviation from the mean. In the case of a normal distribution, about 68 percent of the individuals will be within one standard deviation (plus or minus) of the mean.

The reason this is significant is that when considering a design, one might be inclined to focus on just those who are within one standard deviation of the mean—those in areas C and D in Figure 14.1. Given more time to analysis users and their needs, one might even stretch the coverage to include those in areas B and E, which would cover about 95 percent of the user population.

Now, think about the normal distribution in terms of learner ability as measured by some relevant measure (e.g., prior grades, test scores, etc.). The temptation might be to design curricula, courses, and lessons to meet the needs and expectations of those in areas C and D or possibly in areas B, C, D, and E. One might argue that students in area A (perhaps also area B) will never be able to master the knowledge and skills anyway, so time and effort devoted to them should be minimized. One might further argue that those in area F (perhaps also area E) will do well regardless of whatever instruction and learning activities are designed, so there is no need to focus on them either. These assumptions certainly simplify the task of design. However, they intentionally neglect certain learners in the design process. A similar discussion could be considered with regard to a design team, although the variations in that case are not likely to follow a normal distribution

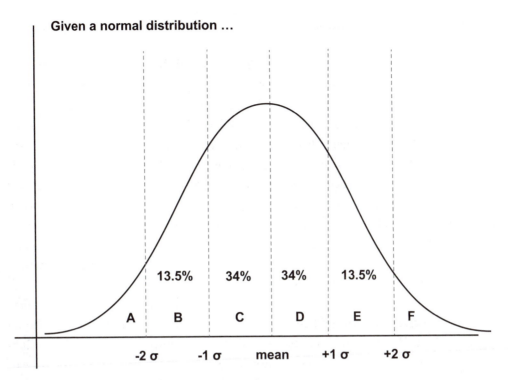

FIGURE 14.1 A normal distribution with standard deviations

given the relatively small numbers of people involved. The point is that focusing on part of the population involved may simplify design, but it may generate other problems, some of which are likely to be related to the goal of the design effort (e.g., improve learning outcomes for all, deliver a quality product on time and within budget, etc.).

How many curricula, courses, and lessons have been designed based on such simplifying assumptions? Are such assumptions pervasive in schools and colleges? Probably so, but this is another issue that is worth discussing in class or in a discussion forum. As a tentative generalization, let us say for now that many education systems intentionally minimize emphasis on poorly performing and exceptional students. Of course there are exceptions, as demonstrated by classes for the gifted, by remediation efforts, and so on.

Again consider Figure 14.1, but this time think about a business or enterprise and worker productivity as the key variable being considered. When one considers potential and actual employees, one could assume a normal distribution with regard to worker productivity. Businesses will typically not focus on those in areas C and D—those within one standard deviation of the mean. Rather, a typical business will place emphasis on avoiding the hiring of those likely to be poor performers (area A and possibly area B); in addition, a typical business will make every effort to reward and further incentivize those demonstrating high productivity (area F and possibly area E).

This difference in emphasis between education and business, while certainly over-generalized, reflects one of many cultural considerations that are worth considering when designing a technology-facilitated learning, instructional, or performance improvement system.

In addition, a central concern involves the relevant stakeholders. It is obvious enough that the end-users (learners and employees) are key stakeholders, and improving their knowledge, skills, and attitudes is always a guiding design issue. However, there are other users and stakeholders who need to be considered relevant to the design process, including teachers or trainers, assessment and evaluation specialists, graphic artists, media and technology specialists, facility personnel, and management. Determining the goals of what is to be designed is paramount, since the design will be evaluated against those goals. Learning and performance outcomes are often not the only goals when all relevant stakeholders are taken into consideration. Obviously costs, access, ease of maintenance, and other considerations should inform a design. Moreover, changes in user attitudes and perceptions are relevant not only to successful implementation, but to long-term success of an effort.

A grading system is a designed artifact. A merit pay system is another designed artifact. What is the intended purpose of these designs? Who are they meant to serve? How should they be evaluated? If these systems are not achieving their intended purpose, how might they be redesigned? These questions are not easily answered. In addition to the issue of identifying relevant user groups and the cultural complexities associated with design, there are often unintended consequences of a particular design. These may emerge in a field test, but some may not become obvious until the system has been in use for some time. In any case, designing for ease of modification is a desirable aspect of an effective design process. What other aspects of effective design might be cited? (Another topic for discussion in class or in an online discussion forum.)

Designed Educational Entities

There are many designed components of a technology-facilitated learning, instructional, or performance system. Typical components include the human-system interface, content materials and media objects, assessments and user feedback, help systems, user guides for teachers/trainers as well as learners, reports, and more. Each of these components has principles to guide effective design (see Gibbons & Brewer, 2005). Moreover, issues of alignment and consistency among and across the various components are important for effective design. Table 14.1 indicates some representative areas of concern with regard to the various designed entities. Each of the design focus areas has a significant body of research and lessons learned which should be explored when confronting critical design issues.

Universal design, which is mentioned in all of the categories in Table 14.1, refers to the notion of creating a system or environment that is free of most of the barriers that users might encounter, particularly users with disabilities (Pliner & Johnson, 2004). Just as ramps are designed to provide easy access to buildings for those in wheelchairs, particular care should be taken in designing support for those with special needs (e.g.,

TABLE 14.1 Educational entities and associated design concerns

Entity class	Representative concern	Design focus areas
Human-system interface	Human interaction with system components	Usability and human use; universal design
Content materials and supporting resources	Coherence and clarity of content	Message design; universal design
Assessments and evaluations	Timely, informative, and fair determination of progress	Alignment of goals and objectives, activities, and measurements; universal design
User feedback	Meaningful feedback on use and activities	Individualized and contextualized messages; universal design
Help systems	Just-in-time and just-in-need support for users	Unobtrusive but readily available help systems; universal design
User guides	Instructions on the use of the system for end users	Comprehensive but easily accessible information for users; universal design
Reports	Data and information on system use for a variety of stakeholders	Timely and flexible reports on use of the system; universal design

the hearing and vision impaired) and from a variety of cultural backgrounds so that they can make effective use of a technology-facilitated learning, instructional, or performance improvement environment (see www.udlcenter.org/aboutudl/udlguidelines).

Design Principles

There are many excellent sources for design principles (see the Resources section below; see also Larson & Lockee, 2013; Merrill, Barclay, & van Schaack, 2008; McKenney & Reeves, 2014; Norman, 1988; Preece, Rogers, & Sharp, 2002; Richey & Klein, 2014; Richey, Klein, & Tracey, 2011). As has been the case in the area of software engineering, user-centered and participatory design are practices that may create initial delays but are likely to result in more robust and more widely accepted solutions (Simonsen & Robertson, 2013). Several of the principles that follow are consistent with efforts to make the users a central consideration in designing effective solutions. In what follows, ten high-level and frequently cited critical design principles are briefly reviewed (Chermayeff, Geismar, & Geissbuhler, 2003). An especially meaningful learning activity would be to expand and elaborate this list.

1. **What is designed can and should be evaluated**. Formulate a measurable design goal based on a thorough analysis of the problem situation and intended purpose; both the implementation and the impact should be evaluated.
2. **Designs should be human centered**. Carefully consider those who will be using the instructional system or learning environment, including their varying

knowledge and abilities, interests, motivation, likely uses, and places of use; involve a broad range of anticipated users in the analysis of the problem as well as in critical stages of the design process.

3. **The use and purpose should drive the design**. In the field of architecture, this principle is generally stated as *form should follow function*; a common error in designing learning environments is to focus on the form and representation first, rather than focusing on the purpose and function first.

4. **A design should be cognitively meaningful**. In other words, the intended use and purpose of that which is designed should be obvious and intuitive to the users as well as the implementation team.

5. **A design should be perceptually attractive**. That is to say, a design should exhibit balance, proportion, emphasis, and other elements that make items clear and distinct, and that are inviting to likely users without losing sight of the purpose and function.

6. **A design should be consistent**. That is to say, things which repeat should appear in familiar and expected places, fonts and other elements should be consistent, and other repetitive items should be designed consistently to help users understand their intended use and emphasis.

7. **A design should be easily modified**. It is likely that instructional designs will change due to ongoing evaluations and feedback from users; the process of changing a design should be relatively simple and straightforward; a persistent problem in educational technology involves failures when an effort is deployed on a large scale.

8. **The design process should consider the broader context and culture**. It is all too easy to make assumptions about the context and culture surrounding an educational environment or instructional system; ignoring such issues can result in confusing activities and misguided expectations; according to principles of universal design for learning, multiple forms of representation and interaction should be included.

9. **The design process should include user testing and field trials prior to dissemination**. In order to discover problems with the design and to uncover unintended uses, it is advisable to have representative users interact with and provide feedback on a prototype or early version; user-centered and participatory design often pays long-term dividends in terms of acceptability and scalability.

10. **Design is both a creative and an engineering enterprise**. Some will argue that design is primarily a creative activity ignoring the engineering aspects of design that can result in a suboptimal result in terms of fulfilling the intended purpose; others argue that design is primarily an engineering activity ignoring the esthetic aspects of design that can result in designs that are uninviting and unappealing to users; a balance of creativity and engineering are likely to result in meaningful and effective designs.

Design Missteps

The ways of violating basic design principles and creating suboptimal learning, instructional, and performance environments are many and varied. A half-dozen anecdotes from research and experience are provided here to suggest the kinds of things that can go badly wrong.

1. Creating a feature simply because it can be done and appeals to the designer can be a mistake. In one case, a programmer decided that one way to fade unavailable menu choices in a computer interface was not only to use a lighter font but to create a blurred image of the unavailable choice. In this case, the programmer was enamored with the technique as it involved having two images, both in a light font, one slightly offset from the other. The result was a blurred text image on the screen. From a user perspective, however, the eye is naturally drawn to the blurred image in an effort to read the blurred word. The cognitive psychology behind this human behavior is that people naturally try to make sense of what they encounter (the kernel principle of a constructivist epistemology). The effect was the opposite of what was intended. The intent was to have the user ignore the blurred word, but the result was that users were naturally drawn to it. Clever programming does not always result in an effective design.

2. When digital media became commonplace in the 1980s, some designers thought it would be clever and appealing to have an audio clip of important text synchronized with the same text scrolling on the screen. While multiple representations are often effective and can provide access to those with certain disabilities (Barron & Kysilka, 1993; Paivio, 1986; Spiro, Feltovich, Jacobson, & Coulson, 1992), in this case the result was again suboptimal. The reason is that most people read faster than a typical speaking rate, so while the user was reading the scrolling text, the audio output was occurring after that text had been read, which created cognitive interference and diminished comprehension (Barron & Kysilka, 1993). In addition, many digital natives like to engage in multitasking while working online. However, research suggests that such multitasking results in increased cognitive load and problems involving split attention problems resulting in suboptimal performance on the tasks involved (Lin, 2009).

3. A computer-based instructional course created for medical technologists was designed so that every screen had a word or phrase highlighted. After every screen or two of text and images, one or two multiple-choice questions were asked. The correct answers were always the words or phrases that had been highlighted. Users quickly caught on to this pattern and quit reading the material; they would simply look for highlighted words and proceed to the quiz. The course was pass–fail and totally dependent on completing the sequence of lessons with all questions answered correctly. When an incorrect answer was entered, the user was returned to the start of that instructional unit. There are many problems with that design,

and it failed to produce any noticeable improvements in knowledge or skills. Discussing the various problems can be the basis for an interesting discussion in class or in an online forum.

4. A computer-based instructional system required the users to make use of the mouse to navigate through the system. As it happened, some users had serious fine motor-control problems and found it difficult to make use of the system. In this case, the system was redesigned so as to provide multiple ways to navigate, including the use of the cursor keys and shortcut keys. The redesign in this case provided increased accessibility for those with motor-control problems.

5. A computer tutorial on statistics was designed to proceed through a series of cleverly crafted problems involving an engaging avatar who interjected humor and spoke informally with many clichés familiar to a local group of users. The program was so successful that an attempt was made to spread its use to a much wider audience, including those in other countries. Not surprisingly, what was meaningful and popular with one group of users failed with others. The humor and clichés were simply not understood outside the country of origin.

6. An introductory online language course was being designed at a large university in an Asian country. The country was rapidly developing and had experienced a large influx of foreigners from many different countries who came with their families to work there for several years. The course was aimed at these newcomers and their families to help familiarize them with the language and culture and make their time as visitors more rewarding. The university had a strong history of success with online courses. However, the content designers were linguists and had no background in how to teach a second or third language. In addition, the university had a practice of using a common framework for all its online courses, most of which were intended for native speakers—at the time, this was the only course not aimed at native speakers. The template included having fairly long intro-ductions to the primary instructors and content specialists—written in the native language—on the opening screen. These introductions were, of course, not meaningful for the intended audience and required a fair amount of scrolling to bypass. Second, the content providers had no sense of how to introduce foreigners to a new language, especially when there could be no assumptions about the native language of the intended learner population, which included Americans, Aus-tralians, Japanese, Koreans, and many others. The resulting course design was simply not usable due to the fact that the introductions and content elaborations were all in the language of that country and not accessible to foreigners. Moreover, because different units were designed by different content specialists, there was no uniformity from one lesson to another, and many lessons were aimed at sophisticated linguistic nuances of little interest to newcomers who simply wanted to learn enough to do grocery shopping and such.

Many other examples could easily be added to this list. An interesting activity would be to have a group tell similar stories and relate those design missteps to a list of basic design principles.

Test Your Understanding

Which of the following are true, which are false, and why (some of these are worth discussion in class or in a discussion forum)?

1. Designs cannot be evaluated.
2. It is possible to identify all types of users and all of their relevant characteristics in a thorough needs assessment and requirements analysis process.
3. Because the perceptual appeal of a learning environment or instructional system will determine motivation and subsequent learner engagement, the emphasis in design should be on esthetics first and foremost.
4. Mastery learning is consistent with a design approach that focuses on students within two standard deviations of the mean score of students on a final test in a required prerequisite course.
5. Design is a balance of creativity and engineering.
6. A program of study specifying required and optional courses is a designed artifact.
7. An organization's mission, vision, and values statements are designed artifacts.
8. An employee's pay rate is a designed artifact.
9. A grading rubric is a designed artifact.
10. A student's grade point average is a designed artifact.
11. Universal design requires focusing on issues involving scalability and multiple platforms.
12. Multitasking improves overall productivity.

A Representative Educational Technology Challenge

Your organization has decided that it wants to have a more meaningful and informative public presence on the World Wide Web. One of the features of this presence will be a portion of the website featuring the key personnel of the organization—who they are, their backgrounds, their responsibilities, and so on. This part of the site should be easily updated as changes in key personnel occur. Initially, the site will be designed and tested internally. When internal users are satisfied with the site and trained in updating their own information, the site will be made public. In addition to determining what the content should be and how it should be represented publicly, there are the additional challenges of designing a back-end system (e.g., a database), a user-interface to update that database, and some means to monitor the content and use of the system to ensure that organizational goals and expectations are met.

Learning Activities

You have been assigned the task of designing the personnel portion of an organizational website and portal. You have decided to begin by creating your own e-portfolio to see what you might include and how a user might interact with what you create.

1. Create a prototype of your e-portfolio; in doing so, indicate who you believe the intended users of the system will be and how they are likely to want to interact with your e-portfolio; identify all relevant assumptions you have with regard to the design.
2. Critique your prototype in terms of the ten design principles indicated in this chapter.
3. Have a colleague or peer also critique your prototype and provide specific feedback on the content, interface, navigation, and other elements of the e-portfolio.
4. Compare your own critique with that of your colleague; document differences, especially those pertaining to unexpected use, ambiguities, and unclear navigation.

Links

Don Norman's websites—www.jnd.org and http://cogsci.ucsd.edu/~norman

The National Center for Universal Design for Learning website—www.udlcenter.org/aboutudl/udlguidelines

Andy Gibbons' Model-Centered Instruction/Design Layers website—www.instructionaldesign.org/theories/design-layers.html

The Design Based Research Collective (funded by the Spencer Foundation) website—www.designbasedresearch.org/

Other Resources

About e-learning instructional design principles website—www.about-elearning.com/instructional-design-principles.html

CAST site for universal design for learning—www.cast.org/udl

The Center for Inclusive Design and Environmental Access at the University of Buffalo—www.ap.buffalo.edu/idea

Charlotte Jirousek's art, design, and visual thinking website—http://char.txa.cornell.edu/language/principl/principl.htm

Dan Calloway's instructional design principles—www.academia.edu/681000/Instructional_Design_Principles

Dave Merrill and colleagues' chapter in the 3rd edition of the *Handbook of Research on Educational Communications and Technology* on prescriptive principles for instructional design—www.aect.org/edtech/edition3/ER5849x_C014.fm.pdf

Design principles website—www.designprinciples.com

The European Design for All e-Accessibility Network—www.edean.org/central.aspx?sId=64I160I3271323I259530&lanID=1&resID=1&assID=99&inpID=3&disID=1&famID=3&skinID=3

Instructional design website—www.instructionaldesign.org

John Lovett's design and color website—www.johnlovett.com/test.htm

Marvin Bartel's composition and design website—www.goshen.edu/art/ed/Compose.htm

North Carolina State Center for Universal Design—www.ncsu.edu/www/ncsu/design/sod5/cud

Rapid e-learning blog on graphic principles for instructional design—www.articulate.com/rapid-elearning/3-graphic-design-principles-for-instructional-design-success

Tanya Elias' journal article on universal instructional design principles published in the *International Review of Research in Open and Distance Learning*—www.irrodl.org/index.php/irrodl/article/view/869/1579

University of Minnesota disability services website on universal design—http://ds.umn.edu/faculty/applyinguid.html

University of Washington website for the universal design of instruction—www.washington.edu/doit/Brochures/Academics/instruction.html

References

Barron, A. E., & Kysilka, M. L. (1993). The effectiveness of digital audio in computer-based training. *Journal of Research on Computing in Education, 25*(3), 277–289.

Chermayeff, I., Geismar, T. H., & Geissbuhler, S. (2003). *Designing*. New York: Graphics.

DBRC (Design Based Research Collective) (2003). Design-based research: An emerging paradigm for educational inquiry. *Educational Researcher, 32*(1), 5–8.

Gibbons, A. S., Boling, E. Smith, K. M. (2014). Design models. In J. M. Spector, M. D. Merrill, M. J. Bishop, & J. Elen, (Eds.), *Handbook for research on educational communications and technology* (4th ed.; pp. 607–616). New York: Springer.

Gibbons, A. S., & Brewer, E. K. (2005). Elementary principles of design languages and design notation systems for instructional design. In J. M. Spector, C. Ohrazda, A. Van Schaack, & D. Wiley (Eds.), *Innovations in instructional technology: Essays in honor of M. David Merrill* (pp. 111–129). Mahwah, NJ: Lawrence Erlbaum Associates.

Larson, M. B., & Lockee, B. B. (2013). *Streamline ID: A practical guide to instructional design*. New York: Routledge.

Lin, L. (2009). Breadth-biased versus focused cognitive control in media multitasking behaviors. *Proceedings of the National Academy of Sciences of the United States of America, 106*(37), pp. 15521–15522.

McKenney, S., & Reeves, T. (2014). Educational design research. In J. M. Spector, M. D. Merrill, M. J. Bishop, & J. Elen, (Eds.), *Handbook for research on educational communications and technology* (4th ed.; pp. 131–140). New York: Springer.

Merrill, M. D., Barclay, M., & van Schaak, A. (2008). Prescriptive principles for instructional design. In J. M. Spector, M. D. Merrill, J. J. G. van Merriënboer (Eds.), *Handbook of research on educational communications and instructional design* (3rd ed.) (pp. 173–184). New York: Routledge.

Norman, D. A. (1988). *The design of everyday things*. New York: Doubleday.

Paivio, A. (1986). *Mental representations: A dual coding approach*. Oxford: Oxford University Press.

Pliner, S., & Johnson, J. (2004). Historical, theoretical, and foundational principles of universal design in higher education. *Equity of Excellence in Education, 37*, 105–113.

Preece, J., Rogers, Y., & Sharp, H. (2002). *Interaction design: Beyond human-computer interaction*. New York: Wiley.

Richey, R. C., & Klein, J. D. (2014). Design and development research. In J. M. Spector, M. D. Merrill, M. J. Bishop, & J. Elen (Eds.), *Handbook for research on educational communications and technology* (4th ed.; pp. 141–150). New York: Springer.

Richey, R. C., Klein, J. D., & Tracey, M. W. (2011). *The instructional design knowledge base: Theory, research and practice*. New York: Routledge.

Simonsen, J., & Robertson, T. (Eds.) (2013). *Routledge international handbook of participatory design*. New York: Routledge.

Spiro, R. J., Feltovich, P. J., Jacobson, M. J., & Coulson, R. L. (1992). Cognitive flexibility, constructivism and hypertext: Random access instruction for advanced knowledge acquisition in ill-structured domains. In T. Duffy & D. H. Jonassen (Eds.), *Constructivism and the technology of instruction*. Hillsdale, NJ: Erlbaum.

fifteen

Integrating Technologies into Activities and Tasks

"Being taken for granted can be a compliment. It means that you've become a comfortable, trusted element in another person's life" (Dr. Joyce Brothers, American psychologist)

Successful integration of an educational technology is marked by that technology being regarded by users as an unobtrusive facilitator of learning, instruction, or performance. When the focus shifts from the technology being used to the educational purpose that technology serves, then that technology is becoming a comfortable and trusted element, and can be regarded as being successfully integrated. Few people give a second thought to the use of a ball-point pen although the mechanisms involved vary—some use a twist mechanism and some use a push button on top, and there are other variations as well. Personal computers have reached a similar level of familiarity for a great many users, but certainly not for all. New and emerging technologies often introduce both fascination and frustration with users. As long as the user's focus is on the technology itself rather than its use in promoting learning, instruction, or performance, then one ought not to conclude that the technology has been successfully integrated—at least for that user.

In Chapter 2, six foundation pillars of educational technology were introduced: communication, interaction, environment, culture, instruction, and learning (see Figure 15.1). One way to think about a technology integration effort is to consider all six foundation pillars. To do so requires a holistic and systemic perspective on education, which has been strongly advocated throughout this volume (see Spector & Anderson, 2000). If any of these pillars are ignored in planning and implementing a technology-enhanced learning, instructional, or performance system, there are likely to be suboptimal

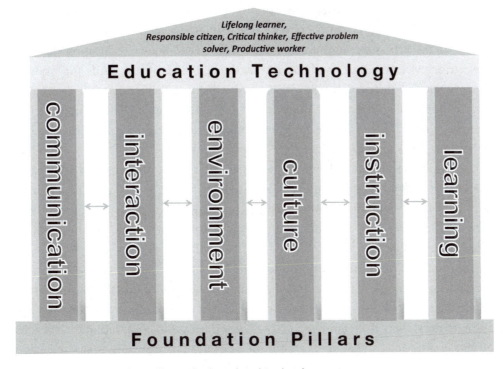

FIGURE 15.1 Foundation pillars of educational technology

outcomes in terms of acceptance by users and impact on learning, instruction, and performance. In other words, technology integration is perhaps the most challenging and complex aspect of designing educational environments and systems of instruction, which is why integration is treated here separately from design, although it is clearly an important design consideration. In the previous chapter, the various aspects of design were treated as if they could be addressed separately, and each of those various design areas (e.g., message design, interaction design, multimedia design, etc.) has separate bodies of research literature and documented lessons learned.

Technology integration is somewhat different than the individual areas of design concern mentioned in Chapter 14. In a sense, when technology is a cornerstone of a new system, as is so often the case, everything is at stake. As discussed in Chapter 11 with regard to the diffusion of innovation, there are many different kinds of concerns and a variety of users to take into consideration. Some of these were discussed in earlier chapters (see also Chapters 5 and 6). In school settings, technology integration is taken up under the rubric of TPACK—technological, pedagogical, and content knowledge (Herring & Smaldino, 2015; Koehler & Mishra, 2015; Mishra & Koehler, 2006). The George Lucas Educational Foundation has a site dedicated to technology integration (see www.edutopia.org/big-list-technology-integration). However, the concern to effectively integrate technology into education is an ongoing concern in every sector and at every level. Some universities now offer advanced degrees and certificates in educational technology integration, and these programs of study are not confined to school settings (professional preparation and training are discussed in a subsequent chapter). Organizations such as the International Society for Technology in Education (ISTE; see www.iste.org/welcome.aspx) and the International Board of Standards for Training, Performance and Instruction (IBSTPI; see www.ibstpi.org) offer standards pertaining to technology integration. The Association for Educational Communications and Technology (AECT; see www.aect.org) and other professional organizations also offer publications pertaining to effective technology integration.

In addition, the educational approaches discussed in previous chapters and emerging technologies such as 3D printing to be discussed in a subsequent chapter have brought about increasing emphasis on integrating technology use in the hands of learners to make their learning both authentic and personal (Honey & Kanter, 2013). The Maker Education Initiative (see http://makered.org) exemplifies one such movement that is gaining traction around the world quite well. The need to effectively integrate technologies into learning and instruction is becoming an imperative for schools, universities, and organizations that wish to remain on the leading edge of effective technology use.

In summary, there is no doubt that technology integration is an important, complex, and challenging topic. What, then, are the major areas of concern and what can be done to ensure effective integration of technology into learning, instruction, and performance?

Technology Integration Cases

To motivate this discussion, let's first consider a concrete example of an educational technology that has been introduced with mixed results—namely, the case of the interactive whiteboard. The interactive whiteboard is a digital display device linked to a computer that projects the computer screen and also allows for input and interactions through the whiteboard (e.g., by touching or using an electronic marker) rather than through a keyboard or mouse. These devices are now commonly found in many classrooms in public schools, colleges, and universities, and also in various business environments.

The intent for their introduction into schools was to promote learner engagement with learning materials through active involvement via the interactive whiteboard. It is certainly true that school children are fascinated with the interactive whiteboard and like to be among those interacting directly with the whiteboard. However, many teachers use the interactive whiteboard merely as a projection device with very limited learner interaction (Kim et al., 2011). The reasons are several and include the fact that allowing more student interaction requires time, and teachers report having to cover a great many topics so that students are properly prepared for mandated tests (Kim et al., 2011). As it happens, teachers are not always well trained in using all aspects of the interactive whiteboard, and fail to recognize that in some situations the interactive whiteboard can both save time and increase student interest (e.g., by using a flipped classroom approach that eliminates a teacher's need to use the interactive whiteboard to present primary instruction and that potentially allows for student use in practicing solving problems in small collaborative groups). In short, the full set of affordances of the interactive whiteboard have yet to be realized in many school settings. As interactive whiteboards evolve to support more distributed input (e.g., from users' personal tablet computers), the culture of use may well change and classrooms may be transformed by this technology, although this has not yet happened on any significant scale in spite of the promise of transforming the classroom when they were introduced. Moreover, as the child's reaction to the interactive whiteboard changes from "please let me touch it" (technology focus) to "see how I solved the problem" (content focus) we can then argue that the interactive whiteboard is being effectively integrated.

As a second case, let's consider word processing. Some may be old enough to remember the early hardware-centered days of word processing that included electronic typewriters with a small memory cache that allowed changes and corrections prior to printing a line. There followed several hardware devices such as the Wang 1200 that kept more text in memory and allowed for format control characters (e.g., bold, italics, underline, etc.) to be entered. As computers spread, software-centered programs began to emerge (e.g., the Unix vi editor and WordStar). Initially, these also allowed format control characters to be entered as part of the text prior to printing. We now have full-featured WYSIWYG (what you see is what you get) word-processing programs in widespread use on many different computer platforms. In summary, word processing has evolved significantly in the last 50 years, and for many users word processing is now fully integrated into their daily lives, representing a familiar, comfortable, and trusted companion for a wide variety of writing activities. Training still occurs for some users, but nowadays word-processing training typically focuses on advanced features of a particular software program since so many users can easily and intuitively perform basic functions without assistance. Nevertheless, one still finds some users pressing the ENTER key multiple times in order to get to the next page rather than making use of the software to perform that function.

A third case is worth mentioning because it focuses on the role of training in effective technology integration—namely, the case of the graphing calculator. Because of the powerful visualization affordances of the graphing calculator and its potential to promote high level mathematical reasoning, New York state mandated its use in high schools and included graphing calculator questions on the New York State Regents Math B exam required for high school graduation, which represented a very serious policy and curriculum design decision around the turn of the century/millennium. However, pre-service teacher training programs have yet to fully embrace the use of the graphing calculator and in-service professional development has not proven adequate in bringing teachers up to a minimal level of competence in its use (Gogus, 2006; see a subsequent chapter on the preparation and training of educational technologists).

The same result has been found in a study conducted by Florida State University's Learning Systems Institute, and it is likely that inadequate preparation and training of teachers in the pedagogical use of the graphing calculator is true elsewhere. The consequences of a failed technology integration effort are leading some to the conclusion that the use of all calculators in classrooms should be banned and that math instruction should return to the days of doing it by hand. The likely consequence of such a change would be to discourage students further from pursuit of studies in mathematics. Meanwhile, technology changes and marches forward. The graphing calculator technology is advancing so that it resembles more and more a personal tablet computer (e.g., the Texas Instruments NSpire device) in terms of size and functionality. At the same time, powerful open-source dynamic mathematics software is now available, along with a great deal of pedagogical support resources that can run on any personal computer (e.g., GeoGebra; see www.geogebra.org/cms). This evolving technology path may parallel that of the word processor with the result that very soon graphing calculator functions will be available on personal handheld computing devices, and easily accessible and usable by both teachers and students—we can hope for that outcome because the potential of visualization to promote serious mathematical reasoning is significant.

Technology Integration Concerns

Given the discussion up to this point, Table 15.1 presents a high-level summary of the kinds of concerns in the form of questions that arise in a technology integration effort. Of course, many other questions could be raised, and the various foundation areas could

TABLE 15.1 Table of representative technology integration concerns

Foundation area	Representative technology integration concerns
Communication	Do all stakeholders fully understand and appreciate the purpose and potential of the technology to be integrated? Are user guides readily available and easily understood? Are robust and personalized feedback mechanisms in place?
Interaction	Does the technology promote active learning engagement with learning materials, other learners, and teachers/trainers? Do learners have sufficient opportunity to create their own materials and share these with others?
Environment	Is the environment in which the technology will be used conducive to its use? Will use of the technology draw undue attention to users or disturb others? Is there adequate support for ongoing use of the technology?
Culture	Does the institutional culture support those willing to be among the first users of a new technology? Is the culture supportive of using technology to promote learning and improve instruction?
Learning	Is there an adequate rationale to believe that the technology will improve learning? Will data be collected and analyzed to determine to what extent learning improves as a result of the use of the technology?
Instruction	Is there evidence to suggest that the technology will improve the quality of instruction? Will the technology be perceived as yet one more thing to be learned to do one's job or as a productivity enhancer? Will data be collected and analyzed to determine the impact on instruction?

easily be subdivided into more specific categories. These activities are potential class activities that can deepen the understanding of the many issues and complexities of technology integration.

Technology Integration Principles

Based on the discussion of technology integration concerns, a preliminary and tentative list of technology integration principles is presented here as a point of departure for further discussion. As with the design principles, these are just a few high-level principles that might deserve elaboration; other principles should certainly be added to this list.

1. **Technology integration in education should enhance learning, performance, and/or instruction**. Data should be collected and analyzed to ensure that the use of a technology does not interfere with but rather supports and facilitates learning, performance, and instruction.

2. **Stakeholders should be informed and key users should be properly trained on new technologies**. Regardless of the context and culture, it is likely that there will be those who will resist the introduction of a new technology; these persons should not be ignored or overlooked with regard to communication and training; teachers and trainers should be adequately trained to the point of fluency prior to deploying a new technology.

3. **Training teachers and trainers how to make effective pedagogical use of a new technology is essential**. Too many technology integration efforts have failed to produce the expected impact due to inadequate preparation of teachers and trainers. This was the case with the introduction of Logo, the graphing calculator and many other technologies which had significant learning affordances but fell short of their promised potential.

4. **Training of users on a new technology is critical**. Prior to introducing a new technology in the context of a key learning sequence, learners need to be familiar with its use so that the focus can remain on the learning content rather than on the technology being used to support learning.

5. **Proper support for a new technology should be in place prior to deployment**. If a new technology begins with breakdowns and failures that require time to correct, the intensity of resistance is likely to increase significantly; ongoing support for a new technology should be planned and implemented.

6. **A systemic representation of the role and use of a new technology should be developed prior to implementation**. In order to anticipate possible collateral or incidental outcomes of introducing a new technology, it is worthwhile to represent within the context of the entire educational system how the new technology will be used and how it might impact other aspects of the system.

7. **Technology costs should not outweigh the benefits**. It is possible to make significant improvements in learning and instruction with large investments,

but it is unlikely that large investments in education will be made or sustained; consequently, it is very important to develop theoretically and empirically based argumentation for a new technology, and to follow through with evidence to show exactly what the benefits are and how they might be valued.

8. **Technology should not be expected to quickly or magically transform learning and instruction**. As a discipline, educational technologists have been overly enthusiastic and promised far too much too soon for nearly every educational technology that has been introduced in the last 50 years; it is better to make more modest promises and collect the data to show that these promises have been kept.

Test Your Understanding

Which of the following are true or false, and why?

1. Technology integration is an aspect of instructional design.
2. A grading rubric is an educational technology.
3. The interactive whiteboard is an educational technology.
4. The graphing calculator has been effectively integrated into a school with which I am familiar.
5. My personal computer represents a technology that is effectively integrated into my life.
6. I have effectively integrated word processing into my writing.
7. Technology integration is the responsibility of managers and not instructional designers.
8. Technology integration is a relative concept in the sense that what is effectively integrated for one person may not be for another.
9. There will always be some who will refuse to use technology in learning and instruction.
10. Those who are the least prepared to make effective use of a new technology are typically those who stand to benefit the most.

A Representative Educational Technology Challenge

As the Dean of a prominent college of education with a highly regarded teacher preparation program, it has recently been brought to your attention that teacher training graduates are going to schools that have far more technology than they used in their college preparation courses; it is commonly reported that recent graduates are not well trained and have little sense of how to make effective use of many available technologies in their new classrooms. How might you transform the teacher training program in your college to improve this situation?

Learning Activities

Select one of the following technologies for this activity—you will need to acquire the technology to complete the activity:

1. slide rule;
2. graphing calculator;
3. spreadsheet program;
4. smart phone with downloadable apps;
5. dynamic mathematics software.

Once you have selected your technology, next select a specific learning goal or objective to be supported using the technology. Ideally, this would be a meaningful goal or objective that can be linked directly to a specific job task or curriculum standard. Next, develop a plan for a unit of instruction that incorporates this technology in support of the targeted learning outcome. Then, document how the teachers/trainers and students will use the technology in that lesson. Finally, document what specific problems you anticipate in the successful deployment of this unit of instruction.

Links

The Association for Educational Communications and Technology—www.aect.org

GeoGebra dynamic mathematics software—www.geogebra.org/cms

The George Lucas Big List of Technology Integration—www.edutopia.org/big-list-technology-integration

The International Board of Standards for Training, Performance and Instruction—www.ibstpi.org

The International Society for Technology in Education—www.iste.org/welcome.aspx

The Maker Education Initiative—http://makered.org

Other Resources

Berglund Center's taxonomy of technology integration—http://education.ed.pacificu.edu/aacu/workshop/reconcept2B.html

Bobi Ash YouTube video clip on technology integration in her classroom—www.youtube.com/watch?v=ANCJPRvHvkE

Center for Information Technology Integration—www.citi.umich.edu

CyberSummit-Kansas 21st century skills YouTube video clip on technology integration—www.youtube.com/watch?v=Iu99aC8YK4Y

Education Week article by Ian Quillen on the real cost of technology integration—http://blogs.edweek.org/edweek/DigitalEducation/2011/01/the_real_cost_of_technology_in.html

Education World's technology integration resources—www.emergingedtech.com/2010/01/education-worlds-technology-integration-resources

Institute for Education Sciences website on technology integration—http://nces.ed.gov/pubs2003/tech_schools/chapter7.asp

Microsoft for Higher Education website—www.pil-tei.com

National Clearinghouse for Education Facilities resources for technology integration—www.ncef.org/rl/technologyII.cfm

National Technology Leadership Coalition—www.ntlcoalition.org

Open Education site on technology integration—technology integration in education LinkedIn site—www.linkedin.com/groups/Technology-Integration-in-Education-108447?mostPopular=&gid=108447

Technology integration in education website—www.technologyintegrationineducation.com

TelEurope (Technology Enhanced Learning: A European Initiative)—www.teleurope.eu/pg/frontpage

The US Department of Education website on K-12 Reforms—www.ed.gov/k-12reforms

References

Gogus, A. S. (2006). *Individual and situation factors that influence teachers' perspectives and perceptions about the usefulness of the graphing calculator on the New York State Math B Regents exam.* Unpublished dissertation. Syracuse, NY: Syracuse University.

Herring, M. C., & Smaldino, S. E. (2015). TPACK (Technological Pedagogical Content Knowledge): Implications for 21st-century teacher education. In J. M. Spector (Ed.), *The encyclopedia of educational technology.* Thousand Oaks, CA: Sage.

Honey, M., & Kanter, D. E. (2013). *Design, make, play: Growing the next generation of STEM innovators.* New York: Routledge.

Kim, C., DeMeester, K., Spector, J. M., Kim, M. K., & Lee, C-J. (2011). Teacher pedagogical beliefs, technology integration, and student learning. Paper presentation at the Annual Meeting of the American Educational Research Association, New Orleans, LA, April 11.

Koehler, M. J., & Mishra, P. (2015). TPACK (Technological Pedagogical Content Knowledge). In J. M. Spector (Ed.), *The encyclopedia of educational technology.* Thousand Oaks, CA: Sage.

Mishra, P., & Koehler, M. J. (2006). Technological pedagogical content knowledge: A framework for teacher knowledge. *Teacher College Record, 108*(6), 1017–1054.

Spector, J. M., & Anderson, T. M. (Eds.) (2000). *Integrated and holistic perspectives on learning, instruction and technology: Understanding complexity.* Dordrecht: Kluwer Academic Press.

Spector, J. M., & Wang, X. (2002a). Integrating technology into learning and working: Introduction. *Education, Technology and Society, 5*(1). Retrieved on April 6, 2011 from www.ifets.info/journals/5_1/editorial.pdf

Spector, J. M., & Wang, X. (2002b). Integrating technology into learning and working: Introduction. *Education, Technology and Society 5*(2). Retrieved April 6, 2011 from www.ifets.info/journals/5_2/editorial.pdf

part four

BROADENING THE CONTEXT

sixteen
Educational Technology Principles and Examples in a Variety of Contexts

"The meaning of a word is its use" (Ludwig Wittgenstein, Philosophical Investigations)

A word all by itself has no meaning, or possibly an indefinite number of potential meanings (Wittgenstein, 1953). According to many modern linguists, it is the use of words in context and within a language community that determines meaning. Use determines meaning. For example, consider the word 'bank.' By itself, it is not clear whether this is a noun or a verb. It could refer to a building, the land next to a river, the fact that a road may not be flat and level, and many other things. Even when presented with a complete sentence, the meaning may be incomplete or impenetrable without knowing the context in which that sentence was used or the statement uttered. Consider the statement 'take it to the bank.' This could be a directive to an employee to take a bag of money to a particular bank; it could also be a kind of affirmation that the preceding statement is well established; and other potential meanings can be constructed around different contexts.

The point for educational technologists and instructional designers is that context of use strongly influences how individuals interpret experience and construct meaning. In the following sections, a brief overview of a representative concern in pairs of the six foundation areas (see Figure 2.2) for major educational settings is provided. In addition, links to websites illustrating good practice are indicated. These sections should be considered a starting point for further discussion and exploration as only very general remarks are provided.

K-12 Education

Primary and secondary education obviously involves children and adolescents who are developing physically, psychologically, and socially. As a consequence, the use of educational technology in K-12 contexts is particularly challenging since developmental concerns are significant.

Communications and Interaction

The key stakeholders in K-12 settings include students, teachers, parents, and school and district administrators. Communicating with stakeholders is always an important consideration when introducing and deploying innovations as previously indicated. In this case, there are many significant differences among these stakeholder groups as well as differences due to subject area and types of activities. The typical approach is to focus on only one or two of these groups—teachers or students—and these two groups are also quite different. Designing specific communication and interaction strategies for different groups of users is quite important. Language appropriate for a 6th-grade student learning earth science is quite different than what would be appropriate for a teacher developing lessons for 6th-grade earth science. Student interactions with learning materials are also quite different from how teachers normally use those same materials. Both students and teachers need to be or become very familiar with the materials, but the goals differ. Teachers require understanding of the materials in order to develop appropriate learning support, anticipate learner difficulties, and respond to student queries. Students require understanding of the materials in order to master objectives, demonstrate proficiency against standards, and move forward with their studies.

Environment and Culture

K-12 environments and school culture are quite diverse. Even within a school district and often within a single school one can find very different environments and cultures. The composition of students in a class can have a strong impact on the culture and environment in a given learning situation. A class with more than 30 students will naturally be quite different from one with less than 10. Classes with second language learners will differ from those without such learners. Many learner characteristics (e.g., gender, age, ethnicity, native language, socioeconomic status, medical and physical conditions, prior performance, etc.) and how a school responds to such diversity is a major aspect of the environment and culture in which learning occurs. Whether learning mostly occurs with whole-class, small-group, or individual activities is another factor. Parent and administrative support also impact school culture. In recent years in the USA, high-stakes testing has created a culture that is focused on learning as interpreted in terms of standardized tests and teaching as interpreted in terms of how well students perform on those tests. Such a narrowly focused culture of learning and teaching while responsive to accountability concerns may not be very responsive to learner needs and can be quite discouraging to teachers as well.

Instruction and Learning

Learning and instruction in K-12 settings typically occurs within the context of standard curricula that are aligned with sets of standards developed by those outside the school setting (e.g., state agencies, national boards, etc.). Instruction is typically directed toward more or less well-defined goals and objectives (or standards), and learning typically involves a mixture of whole-class (e.g., teacher-led lectures and discussions), small-group (e.g., in-class collaborations) and individual activities (e.g., homework). Students may be grouped heterogeneously (e.g., students at different levels and with a variety of characteristics) or homogeneously (e.g., classes for the gifted, differentiated instruction, etc.). Pacing is typically determined by the standard curriculum regardless of individual student performance or readiness; remediation is quite often offered to those who fall behind the scheduled progression of instructional units, but those who progress more rapidly may not be offered new learning opportunities while they wait for classmates to catch up.

While primary and secondary education appears aimed at specific learning goals, there are other goals that educational technologists and instructional designers need to keep in mind. *The goal of public education is to develop informed and responsible citizens.* Ethical and social development are just as important as learning when that overarching goal is taken into consideration. It is quite easy for curriculum and instructional designers and developers to overlook ethical and social development and focus only on the content and learning materials. It is probably natural for parents and those who fund public education to be just as concerned with ethical and social development as they are with developing knowledge and understanding. This is why values are represented as the top layer of instructional design concerns (see Figure 2.1).

K-12 Examples

The Web-based Inquiry Science Environment (WISE; see http://wise.berkeley.edu) is a free online set of resources for science education in grades 5 through 12. It is designed for both students and teachers, and allows anyone to join.

In South Korea, a smart school opened in Sejong City in 2012 that is likely to be a model for future developments in K-12 education around the world (see www.korea.net/NewsFocus/Sci-Tech/view?articleId=99412). This school has new technologies and embraces new approaches to teaching and learning with and without technology.

Higher Education

Tertiary education includes post-secondary contexts such as community, technical, and vocational colleges as well as universities and graduate institutes. The learners in higher education contexts are often considered adults, but many are young adults and still developing in many ways. Many of these young adults are searching for a professional path to pursue while still developing a personal identity and social skills; others are mature adults seeking to continue their education or perhaps develop new knowledge and skills to support a career change.

Communications and Interaction

The key stakeholders in higher education contexts include learners (adults at different stages of maturity), faculty (scholars with specific areas of expertise), administrators (adults who manage facilities and personnel), and sponsors (funding agencies, alumni and donors). College students are presumably mature adults capable of self-direction and responsible behavior—an assumption that is not always warranted, especially with regard to students just arriving from high school. In any case, students in tertiary settings are responsible for taking personal responsibility for their educational goals (e.g., identifying a major program of study, selecting courses, enrolling, paying fees, buying required materials, etc.). Parents are not involved in a central way, although they may visit initially with the prospective student and periodically thereafter. Faculty members provide the major points of contact with students; college and university faculty are generally recognized specialists with established academic credentials who can operate independently with regard to teaching in specific content areas.

While student performance is typically graded, the omnipresent standardized tests are no longer the primary driving force in assessing individual progress. Faculty typically have a great deal of freedom to support individual learners and assess their progress. Some subject areas do require a standardized graduation exam in order to be certified according to a professional organization (e.g., architects, lawyers, nurses, etc.), but for many the degree in the chosen subject area is the mark of success. The degree, the granting institution, a strong résumé, and letters of recommendation are much more important than a transcript and grades to most prospective employers.

Given that context, communication between faculty and students should be structured accordingly; for example, students should be encouraged to ask for elaboration, and faculty should be encouraged to be responsive to and supportive of individual learning needs. The language should be that of respectful academic discourse. Interactions should be designed to promote increasing deeper inquiry into an area and centered around increasingly challenging problems which are representative of the central problems within a discipline.

Environment and Culture

Learning environments and cultural contexts associated with colleges and universities are quite varied. In some colleges and universities, an overt attempt is made for students to address faculty using their first name as a way to foster meaningful and open relationships of the kind to be encountered after graduation. In other colleges and universities, an overt attempt is made for students to address faculty by their degree or university status and the last name as a way to foster a respectful environment.

Such local practices may require adjustment on the part of both faculty and students. As with most situations, it is generally wise to follow local practice and customs.

Higher education institutions are places where students can explore a variety of academic and nonacademic pursuits, and this is generally encouraged. It is not uncommon for a particular faculty member to believe that students should be devoting the majority of their waking life to that faculty member's course and learning materials. This may happen when a particular instructor has fallen in love with the subject and expects all students to be so enamored with the subject that most waking hours will be devoted in some way to that subject. The reality, of course, is that students have a variety of interests and obligations, and some may be enrolled in the course only as a result of a general requirement. Such different outlooks on the value of the course and subject can create serious misunderstandings between instructors and students, and may even result in students losing interest in the subject as a result of unrealistic expectations on the part of the instructor. In any case, the environment and culture in higher education settings vary widely and from course to course, from instructor to instructor, and from the composition of one class to that of another.

Instruction and Learning

Higher education courses are focused primarily on learning outcomes associated with progressing through a sequence of courses within a discipline that may begin with an overview or introductory course followed by in-depth explorations of specific areas within the discipline, and then advanced problems and issues associated with professional practice in that discipline. As a consequence, instruction is typically structured around a variety of learning activities intended to support the level of desired understanding. While learning activities may involve whole-class, small-group, and individual activities, grades are usually assigned based on individual performance (although performance in the class and small groups are often components of individual performance). In higher education settings, it is somewhat rare to find professional instructional designers and educational technologists involved in course planning and implementation.

While some programs of study require a certification examination in order to graduate, others require only a passing average grade in a certain number of courses. As students progress further in an area of study, they are expected to take more responsibility for monitoring and directing their own progress and to become increasingly self-reliant in developing their higher-order reasoning and problem-solving skills. Ironically, when one considers the typical experience of students in primary and secondary settings, higher education students are typically not adequately prepared for such a transition to self-directed studies having been trained thus far in more structured and teacher-directed learning activities. Educational technologists and instructional designers should realize that it is probably unreasonable to expect every student to immediately become self-directed with highly evolved meta-cognitive skills. Some higher education students will want and require structured learning activities for many years still. One cannot expect a learner to suddenly become a successful, self-directed learning with appropriately developed meta-cognitive skills any more than one can expect a faculty member to suddenly switch entirely from using only lectures to fostering problem-centered learning with mostly small-group activities. Such transitions take time.

Higher Education Examples

The open learning initiative at Carnegie Mellon University provides access to a number of free online courses. One such course is in causal and statistical reasoning—http://oli.web.cmu.edu/openlearning/forstudents/freecourses/csr.

The master's program in system dynamics at the University of Bergen is considered one of the best in that area in the world (see www.uib.no/en/studyprogramme/MASV-SYSDY). That residential program represents an excellent mix of system dynamics theory, modeling methodologies, and applied work in various fields including development issues, natural resources management, and socioeconomic problems.

Business and Industry

Of course education and training is a major concern in business and industry, and many organizations make extensive use of educational technology at the workplace so as to provide cost-efficient training. In addition, there are many enterprises which develop and deploy training and education primarily for the business sector. Many courses for business and industry are targeted at specific learning outcomes and consist of a number of webinars, demonstration sessions (often online), individual activities, and group discussion and critique. These courses are typically proprietary and cannot be exemplified in this volume, but many adults will have had such a corporate training experience and can share that experience with others in class or through a discussion forum. In addition to proprietary courses, those which are offered for employees within the organization may contain sensitive or confidential information which should not be released to the public, which creates a security issue when planning and implementing such courses.

Communications and Interaction

The key stakeholders in business and industry include the employees, management, clients, and the general public. This constellation of stakeholders creates specific requirements for communication and interaction. When clients and the public are involved, a great deal of effort is taken to carefully formulate communications and interactions associated with learning activities. An organization selling a product may offer potential clients a free short course on the use of that product. Such a course may have a targeted learning outcome, but it is also likely to have a targeted public relations outcome (e.g., interest in the product).

Environment and Culture

Organizational cultures vary significantly. Some organizations actively support employees in their desire to pursue further and ongoing education based on a belief that well-educated and highly skilled workers will result in a more productive enterprise. Other organizations are reluctant to support employees in furthering their education and training for fear that the best of these employees will leave and take jobs in competing organizations. In some countries (Norway, for example), it is the right of employees to pursue additional studies and employers are obligated to allow time for such life-long education. Much has been written in recent years about the learning organization (Argyris & Schön, 1996; Spector & Davidsen, 2006). An organizational culture that fosters independent thinking and values a highly skilled and knowledgeable workforce accounts in large part for a company's ability to develop and maintain the status of a superior organization (Collins, 2001).

Instruction and Learning

Instruction and learning in business and industry may have multiple goals. The obvious goal is to develop and maintain a highly skilled workforce. However, some organizations use training as a way to develop positive worker attitudes and to reward exceptional employees. For example, an organization may schedule a retreat for all or part of the staff to spend a day off-site at an attractive setting to talk openly about how organizational issues. A sales organization may offer training at a resort setting for those who have met their annual sales quotas. In such cases, a primary outcome of the training is improved motivation, which can and should be measured along with any desired learning outcomes.

In any case, corporate training often makes use of instructional design experts to plan and implement courses. The pros and cons of having instructional design experts involved in course planning and implementation, comparing representative higher educational courses with those found in business and industry, is an excellent topic for a class discussion or a discussion forum.

Business and Industry Examples

ALISON (Advance Learning Interactive Systems Online) provides free online courses in a number of areas pertinent to life-long learning and workplace contexts. To explore a course follow this link: http://alison.com.

Allen Communication (see www.allencomm.com/about-allen) is a recognized leader in corporate training. The focus of that enterprise is on customized training to improve human performance.

Strategy Dynamics (see www.strategydynamics.com) offers a number of micro-worlds and interactive simulations to support a variety of training requirements. In addition to online courses and micro-worlds (some are free), Strategy Dynamics has a planning and modeling tool called Sysdea (https://sysdea.com) that offers many of the capabilities of PowerSim (www.powersim.com) and Stella/iThink (www.iseesystems.com) and perhaps more.

Governmental Agencies

As with the other sectors, there is a great deal of variety in the governmental agency sector, which includes different levels (national, state/province, local) as well as different types (budget and finance, defense, education and welfare, legislative, judicial, etc.). Some training is aimed at employees within the agency and some is aimed at the community being served by the agency. Many government agencies have required training for employees to satisfy various regulations and accountability concerns. Much of this training involves having employees attend a required number of lectures or read an assigned text followed by a simple knowledge test (in some cases only attendance is required). By most standards, such training might be considered more properly as information dissemination and not training. Training involves learning, which involves stable and persisting changes in abilities, beliefs, knowledge, or skills. If no such changes occur or can be documented, then it is legitimate to question calling such information dissemination sessions training.

On the other hand, many government organizations take training quite seriously; this is especially true in the defense and public health sectors since lives are at risk when training is not adequate.

Communications and Interaction

The key stakeholders may be employees and managers in the agency, other agencies and organizations, the general public, or a combination of these. In nearly all cases, learners are expected to be adults, as was the case for business and industry. Governmental agencies may prescribe the use of specific words and associated meanings, and these should be noted and followed in learning materials. For example, 'tornado watch' and 'tornado warning' have different meanings and knowing that difference might make a life-saving or life-changing difference (i.e., a tornado warning indicates that a tornado has been detected nearby and precautions must be taken immediately).

A challenge when communicating with many people with very different backgrounds is that it is difficult to know what they already know and understand. This situation occurs with any instructional system or learning environment or tutorial course aimed at the general public. Developers are advised to test a near-final prototype with a wide variety of representative users to minimize the need to revise immediately due to improper or inaccessible language in the instructional and learning materials.

Environment and Culture

As noted in other sectors, the environment and culture are likely to vary significantly from one organization to another. In some cases, a very formal culture dictates how individuals interact and communicate with each other (e.g., military organizations). In other cases, the environment and culture are quite open and fluid. Organizing learning activities and materials to align with the environments and cultures in which they will be used is highly desirable. The tradeoff in doing this may be reduced portability of courses and learning materials to agencies with a different environment and culture.

Instruction and Learning

Many governmental agencies mandate specific courses and programs of study in order to advance within that agency. Many such courses are performance-based, requiring the individual to perform at a specified level prior to advancing to the next level. Such mastery-based learning is much more common in governmental agencies than in higher education, where a fixed period of study is involved followed by some measure of what was learned in that fixed time period. In a mastery-based instructional approach, the student is allowed as much time as required in order to achieve proficiency.

Government Agency Examples

The National Environmental Health Association (NEHA) offers a number of free online public health courses sponsored by the Center for Disease Control (CDC). Follow the following link for access to these courses—www.nehacert.org/catalog/index.php?cPath= 28&main_page=index.

OpenupED (see www.openuped.eu) is a pan-European project hosting a number of MOOCs (massive open online courses) in various topical areas in an effort to make education more broadly available across Europe. MOOCs and other emerging technologies are discussed in the final chapter.

The National Taiwan Normal University's Mandarin Training Center Online (see http://online.mtc.ntnu.edu.tw/?menuid=127) offers a number of courses aimed at professionals wanting to learn Chinese and work in Taiwan. Similar courses are appearing in other Asian countries and other parts of the world.

Nonprofit and Nongovernmental Organizations

A nonprofit organization (NPO) is one that does not distribute its earnings to owners or shareholders; examples include charities, educational organizations, professional and trade associations, and organizations aimed at a public interest such as the arts or science. A nongovernmental organization (NGO) is created typically to serve a public or social interest not addressed (adequately) by the government; an example of an NGO is the International Red Cross. NGOs are typically also NPOs but not every NPO is an NGO recognized by the United Nations or the World Bank with a humanitarian mission. In any event, such organizations often offer training and education for employees as well as the general public. This, of course, introduces many challenges and complexities for educational technologists and instructional designers.

Communications and Interaction

The key stakeholders may be employees and managers with the organization or those outside the organization—specifically, the general public. Because these organizations often have a global mission, the language and forms of interaction involved must be carefully crafted. What might work well in a highly developed and well-organized society might not work at all in a developing country with minimal infrastructure. Of course, communication and interaction are closely intertwined with the other foundation areas, as should be obvious from previous sector elaborations and from the discussion in Chapter 2.

Environment and Culture

When a global community of users is involved, it is quite difficult to make assumptions about the environment and culture surrounding the use of instructional materials and learning environments. If the means of providing instructional materials involves a smart phone device, the situation surrounding the user at the time of use can make a difference. For example, if the user is alone at home in a comfortable and safe setting with a stable connection, then longer sequences can be designed. When learners are in a public setting or in remote areas with unstable connections, then shorter instructional sequences make more sense. The challenge is to find a design that is likely to satisfy most of the anticipated users in their various contexts of use.

Instruction and Learning

NPOs and NGOs are involved with both training and education for a wide variety of audiences. This makes it quite difficult to offer very much in the way of meaningful generalizations beyond what has been said along these lines with the other sectors. It is perhaps worth emphasizing that the larger the instructional system or learning environment being developed and the wider the audience, the more important it is to conduct a thorough needs assessment and requirements analysis involving all stakeholder groups. It is also important to develop and test early prototypes with representative end users so as not to waste valuable development time and effort. Having reliable data on effectiveness and impact is an obvious way to satisfy sponsors.

Nongovernmental Agency Examples

The International Federation of Red Crescent Societies offers a number of free courses ranging from public health issues to disaster preparedness and recovery. These courses can be found at the following URL: https://ifrc.csod.com/client/ifrc/default.aspx.

The United Nations World Health Organization (WHO) might be considered an example in this category (see www.who.int/en). Included within the wide variety of WHO programs are courses open to anyone on topics ranging from aging to project planning.

Test Your Understanding

Which of the following statements are true and why?

1. Using British spelling for a course to be used primarily in the USA is not problematic.
2. The color scheme selected for use in a course to be delivered in South Korea can be used without change in many other countries.
3. A private development company can use an official government seal without obtaining prior permission in a course being developed for that agency.
4. If there are no assessments involved in a required tutorial, then that tutorial should be regarded as information dissemination and not as training.
5. Knowledge and skills involved in designing and developing learning and instruction in one sector are likely to transfer easily to a different sector.
6. University professors typically perform the tasks of instructional design and development.
7. K-12 teachers typically have a great deal of flexibility in choosing instructional goals and learning materials.
8. Mastery-based learning is most common in a college or university context.
9. When planning educational technology use by the general public one should focus on a single common language to be used in all contexts.
10. "Half of the people can be all right part of the time. Some of the people can be all right part of the time. But all of the people can't be all right all of the time."[1]

A Representative Educational Technology Challenge

In one of the sectors[2] discussed briefly in this chapter, it has become evident that computer security is a major issue. Users have been infected by many computer viruses and many files lost as a consequence. Given such a problem, you have been asked to identify policy changes that might be appropriate to consider as well as training that might be needed for computer users. The specific task at hand is to draft a computer security plan that includes both policy and training recommendations along with the accompanying rationale.

Learning Activities

Find a lesson designed for a middle or high school writing class on a topic you understand. Redesign that lesson for use in a college or university context for students still struggling with writing skills. Once you have done this, identify the factors that you thought most relevant to the redesign effort and why they were relevant. Explain if and how these factors were interrelated.

Links

ALISON website with access to a variety of free online courses—http://alison.com

Carnegie Mellon University's open learning initiative—http://oli.web.cmu.edu/openlearning/forstudents/freecourses/csr

The International Federation of Red Crescent Societies and publicly available courses—https://ifrc.csod.com/client/ifrc/default.aspx

WISE science education website—http://wise.berkeley.edu

Smart school in South Korea—www.korea.net/NewsFocus/Sci-Tech/view?articleId=99412

System Dynamics Master's Program at the University of Bergen—www.uib.no/en/studyprogramme/MASV-SYSDY

Strategy Dynamics website—www.strategydynamics.com

The Mandarin Training Center Online—http://online.mtc.ntnu.edu.tw/?menuid=127

The WHO programs—www.who.int/en

Other Resources

The learning organization website—www.infed.org/biblio/learning-organization.htm

The open learning initiative—http://oli.web.cmu.edu/openlearning

The Open University's free learning website called OpenLearn—www.open.ac.uk/openlearn/?gclid=CO6MyZu_sKgCFQpm7Aodd2biIw

Notes

1. From Bob Dylan's "Talkin' World War III Blues."
2. The sector is intentionally omitted so that students can imagine a context close to their current or anticipated work environment.

References

Argyris, C., & Schön, D. (1996) *Organisational learning II: Theory, method and practice*. Reading, MA: Addison Wesley.

Collins, J. (2001). *Good to great: Why some companies make the leap . . . and others don't*. New York: HarperCollins.

Spector, J. M., & Davidsen, P. I. (2006). How can organizational learning be modeled and measured. *Evaluation and Program Planning, 29*(1), 63–69.

Wittgenstein, L. (1953). *Philosophical investigations* (G. E. M. Anscombe & R. Rhees (Eds.); G. E. M. Anscombe (Trans.)). Oxford: Blackwell.

seventeen
Professional Preparation and Training

"We judge ourselves by what we feel capable of doing, while others judge us by what we have done" (Henry Wadsworth Longfellow, Kavanagh: A Tale*)*

The goal of a training regimen in general is to prepare someone to regularly perform anticipated tasks with competence and skill. Given the increasing rapidity with which new technologies are being brought into education and the workplace, it is appropriate to examine how educational technology professionals are being trained. The basic line of reasoning followed herein is that new technologies often require new competencies in the form of knowledge, skills, and attitudes (see www.ibstpi.org). Requiring new competencies has the associated requirement of training those involved appropriately and probably differently.

One example of these changes concerns what might be called competency in facilitating discussions in secondary and tertiary education and also in adult training. In a classroom setting, that competency is typically addressed when preparing teachers and trainers; there are well-established skills involved (see, for example, Bloom, 2006; Hassard & Dias, 2009; Herbel-Eisenmann & Cirillo, 2009). The International Board of Standards for Training, Performance and Instruction includes effective facilitation skills as a fundamental instructor competency (see www.ibstpi.org). For ibstpi, facilitation includes engaging all participants, keeping participants focused on an issue, encouraging and supporting collaboration, bringing discussions to closure, monitoring and assessing progress, and adapting to the dynamics of the discussion. Facilitation strategies include setting clear expectations, allowing informal discussions to proceed when relevant, posing good questions, maintaining eye contact, and so on. These are skills that can be practiced in teacher training programs and competencies that can be developed and tested as part of certification.

However, there are two critical points to be made. First, online discussions are much different from classroom discussions. There is no eye contact possible in asynchronous discussion forums, for example. Moreover, the time constraints are quite different as is the form of expression. Someone who is comfortable in vocalizing their thoughts might not be as comfortable in entering those thoughts in text format in a discussion forum, especially if that person's writing skills are not at the same level as his or her speaking skills. Moreover, many who might be reluctant to speak out in class (perhaps they like to formulate thoughts before speaking) might be more inclined to be active in an asynchronous discussion forum that allows time to prepare a response. In short, there are many differences between real-time, face-to-face discussions and asynchronous online discussions (synchronous video-conferencing is sufficiently similar to face-to-face discussion to be less relevant to the point being made here, although there are critical differences there as well). Not only are there significant differences involved, those differences affect different learners differently.

In addition to there being new competencies associated with new forms of instruction such as distance learning, there are new competencies associated with new approaches to learning both in and out of a classroom setting. The notion of flipping the classroom dates back to the previous century and involves having students do things previously done in the classroom (e.g., reviewing resources and primary presentations) outside the class, while focusing on problem solving and things previously done outside the classroom (e.g., homework) inside the classroom (see Lage, Platt, & Treglia, 2000; Walvoord & Anderson, 1998).

Flipping the classroom involves a number of interesting things. It shifts the emphasis from teaching styles to learning styles, since the primary presentations take place outside the classroom with individual learners approaching problem solving in very different ways. Flipping the classroom also can promote inclusive, differentiated, and personalized instruction not really possible in a traditional classroom. However, along with those new opportunities come new requirements and competencies for teachers. While the notion of flipping the classroom has been around for at least a generation, there are still very few examples of it being done on a large scale or throughout a school system. Assuming that claim is correct, why might it be so? (This is another good question for a classroom or online discussion.)

In addition to such requirements as facilitating online discussions and flipping the classroom, new technologies are being introduced into classrooms and work environments that teachers and instructors must master in order to use them effectively. Engineering instructors need to know how to integrate 3D printing into their instruction. Science teachers need to know how to use digital microscopes and a host of digital probes. Mathematics educators need to master Geometer's Sketchpad (see www.dynamicgeometry.com) and Geogebra (see www.geogebra.org) to support many of their classes. Those teachers who wish to have students create engaging multimedia need to develop competence with a variety of Maker technologies (see http://makerfaire.com/maker-movement and http://makermedia.com). In short, new technologies and new approaches to learning and instruction have brought new requirements for teachers.

Teachers require new competencies for a variety of reasons, including having to make effective use of new technologies. This means that traditional means of preparing teachers and instructors need to change in order to accommodate these changes. Which teacher preparation programs are making changes and what changes are proving to be beneficial? What are the implications for professional development? These questions are addressed in the remaining sections of this chapter. (They are also good questions for a discussion forum.)

Leading Programs

It is perhaps misguided to identify a small number of leading programs in the area of educational technology. First, educational technology programs focus on different aspects and emphasise different things. In the 1950s, when there were not so many programs and when there were many fewer information and communications technologies available, one could identify leading programs in North America and elsewhere. Programs that have evolved from leading programs of an earlier era include the following: (a) the Instructional Systems Technology program at Indiana University (see http://education.indiana.edu/about/departments/instructional), (b) the Instructional Systems program at Florida State University (see http://coe.fsu.edu/insys), and (c) the Instructional Design, Development, & Evaluation Department at Syracuse University (see http://soe.syr.edu/academic/Instructional_Design_Development_and_Evaluation). Of course, other such programs could be listed, as there were many and now there are many more. The point to be made here is that graduate programs in the area of educational technology have evolved significantly in the last 50 plus years, just as have the technologies being integrated into learning, performance, and instruction.

Many early educational technology developments occurred in university settings, and these were often associated with various computer technologies. One such example is PLATO (Programmed Logic for Automatic Teaching Operations), which was developed in the 1960s at the University of Illinois and which hosted many courses for some 40 years. More recent developments can be found at the Centre de Recherche LICEF, Télé-Université, Université du Québec (see www.licef.ca) which developed a number of tools to support the design, development, and deployment of learning environments.

While universities were making great strides in developing educational technologies, a great deal of research on educational technology was being conducted by government laboratories—notably, the U.S. Navy Personnel Research and Development Center, the U.S. Army Research Institute, and the U. S. Air Force Armstrong Laboratory. Whereas university research often focused on research and development (R&D) of technologies for use in higher education, the Department of Defense focused on R&D pertaining to adult learning of technical skills. NATO (the North Atlantic Treaty Organization) also promoted research on advanced learning for a number of years.

Not surprisingly, a third area of application developed around the use of technologies in primary and secondary schools. The growth in this area was certainly spurred by the introduction of personal computers. The Minnesota Educational Computing Consortium (MECC; see www.mecc.co) was founded in 1974 and survived until 1999. Many new educational technologies have since been founded, and provided many tools and technologies for schools as well as for colleges, universities, and private enterprises.

This short overview of the growth of educational technology R&D is pertinent to graduate programs preparing adults for careers in the broad area of educational technology because it provides one way to characterize such programs and their various areas of emphasis. Undergraduate programs are not included in this discussion as there are too few of these in existence. One of the most prominent undergraduate programs was at the University of Freiburg in Germany (Educational Science), but it has since been eliminated. Hartley and colleagues (2010) developed an undergraduate curriculum for advanced learning technologies but it has not yet been implemented anywhere. In short, while there are many opportunities for undergraduate programs in educational technology, few such programs have been developed.

Table 17.1 depicts one way to characterize existing educational technology graduate programs around the world. The programs indicated are meant to be representative rather than the most highly regarded programs in an area. The program areas in Table 17.1 are not mutually exclusive and a number of programs address multiple program areas and levels (see, for example, Spector et al., 2014).

Nearly all the programs in Table 17.1 offer courses and specializations outside the indicated program area, and many other good programs exist at other universities around the world. An in-class or online activity might involve expanding this table to include different program areas and representative programs. Given a wide variety of graduate programs involved in the preparation and training of educational technologists, it is reasonable to look at how programs have changed and what changes are likely to occur in the future.

Programmatic Changes

As suggested previously, early college and university programs in educational technology typically covered multiple sectors (K-12, higher education, business, government) with a strong emphasis on instructional design and technology integration. The emphasis on instructional design and technology integration are still quite strong, as Table 17.1 suggests. However, due to the variety of contexts and technologies involved, programs have begun to focus on (a) specific technologies (e.g., online environments, mobile technologies, etc.), (b) specific aspects of instructional design (e.g., lesson and curriculum development, program evaluation, etc.), (c) specific domains of application

TABLE 17.1

Program Area	Level(s)	Example Programs
Primary and Secondary Teacher Training	Masters	Faculty of Education at Universitas Terbuka, Indonesia; Learning Design and Technology, San Diego State University; Ontario Institute for Studies in Education; Teacher Education, University of Michigan
Media Specialists and School Technologists	Masters	Instructional Technology, Georgia Southern University; Media Studies, University of Bergen, Norway; Curriculum and Instruction, Texas A&M – Corpus Christie
Educational Technology in Higher Education	Masters, Doctoral	Learning Technologies, University of Texas @ Austin; Ewha Womans University, Korea; Educational Psychology, University of Wisconsin;
Corporate/Government Training & Performance	Masters	Applied Technology and Performance Improvement, University of North Texas; Information Sciences and Technology, Penn State University; Workforce Education, University of Georgia
Educational Technology and Tools R&D	Masters, Doctoral	East China Normal University, Shanghai, China; Learning Sciences and Technology Design, Stanford University; School of Engineering and Applied Science, University of Virginia
Educational Technology Research and Evaluation	Masters, Doctoral	School of Information and Communications Technology, Piraeus University, Greece; Beijing Normal University, Beijing, China; Faculty of the Sciences of Education, University of Quebec, Canada
Instructional Design and Development (multiple sectors)	Masters, Doctoral	Instructional Design, Development and Evaluation, Syracuse University; Instructional Psychology and Technology, Brigham Young University; Instructional Systems, Florida State University
Learning Sciences	Masters, Doctoral	Learning Sciences, Indiana University; Educational Psychology and Educational Technology, Michigan State University; Mind, Brain and Education, Harvard Graduate School of Education
Cross-cutting Programs	Masters	Information Science and Technology, Hong Kong University; Instructional Technology, University of Twente; Information Management, National Sun Yat-sen University, Taiwan

(e.g., Science, Technology, Engineering, and Mathematics applications), (d) specific approaches to learning and instruction (e.g., inquiry learning, experiential learning, etc.), (e) specific sectors (e.g., corporate training, leadership development, etc.), and so on.

Another change that has occurred in the last 50 years pertains to divisions within the field of educational technology. Teacher training is now emphasizing what is called TPACK (Technological, Pedagogical, Content Knowledge) (Herring & Smaldino, 2015; Koehler & Mishra, 2015; Mishra & Koehler, 2006). Technologies for use in primary and secondary education are far too numerous to list and beyond the mastery of any one individual. Many professionals associate themselves with specific approaches or areas of scholarship, such as instructional design, learning science, or performance technology. Specific associations and journals exist to support these professionals (see Appendices B and C). These divisions within the broad area of educational technology introduce both benefits and challenges. The benefits involve opportunities to form collaborations, conduct research and publish findings with those working in closely related areas. The challenges involve the fact that there is a great deal of overlap among these various areas. Research, development, and practice might well advance more rapidly were there more cross-collaboration across those somewhat arbitrary divisions. This speculative remark is worthy of discussion in class or in an online forum.

Professional Development

Given the rapid rate of change with regard to information and communications technologies, there is an obvious need for ongoing professional development in every sector (K-12, higher education, business, government, etc.). Some of the very technologies that result in this requirement are also playing a role in how professional development is planned, implemented, and evaluated. For example, online environments and mobile technologies allow some professional development to occur in the work environment. However, much of that training lacks some of the critical components of instruction. All too often, such online and mobile training involve mostly information dissemination with too little emphasis placed on skill development and deep understanding of complex phenomena.

Collaboration tools are among the technologies that can be used to promote reflection and understanding (e.g., peer assessments, structured observations, and critiques). Virtual and augmented realities can be used to engage learners in practice with some automated feedback, which can result in skill development as well as understanding. However, the temptation is to believe that online and mobile professional development will be an inexpensive alternative to face-to-face training sessions, which involve travel costs as well as lost work time. The reality is that online and mobile professional development courses require time, expertise, resources, and effort to develop, and they may not always yield all of the expected benefits.

The point here is only to highlight increased requirements for professional development due to new and changing technologies along with the possibility of using some of those technologies to meet that challenge. As Collins (2005) argued, the solution is not in traditional business thinking and trying to minimize costs. Rather the solution involves planning for the future.

Test Your Understanding

Answer the following questions as indicated:

1. The competencies for being an effective classroom instructor are roughly the same as those for being an effective online instructor. (T/F). Explain your answer.

2. In a flipped classroom environment, the teacher becomes the student, and students become the teacher. (T/F). Explain your answer.
3. The U.S. Department of Defense has been responsible for a great deal of research and development in the area of educational technology. (T/F). Explain your answer.
4. Preparing a person to integrate technology in a K-12 environment is quite different than preparing an instructional designer for the corporate sector. (T/F). Explain your answer.

A Representative Educational Technology Challenge

Suppose you have been appointed the incoming Dean of Education for a prominent university preparing teachers for careers in K-12 schools. You have been given a free hand in redesigning the entire curriculum for pre-service teacher training, including options to (a) require a bachelor's degree in an area of specialization, (b) require a one-semester long teaching internship the second semester of the first year of the program in addition to a longer internship toward the end of the program, (c) require specific training in designing, developing, and evaluating technology-intensive lessons, and more. You have been given a generous budget (US$1 million per year for the next five years) that allows hiring additional faculty and acquiring new technologies. What changes would you propose, why, and how would you go about implementing those changes?

Resources

Centre de Recherche LICEF, Télé-Université, Université du Québec—see www.licef.ca

Dynamic geometry software—see www.geogebra.org and www.dynamicgeometry.com

Knewton—an educational technology enterprise that specializes in personalizing learning—see www.knewton.com/about

Minnesota Educational Computing Consortium (MECC)—see www.mecc.co

The Maker Movement—integrating do it yourself technologies into learning and instruction—see http://makermedia.com and http://makerfaire.com/maker-movement

References

Bloom, J. W. (2006). *Creating a classroom community of young scientists*. New York: Routledge.

Collins, J. (2005). *Good to great and the social sectors: A monograph to accompany good to great*. New York: Harper.

Hartley, R., Kinshuk, Koper, R., Okamoto, T., & Spector, J. M. (2010). The education and training of learning technologists: A competences approach. *Educational Technology & Society, 13*(2), 206–216.

Hassard, J., & Dias, M. (2009). *The art of teaching science: Inquiry and innovation in middle and high school* (2nd ed.). New York: Routledge.

Herbel-Eisenmann, B., & Cirillo, M. (Eds.) (2009). *Promoting purposeful discourse*. Reston, VA: National Council of Teachers of Mathematics.

Herring, M. C., & Smaldino, S. E. (2015). TPACK (Technological Pedagogical Content Knowledge): Implications for 21st century teacher education. In J. M. Spector (Ed.), *The encyclopedia of educational technology*. Thousand Oaks, CA: Sage.

Koehler, M. J., & Mishra, P. (2015). TPACK (Technological Pedagogical Content Knowledge). In J. M. Spector (Ed.), *The encyclopedia of educational technology*. Thousand Oaks, CA: Sage.

Lage, M. J., Platt, G. J., & Treglia, M. (2000). Inverting the classroom: A gateway to creating an inclusive learning environment. *Journal of Economic Education, 31,* 30–43.

Mishra, P., & Koehler, M. J. (2006). Technological pedagogical content knowledge: A framework for teacher knowledge. *Teacher College Record, 108*(6), 1017–1054.

Spector, J. M., Yuen, H. K., Wang, M., Churchill, D., & Law, N. (2014). *Hong Kong perspectives on educational technology research and practice.* Englewood Cliffs, NJ: Educational Technology Publications.

Walvoord, B. E., & Anderson, V. J. (1998). Effective grading: A tool for learning and assessment. San Francisco, CA: Jossey-Bass.

eighteen
Scalability and Replication Studies

"The electronics industry has not solved a single problem;
it has only created the problem of using its products"
(Edsger Dijkstra, The Humble Programmer*)*

What works in a small and tightly controlled environment may well not work in other environments without substantial modifications and adequate support. For example, a demonstration or proof-of-concept project in a particular school or organization typically has substantial support in the form of developers, technicians, and researchers along with ongoing training and preparation of local personnel. When the demonstration project is implemented and evaluated, the results are often promising, although not always to the extent expected or predicted. As a result of promising outcomes in the demonstration project, follow-on efforts may ensue involving more schools and organizations that often have quite different circumstances and constraints. When these follow-on efforts are evaluated, which is all too rare, the results are quite often much less promising than the original demonstration project (Blumenfeld, Fishman, Krajcik, Marx, & Soloway, 2000).

Many of the challenges of bringing a promising demonstration project to scale occur in other disciplines as well as in the field of educational technology. These challenges essentially involve the need for a holistic and systemic view (Quint, Bloom, Black, Stephens, & Akey, 2005). What makes scalability such a challenge in education is the somewhat amorphous nature of the targeted systems, which involve a wide variety of students, teachers, parents, administrators, school board personnel, community activists, and regulations at the school, district, state, and national level. It should not be a surprise that bringing about systemic reform on a large scale in the domain of education remains a pressing and formidable challenge. Nor should it be a surprise to conclude that technology is not necessarily the solution. As in other instances, technology can be a help or a hindrance. What is essential is a systems perspective (see the discussion in Chapter 6 on this topic). In this chapter, a definition of scale is offered along with a discussion of particular issues involving bringing demonstration projects to scale. The need for replication studies is a central aspect of scalability and is addressed as part of a general solution approach.

Defining Scale and Scalability

As noted by Clarke and Dede (2009), scaling up involves taking a project designed for a particular setting and implementing it in a much wider range of situations. In the context of educational applications, this typically requires significant adaptation and support in order to achieve results similar to those of the initial demonstration effort (Clarke & Dede, 2009; Dede, Honan, & Peters, 2005).

Within the context of formal education, taking a project to scale can mean taking what worked with one subject area at one grade level to other subject levels and grade levels within the same school. This level of scaling can present challenges associated with different subject areas, different grade levels, different students, and different teachers. Adapting the application to take into account those concerns is required. Pilot testing of refined applications is then needed, as is training teachers and other support personnel. Those teachers (often lead teachers or early adopters) involved in the initial effort often serve in training and support roles and often provide rationale, lessons learned, and motivation from a teacher's perspective to new teachers becoming involved. While this level of scaling up is not trivial, it is often manageable given proper support from school administrators (Kim, Kim, Lee, Spector, & DeMeester, 2013).

Taking an effort shown to be effective in one school and implementing it throughout a school district involves additional challenges. School cultures differ as do the support offered by different school principals, headmasters, and other administrators. Moreover, the school district introduces a new layer of bureaucracy that must be taken into account. This level of scale will typically involve parents and voters much more than is the case at the local school level.

Taking an effort shown to be effective at the district level to the state level in the USA introduces still more challenges. State standards must be explicitly acknowledged along with ongoing financial support required. Adapting the effort for nationwide use and expecting systemic national reform and significant improvements in learning is the most serious challenge of all. To the best of this author's knowledge, there has been very little success at that level beyond such efforts as Head Start that was initiated in 1965 in the USA (see www.acf.hhs.gov/programs/ohs). An interesting discussion topic would be to cite and discuss other success stories about large-scale educational innovations in the

USA and in other countries. (There is evidence of this in South Korea as noted in an earlier chapter.)

Similar issues of scale pertain to organizations other than schools. As discussed in Chapter 6 with regard to integrative approaches, a systemic view that takes into account a variety of values, cultural perspectives, work practices, and prior experiences is required to achieve success in scaling up promising efforts.

Scalability can be defined as the effort (time, money, expertise, etc.) required to take a project implemented at one level to a higher level. Dede and colleagues (2005, 2009) identified these areas of concern with regard to scaling up: (a) *depth* (the extent and kinds of changes required), (b) *sustainability* (the resources required for adaptation and ongoing support), (c) *spread* (the different types and numbers of users and their backgrounds), (d) *shift* (the fact that ownership is likely to shift from project managers and principal investigators to others such as school and district administrators), and (e) *evolution* (the reality that systemic change typically requires gradual and steady progress rather than radical reconstruction). A topic for discussion might focus on elaborating these areas or identifying other areas of concern.

Issues Related to Scale

Each of the five areas of concern outlined by Dede and colleagues (2005, 2009) are echoed by Kim and colleagues (2013), who emphasized school and district culture and leadership as key points of leverage at the school and district levels. In addition to those concerns when taking a project or effort to scale, issues associated with the diffusion of innovation arise. One approach is to target early adopters at the school level (Ellsworth, 2015). This approach has the advantage of having those most willing and anxious to explore innovative new technologies lead the way for others to follow. A potential drawback is that middle-to-late adopters may become intimidated and reluctant to embrace what they may see as something beyond their capacity or expertise. As a result, there is increasing interest in having those who would be considered middle adopters or representative end-users involved early in an effort.

Design-based research, participatory design, and user-centered design are approaches which advocate having representative users at various levels of readiness involved early, and often when planning and implementing educational technology innovations.

Solution Approaches

Many have argued that assessment of learners is central to learning (Andrews & Wulfeck, 2014; Jonassen, 2014; Luschei, 2014; Spector, 2010). The basic reasoning is that learners need to be aware of their progress (e.g., via formative assessment and feedback), and instructors, designers, and decision makers need to be aware of how well lessons, courses, and curricula actually support targeted learning goals.

In a similar manner, evaluation of programs and projects is central to their success (Hamilton & Feldman, 2014; Spector, 2015a). Just as formative assessment (aimed at improving student performance and understanding) is critical in ensuring student learning, formative evaluation (aimed at improving the quality of a project or program as it evolves) is critical in ensuring the success of an effort. Evidence suggests that as the scale of an effort increases, the involvement of users (as in a design-based approach, participatory design, or user-centered design) becomes increasingly important. Evidence-based decision making before, during, and subsequent to an educational technology innovation is a critical factor, especially when scaling up (Hamilton & Feldman, 2014; Luschei, 2014).

The reason formative evaluation is especially critical is that educational technologists have a tendency to become advocates for an innovation they have helped implement. An advocacy-based approach to decision making is not always the wisest path to follow when scaling up demonstration efforts. In general, the practice of conducting replication studies to confirm (or refute) the findings of prior implementations, and conducting ongoing and rigorous fidelity of implementation studies, is vital to the cumulative understanding of what works and why in the broad area of educational technology.

Replication Studies

The basic question that arises when scaling up involves the extent to which prior findings will generalize to a new setting or context. Replication studies represent a systematic approach to addressing that question as they typically apply an approach, methodology, and instrumentation used in a prior study to a new population or context. These studies can help to build confidence in the initial findings and serve as a way to determine the generalizability of those findings.

Basically, there are three types of replication studies: (a) *exact* or literal replications (hardly ever feasible), (b) *operational* replication studies (testing the validity of the original findings), and (c) *constructive* replication studies (testing the primary constructs in the original study) (Lykken, 1968). Schmidt (2009) recategorized replication studies as those aimed at repeating the experimental procedure in a new setting (*direct*) and those aimed at the underlying hypotheses using different experimental procedures (*conceptual*). Both direct and conceptual replication studies, along with meta-analyses, can contribute to the generalizability of findings and thereby justify scale-up efforts.

While replication studies are widely encouraged and standard practice in the medical domain, they have not been embraced or strongly encouraged in the education domain. Part of the reason for the importance of replication of studies in the healthcare and medicine is the confidence that the public demands with regard to medical practice. In addition, medical researchers receive approach recognition as those studies are valued by the professional community as well as by the general public. However, in education, scholars have not typically received proper recognition for conducting such studies, and much more emphasis has historically been placed on developing new approaches, methods, and instruments than in confirming those developed by others. At the 2014 National Technology Leadership Summit (NTLS; see www.ntls.info) meeting in

Washington, DC, the significance of replication studies was emphasized and a number of prominent journal editors accepted the challenge of encouraging the publication of replication studies in their journals. Hopefully this will happen.

Test Your Understanding

Indicate your response to each of the following questions:

1. Participatory design is the practice of having designers engaged as simulated end-user during the development process. (T/F)
2. A replication study involves repeating an experiment or study with the same participants, methodology, and instrumentation after a significant delay. (T/F)
3. Scalability refers to the time, expertise, and other resources required in order to take an innovation or program implemented at one level to a higher level. (T/F)
4. A project that conducts a survey of the early adopters of an effort with regard to their likes and dislikes concerning the effort soon after it was implemented is an example of a user-centered design practice. (T/F)
5. Name as many examples as you can of educational technology innovations that have been successfully scaled up to a national level. (Open-ended response; at least one good example is required to be successful on this question.)

A Representative Educational Technology Challenge

Suppose that you are a tenured faculty member in science education at a prestigious university. You previously received a small grant from the National Science Foundation to create and demonstrate how you would use innovative technologies to support the implementation of next generation science standards at the 8th grade level. Your first project focused on the use of inexpensive 3D printers (digital fabricators) in support of a unit of instruction that involved electro-magnestism intended to be aligned with the following standard (see www.nextgenscience.org):

Motions and Stability: Forces and Interaction. Determine the factors that affect the strength of electric and magnetic forces. Examples of devices that use electric and magnetic forces include electromagnets, electric motors, or generators. Examples of data include the effect of the number of turns of wire on the strength of an electromagnet, or the effect of increasing the number or strength of magnets on the speed of an electric motor. Assessment about questions that require quantitative answers is limited to proportional reasoning and algebraic thinking.

The initial project involves groups of six students at four different schools in different school districts working for one month during the summer vacation. Students were recommended by their principals and participated on a voluntary basis without incentives other than the opportunity to work on an interesting project. Student groups were given access to a digital fabricator and both a content specialist (Ph.D. in science or engineering education) and a technical specialist along with the specifications for a general-purpose electric motor and appropriate support materials. Students had the task of constructing a working motor and testing its performance with variations in wiring and location of magnets. All four student groups succeeded in building and testing the motor and reported their findings to the involved project faculty. Students also complete a standardized test based on understanding of the underlying principles of magnetism and the electric motors. All students scored very high on that test and reported high enthusiasm for the project on an end-of-task survey.

You are now developing a proposal for a follow-on scale-up grant to NSF to extend your findings with these four groups of students to the four different school districts that they represented. The effort will involve all 8th-grade science classes in the four districts, and all units of instruction related to electric and magnetic forces. One part of your proposal involves an implementation plan in which you are specifying the issues involved in scaling up and how you will address those issues. What specific issues would you identify? How do you propose addressing those issues? How will you evaluate progress and success in addressing those issues? How will you respond to identified areas of deficiency as the scale-up effort evolves?

Resources

The Head Start Program—see www.acf.hhs.gov/programs/ohs

The National Technology Leadership Summit—see www.ntls.info

The National Science Teachers Association—see www.nsta.org/about/positions/ngss.aspx

The Next Generation Science Standards—see www.nextgenscience.org

References

Andrews, D. H., & Wulfeck, W. H., II (2014). In J. M. Spector, M. D. Merrill, J. Elen, & M. J. Bishop (Eds.), *Handbook of research on educational communications and technology* (pp. 303–310). New York: Springer.

Blumenfeld, P., Fishman, B. J., Krajcik, J., Marx, R. W., & Soloway, E. (2000). Creating usable innovation in systemic reform: Scaling up technology-embedded project-based science in urban schools. *Educational Psychologist, 35*(3), 140–164.

Clarke, J., & Dede, C. (2009). Robust designs for scalability. In L. Moller, J. B. Huett, & D. M. Harvey, *Learning and instructional technologies for the 21st* century (pp. 27–48). New York: Springer.

Dede, C., Honan, J., & Peters, L. (Eds.) (2005). *Scaling up success: Lessons learned from technology-based educational innovation.* New York: Jossey-Bass.

Ellsworth, J. B. (2015). Early adopters. In J. M. Spector (Ed.), *The encyclopedia of educational technology.* Thousand Oaks, CA: Sage.

Hamilton, J., & Feldman, J. (2014). Planning a program evaluation: Matching methodology to program status. In J. M. Spector, M. D. Merrill, J. Elen, & M. J. Bishop (Eds.), *Handbook of research on educational communications and technology* (pp. 249–257). New York: Springer.

Jonassen, D. H. (2014). Assessing problem solving. In J. M. Spector, M. D. Merrill, J. Elen, & M. J. Bishop (Eds.), *Handbook of research on educational communications and technology* (pp. 269–288). New York: Springer.

Kim, C., Kim, M., Lee, C., Spector, J. M., & DeMeester, K. (2013). Teacher pedagogical beliefs and technology integration. *Teaching and Teacher Education, 29*, 76–85.

Luschei, T. F. (2014). Assessing the costs and benefits of educational technology. In J. M. Spector, M. D. Merrill, J. Elen, & M. J. Bishop (Eds.), *Handbook of research on educational communications and technology* (pp. 239–248). New York: Springer.

Lykken, D. T. (1968). Statistical significance in psychological research. *Psychological Bulletin, 70,* 151–159.

Quint, J., Bloom, H. S., Black, A. R., Stephens, L., with Akey, T. M. (2005). *The challenge of scaling up educational reform: Findings and lessons from first things first* (Final Report; ERIC Number ED485680). New York: MDRC. Retrieved from http://eric.ed.gov/?id=ED485680

Schmidt, S. (2009). Shall we really do it again? The powerful concept of replication is neglected in the social sciences. *Review of General Pscyhology, 13,* 90–100.

Spector, J. M. (2010). Mental representations and their analysis: An epistemological perspective. In D. Ifenthaler, P. Pirnay-dummer, & N. M. Seel (Eds.), *Computer-based diagnostics and systematic analysis of knowledge* (17–40). New York: Springer.

Spector, J. M. (2015). Program evaluation. In J. M. Spector (Ed.), *The encyclopedia of educational technology.* Thousand Oaks, CA: Sage.

nineteen
Emerging Technologies

"Men have become the tools of their tools" (Henry David Thoreau, Walden *and* On the Duty of Civil Disobedience*)*

As with most things, technologies change. One common representation of changes in education technologies is that devices are getting smaller, more powerful, and less expensive (Spector, 2014b, 2015). This is obvious when focusing on physical devices and their capabilities. Here's an activity worth considering in a group discussion: What was the first computer you remember using? Do you recall its size, internal memory capacity, external storage medium and capacity, and its approximate cost? What computing device are you now using? How big is it? What are its memory and storage capabilities? How much did it cost? Some may recall starting on a mainframe computer that was the size of a large filing cabinet (or larger), which cost US$300,000 or more.

The revolutionary IBM 360 mainframe computer was announced in April 1964. It took three years and about US$5 billion to develop. A high-end IBM 360 sold for about US$500,000 in the mid-1960s. It had between 8 Kb and 8 Mb of internal main memory. External storage was primary on removable disk packs with a capacity of 7.25 Mb each disk pack (roughly the size of a small automobile tire); high-density tape drives were used for archiving. Many innovations made their first appearance in the IBM 360 family of mainframe computers. IBM net revenues more than doubled in the first five years the IBM 360 was on the market (see www.computerhistory.org/revolution/mainframe-computers/7/161). Figure 19.1 depicts a typical IBM 360 facility in the late 1960s.

FIGURE 19.1 IBM 360 Model 40, from the IBM archives (see www-03.ibm.com/ibm/history)

Compare the IBM 360, which is about 50 years old, with your current computing device. Is that not remarkable progress in a very short time period? Compare and contrast the progress in computing technologies in the last 50 years with progress in automotive technologies in the same time period. What might you conclude from such an analysis about those technologies with regard to the values of and benefits to society in general and to you personally?

Next, consider one of the promising areas of emerging technologies—namely, wearable computers. Smart watches are now appearing which communicate with your smartphone, tablet computer, and other computing devices (see Figure 19.2).

Would anyone in 1914 have imagined such watches? Perhaps. A comic strip character named Dick Tracy first appeared in 1931. In 1946, a wrist-worn two-way communication device was added to the comic strip, and in 1964 that device became a two-way video-communicator. So, about 50 years ago a few people were imaging devices that are now becoming everyday technologies.

There are several points to be made here. First, it is quite difficult to imagine which technologies with what capabilities will be available in 50 years. However, it is worthwhile to pay attention to what science fiction writers and futurists are thinking about. In addition, it is possible to look at the technologies now emerging and consider how they might evolve and influence learning, performance, and instruction.

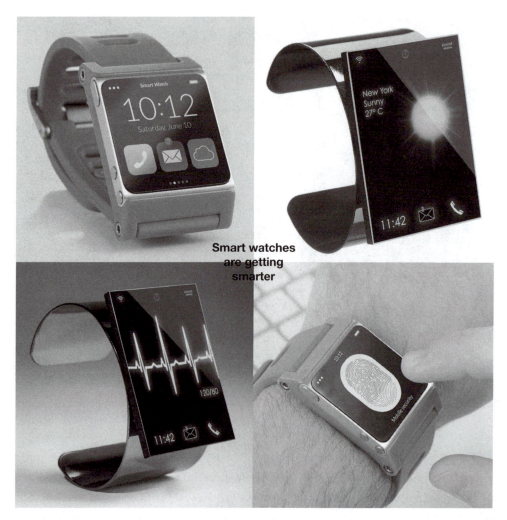

Smart watches
are getting
smarter

FIGURE 19.2 Smart watches are getting smarter

Identifying Emerging Technologies

A good place to begin examining emerging technologies likely to impact learning, performance, and instruction is the New Media Consortium's *Horizon Reports* (see www.nmc.org). Since 2002, the New Media Consortium (NMC) has been charting the landscape of emerging technology that has the potential to have significant influence on teaching, learning, and creative inquiry. All of these annual reports are available at no cost on the NMC website. As the project has evolved, reports are now being issued for specific contexts, such as higher education, Asian and European schools, libraries, Australian tertiary education, and more.

In the higher education edition, technologies are considered in terms of (a) trends (near-term, mid-range, and long-range), (b) challenges (solvable, difficult, and wicked), and (c) important developments (one year or less, two to three years, four to five years).

One can then look back over prior reports to see how the trends, challenges, and developments have been changing.

In the *2014 NMC Horizon Report Higher Education Edition*, the near-term trends include the ubiquity of social media and the integration of online, hybrid, and collaborative learning. Social media have broad implications outside the education sector and have played a significant role in economic and political events. As with many technologies, not all uses of social media have been positive or desirable. Cyberbullying might also be cited as a growing trend, although many educational technologists are inclined to downplay or ignore the negative side of emerging technologies. Residential college and university courses are now being designed to include social media and other online resources, so hybrid courses are already the norm in many colleges and universities. As with all of the technologies to be mentioned in this chapter, there are benefits but also potential problems. These are worth discussing in each case.

Mid-range trends (three to five years) cited in the *2014 Horizon Report Higher Education Edition* (see http://cdn.nmc.org/media/2014-nmc-horizon-report-he-*EN-SC*.pdf) include data-driven assessments and a shift from students as consumers of educational resources to students as creators of educational artifacts. The Maker Movement (see http://makerfaire.com/maker-movement) launched in 2005 is representative of this emphasis on education centered on artifacts and products designed and developed by students. Specific technologies mentioned in previous *Horizon Reports*, such as 3D printing and digital fabrication, support this ongoing trend.

Solvable challenges include the low level of digital fluency among faculty and the lack of appropriate rewards for innovative and effective teaching. A difficult challenge cited in the *Horizon Report* involves scaling up innovations, which has been discussed in the previous chapter and which remains an ongoing serious challenge.

Important short- and medium-term developments cited in the *Horizon Report* include the flipped classroom, learning analytics, 3D printing, and games and gamification. As suggested by the rapidly expanding Maker Movement, 3D printing is probably a short-term technology already having an impact in many colleges and universities. While NMC indicates that learning analytics is a short-term technology development, its use and widespread implementation suggest that it might better be considered as a medium-term development, not yet fully implemented and not yet with noticeable impact on learning and instruction. In any case, a worthwhile discussion activity would be further discussion of the various trends, challenges, and developments mentioned in the various *Horizon Reports*.

Additional information about emerging educational technologies can be found at the following websites:

- www.emergingedtech.com/about
- www.educatorstechnology.com/2014/01/the-5-emerging-educational-technologies. html
- www.ifets.info/journals/16_2/3.pdf

Selected Technologies

In this section, some promising shorter term technologies are singled out for additional elaboration. Other emerging technologies and their likely impact might be discussed in class or in an online discussion forum. Many have argued that new technologies are changing the nature of learning and instruction (Becker, 2010; Clark, 1994; Kozma, 1994; McLuhan, 1964). This debate might be traced to Marshall McLuhan work in the 1960s in which emphasis shifted from the message (e.g., information and content) to the medium used (see, for example, McLuhan, 1964). Richard Clark and Robert Kozma engaged in a widely publicized and published debate in the 1990s with regard to the influence of media on learning and instruction (see, for example, Clark, 1994; Kozma, 1994). Becker (2010) summarized that debate in terms of twenty-first-century technologies, emphasizing the role of games and informal learning environments.

This debate is worthy of serious discussion in class or in an online forum. To frame such a discussion, one might begin by exploring (i.e., elaborating, defending, challenging) the following claims:

- New media have changed the ways that information can be designed and disseminated.
- New technologies have made possible learning activities that were not previously practical or feasible.
- The things that primarily account for learning outcomes include (a) prior knowledge, (b) the time spent on a learning task, (c) timely, informative, and supportive feedback, and (d) the selection and sequencing of learning resources and activities.
- New media and new technologies have changed the fundamental nature of how people learn and develop expertise.

In the course of such a discussion, one might consider the following widely accepted and long-established principles:

- People construct internal representations to make sense of their experiences (the core concept of a constructivist epistemology; Jonassen, 2006; Spector, Lockee, Smaldino, & Herring, 2013).
- People learn what they do (the core concept of active learning; Dewey, 1938; Merrill, 2013).
- The design of learning activities in a learning environment or situation is critical for the development of knowledge and understanding (Bransford, Brown, & Cocking, 2000; Jonassen and Land, 2012).

The position taken in this volume is that the nature of learning has remained relatively constant for thousands of years, although much more is now known about how learning occurs in the brain and how learning can be facilitated by appropriate activities and support. Learning is characterized by stable and persistent changes in what a person (or group) knows and is able to do. What has changed in the last 50 years or so is how best to facilitate learning using available technologies and new instructional approaches based on a deeper understanding of how the mind works. Some technologies are now called *mindtools* because they extend what a person can do or they facilitate and accelerate the acquisition of knowledge and the development of expertise (Spector, Lockee, Smaldino, & Herring, 2013).

New approaches include using technology to promote interest and inquiry. Increased interest in an activity can result in a learner spending more time on a learning task. Getting students to have questions and explore alternative answers to those questions can result in more time on a task. Learning is not fundamentally about teachers telling students information or about students asking questions, although those activities can support learning. Learning involves an individual engaging in an exploration to find out something new or understand something puzzling—that is to say, learning is about *having* questions, exploring alternative answers, and evaluating what seems to be the most reasonable resolution of that which the student is trying to understand. This inquiry-based approach seems to be what has emerged as a prominent approach to learning in the last 50 years or so (Bransford, Brown, & Cocking, 2000).

Given that an inquiry-based approach is central to learning, the primary role of a teacher then becomes that of helping learners to *have* questions. A few recent technologies are discussed next, especially with regard to their ability to support inquiry-based learning and develop knowledge and understanding.

Personalized Learning

Personalized learning in a sense is not a new technology if one thinks about such things as individual tutoring or apprenticeship. However, with new technologies, a new kind of personalized learning is emerging. In the context of twenty-first-century technologies, personalized learning involves the dynamic configuration of learning activities, assignments, assessments, and resources to fit individual needs and expectations, based on an automated analysis of student profiles, past performance, current learning needs and difficulties, and what has worked for similar students with similar learning needs and difficulties.

What are new are digital technologies, such as learning management systems and learning object repositories, which provide the potential to develop large sets of data about a variety of learners, learning resources (e.g., learning objects, learning activities, digital representations), and the outcomes of learners engaging with those resources using specific assessments. Learning analytics can provide the means to analyze those large data sets and use the outcomes to customize a learning experience for a specific learner. As yet, this has not been accomplished on a large scale, so personalized learning has yet to become a mainstream technology, although the potential to improve learning certainly exists and that potential may be realized in the next five years or so. Obstacles include issues of scale (discussed in the previous chapter) and privacy. Preserving the anonymity of learners outside the scope of their activities and courses is an issue in many countries.

MOOCs

Massive open online courses refer to those which provide access to nearly anyone with an internet connection at no cost to those who enroll (Spector, 2014a). An early MOOC appeared in 2008 in Canada (Downes, 2008) and was inspired by a connectivist approach that allowed anyone to participate in course discussions and access course resources. Subsequent approaches often emphasized the notion of connecting large groups of individuals to share and exchange ideas and insights; these are generally referred to as cMOOCs to emphasize the role of connecting a large and distributed community who have common interests. The original Canadian MOOC is a good example of a cMOOC.

A somewhat different approach to MOOCs has developed that emphasizes the ability to share traditional learning resources and activities centered around a distinguished educator; these are often referred to xMOOCs. xMOOCs often involve access to readings and other resources in an online repository as well as digitized lectures streamed over the Internet. Companies such as Udacity, Coursera, and edX have arisen to spread xMOOCs around the world.

In both approaches, only those few learners at the home institution who pay for the MOOC receive individual feedback and course credit. The vast majority who sign up for the MOOC on a noncredit basis and pay no course fee do not receive a grade or course credit, and they receive only minimal or superficial feedback and assessments. The basic idea of MOOCs is to make education available to everyone at no cost. However, recalling the definition of learning as involving stable and persisting changes in what a person knows and can do, there is no basis to claim that learning is occurring in these MOOCs except for the few who pay tuition, are assessed, and graded. MOOCs can be considered collections of learning objects, but they typically lack the ingredients needed to be considered collections of instructional objects (e.g., feedback on learning activities, formative, and summative assessments). It would be more appropriate to have the 'C' in 'MOOC' refer to 'community' rather than 'course' (Spector 2014a), consistent with the early MOOCs.

The development and deployment of MOOCs typically have not involved instructional designers. Rather, MOOCs have been based on what a particular person (typically a famous scholar) believes is relevant and how those resources should be structured and made available. Given the large number of participants in a MOOC, providing timely and informative feedback and assessment is a challenge, especially for courses involving complex learning tasks and problem-solving activities. In those courses (e.g., artificial intelligence, engineering design, environmental planning, macroeconomics, etc.), performance and progress are not easily determined using simple objective tests, and providing timely and informative feedback on portfolios, projects, or research papers is a serious challenge in a MOOC or in any large enrollment course.

MOOCs are likely to evolve given the challenges just mentioned. One promising direction is toward the notion of academic or educational *badges*. The notion of badges in education involves decomposing a course or program into sets of competencies. A badge is awarded to a student who demonstrates mastery of a particular competency. When a student has all of the badges associated with a course or program, then credit and certification are awarded. Badges are often found in informal or noncredit-bearing learning contexts; there is an effort to incorporate competency-based badges into some formal learning contexts (see http://net.educause.edu/ir/library/pdf/eli7085.pdf).

Serious Games

The notion of integrating games into teaching and learning has existed for a long time. Games have often and effectively been involved in primary education. They can be used to engage children and support specific learning goals, such as associating words with objects and mastering simple arithmetic. Games can be competitive or cooperative; they have rules to guide game-play; they often have an associated narrative; and they typically have well-defined ways to assign a score or determine a winner. Games are popular and can be used for entertainment or distraction or they can be used to directly or indirectly support a learning activity or goal.

Serious games have many of the typical characteristics of games but are aimed at supporting educational or training goals rather than entertainment. A serious game is one in which the goal of the game is closely aligned with a specific learning goal such that the degree to which an individual succeeds in the game can be associated with the degree to which that person has mastered the learning objective. Examples and elaborations of serious games can be found at the Serious Games Initiative (see www.seriousgames.org) and at the Games and Learning Alliance (see www.galanoe.eu).

Many serious games have characteristics that are found in interactive simulations that have existed for 20 or 30 years. Both make use of sophisticated technologies (e.g., 3D representations, dynamic interactions, narratives to motivate engagement, etc.). One important distinction is that interactive simulations are typically used to support a unit of instruction rather than replace it entirely. The notion of serious games emerged from the success of highly interactive simulations developed since the 1980s and the dramatic expansion of the video-game industry in that same time frame. There are many serious games now available in a variety of categories (see http://serious.gameclassification.com).

As educational games began to be developed for adult learners for complex and challenging learning tasks, it became clear that it was more reasonable to include aspects of games in support of other learning tasks. The general strategy of including aspects of games in a learning environment is now referred to as *gamification*. It appears from early research that gamification can be effective in promoting interest and motivation, and in supporting the mastery of ill-structured problem-solving tasks. The general strategies of game-based and game-supported learning are likely to be of strong interest to educational technologists for many years, although having a game completely replace a unit of instruction remains an elusive goal.

Wearable Devices

The general trend of digital devices becoming smaller, more powerful, and more affordable was mentioned earlier in this chapter. When one considers the evolution of the personal computer from early products in the 1970s (e.g., the Apple II, the Commodore PET, and the Tandy Corporation TRS-80) to tablet devices and smartphones now available, the trend is obvious. People might have carried an early personal computer from one room to another on a rare occasion. Now, many people will not leave home without their smartphones.

It is clear that this trend is leading to wearable devices that have some of the same capabilities of smartphones, tablet devices, and laptop computers. As mentioned previously, watches that communicate with a smartphone are already on the market. More are coming. Heads-up displays that can be worn like eyeglasses are already available; Google Glass is one example (see www.google.com/glass/start). Clothing with embedded electronics is being developed as are smart electronic devices that interact with parts of the body. Long-range technologies include brain-computer interfaces that will send, receive, and analyze information from a person's brain with the potential of enabling a person to perform tasks previously not possible for that individual.

Potential and Pitfalls

Clearly, there is great potential to use technology to improve learning, performance, and instruction. This has been the case for nearly every educational technology introduced in the last 100 years. Only a few years after television appeared was its potential use in schools advocated. Educational television was then declared to be a technology that would transform schools and dramatically improve learning and performance. While there were and still are reasonable uses for educational television, no such transformation occurred. This story has been repeated many times since then. Personal computers would revolutionize education. The internet would make high-quality education available to everyone. Discussing other such claims for new technologies and how these technologies fell short of the promises and predictions might be worthwhile in class or in an online forum.

The potential is often clear. Pilot projects often show great promise. Why have so many educational technologies fallen far short of predicted outcomes? Why do so many educators and technologists continue to become such strong advocates of a particular technology as one that will dramatically transform learning and instruction? The lesson from the Clark–Kozma debates (Clark, 1994; Kozma, 1994) should be that clearly a new technology may facilitate a new kind of learning experience, but the issues of appropriate use, effective design, and the ability to take the technology to scale are critical factors in making good use of a new technology. The history of new and emerging educational technologies suggests that promises of significant and sustained improvements on a large scale that will dramatically transform learning are unlikely to occur as promised. Some improvements can certainly occur when there is support for design, training, deployment, refinements, and so on. In the world of education, that level of support is rare. When one considers the commercial success of video games and compares the support available for design, redesign, deployment in that sector with the support available in the education sector, one should not be surprised that promises made for radical change due to educational technology fall short so often.

Test Your Understanding

Indicate your response to each of the following questions:

1. Browsing through the online Encyclopedia Smithsonian is an example of an informal learning experience (T/F) (see www.si.edu/Encyclopedia).
2. Viewing the *River of Wisdom* animation at the China Art Museum and then reporting how it exemplifies Zhang Zeduan's *Along the River During the Qingming Festival* masterpiece is an example of an informal learning experience (T/F) (see http://en.wikipedia.org/wiki/China_pavilion_at_Expo_2010#River_of_Wisdom).
3. Technologies have changed the fundamental nature of learning (T/F). Explain why you answered as you did (open-ended).
4. What do you believe accounts for the most variance of learning in a course you teach or have taken? Explain why you answered as you did (open-ended).

A Representative Educational Technology Challenge

Suppose that you have a Ph.D. in History and have been teaching a face-to-face World History course for college/university first-year students for the last 20 years. You are regarded as the best history teacher at your institution, which now wishes to make that course available to anyone anywhere in the world with internet access who wishes to sign up at no cost in addition to those at your institution who sign up for course credit. How would you go about redesigning the course for that new context? What are the key things to take into consideration? How would you briefly describe each one? How are those things related to each other? How would you characterize the various relationships? (Note: You are not allowed to decline the task or retire early.)

Resources

Games and Learning Alliance (GaLA): A Network of Excellence for Serious Games—see www.galanoe.eu

The Maker Movement—see http://makerfaire.com/maker-movement

MOOC Research Hub—see www.moocresearch.com

The New Media Consortium—see www.nmc.org

Reimagining the Computer at ComputerHistory.org—see www.computerhistory.org/revolution/mainframe-computers/7/162

The Serious Games Initiative—see www.seriousgames.org

Things you should know about badges—see http://net.educause.edu/ir/library/pdf/eli7085.pdf

Emerging Technologies—www.emergingedtech.com/about

Educators' Technologies—www.educatorstechnology.com/2014/01/the-5-emerging-educational-technologies.html

Article in *Educational Technology and Society* on emerging technologies—www.ifets.info/journals/16_2/3.pdf

References

Becker, K. (2010). The Clark–Kozma debate in the 21st century. Retrieved from www.academia.edu/462857/The_Clark-Kozma_Debate_in_the_21st_Century

Bransford, J. D., Brown, A. L., Cocking, R. R. (Eds.) (2000). *How people learn: Brain, mind, experience and school* (expanded edition with additional material from the Committee on Learning Research and Educational Practice). Washington, DC: National Academy Press. Retrieved from www.nap.edu/openbook.php?isbn=0309070368

Clark, R. E. (1994). Media will never influence learning. *Educational Technology Research and Development, 42*(2), 21–29.

Dewey, J. (1938). *Experience and education.* New York: Kappa Delta Pi.

Downes, S. (2008). *CCK08—The distributed course: The MOOC guide.* Retrieved from https://sites.google.com/site/themoocguide/3-cck08—-the-distributed-course

Kozma, R. B. (1994). Will media influence learning? Reframing the debate. *Educational Technology Research and Development, 42*(2), 7–19.

Jonassen, D. H. (2006). *Modeling with technology: Mindtools for conceptual change.* Columbus, OH: Merrill/Prentice-Hall.

Jonassen, D. H., & Land, S. M. (Eds.) (2012). *Theoretical foundations of learning environments: Theory into practice* (2nd ed.). New York: Routledge.

Merrill, M. D. (2013). *First principles of instruction: Identifying and designing effective, efficient, and engaging instruction.* San Francisco, CA: Wiley & Sons.

McLuhan, M. (1964). *Understanding media: The extensions of man.* New York: Mcraw-Hill.

Spector, J. M. (2014a). Conceptualizing the emerging field of smart learning environments. *Smart Learning Environment, 1.*

Spector, J. M. (2014b). Remarks on MOOCs and mini-MOOCs. *Educational Technology Research & Development, 62*(3), 385–392.

Spector, J. M. (Ed.) (2015). *The encyclopedia of educational technology.* Thousand Oaks, CA: Sage.

Spector, J. M., Lockee, B. B., Smaldino, S. E., & Herring, M. C. (Eds.) (2013). *Learning, problem solving and mindtools: Essays in honor of David H. Jonassen.* New York: Routledge.

Appendices

Appendix A: Effective Communication Guidelines

- Use simple descriptive sentences whenever possible; a complex story can be told using very simple sentences; say it simply and directly.
- Avoid long sentences that contain multiple clauses and phrases that modify previous parts of a long sentence.
- Try to express just one idea in each sentence; writing is quite different than speaking; write for maximum comprehension by a wide audience; minimize cognitive load placed on readers.
- Avoid doubly modified nouns and exaggeration; understatement is often more effective than grandiose claims, especially with academic readers.
- Include concrete and specific examples to clarify and elaborate key points; avoid vague generalizations; define each new term introduced.
- Minimize the introduction of unnecessary concepts; use the same word or phrase to consistently refer to the same concept or construct; introducing apparent synonyms tends to create misunderstanding.
- Avoid sentences with multiple independent and dependent clauses; complex sentences are difficult to follow and create unnecessary cognitive load; aim for comprehension by a wide variety of readers.

- Avoid the use of relative pronouns as they tend to create ambiguity and place a cognitive load on the reader; better to use a noun or noun phrase even when repetitive (except within a single sentence).
- Avoid sweeping generalizations and words such as 'all,' 'none,' 'always,' 'never,' 'proves,' and so on as these will create a natural response in the reader to find a counter-example and they are rarely needed to make the intended point or argument.
- Be familiar with the guidelines and requirements of the publication venue and follow those very carefully.
- Proofread your work more than once, and have a colleague read your work and give you feedback.
- Be responsive to feedback from readers and reviewers; what is important is what readers understand or fail to understand; treat a failure to understand or a misunderstanding as your responsibility rather a reader's or reviewer's fault.
- Proofread your work more than once, and have a colleague read your work and give you feedback.
- There are many good resources available at no cost online to support academic writing; one example is the Purdue Online Writing Lab—http://owl.english.purdue.edu/owl.

Appendix B: Professional Associations

AACE: The Association for the Advancement of Computing in Education; see www.aace.org

AECT: The Association for Educational Communications and Technology; see www.aect.org

AERA: The American Educational Research Association (several relevant SIGs); see www.aera.net

ASTD/ATD: Association for Talent Development (formerly the American Society for Training Development); see www.astd.org

EARLI: The European Association for Research on Learning and Instruction; see http://earli.org

EERA: The European Educational Research Association; see www.eera-ecer.de

IADIS: The International Association for the Development of the Internet Society; see www.iadisportal.org

IEEE Computer Society: The Computer Society is focused on educational computing; see www.computer.org/portal/web/guest/home

ISLS: International Society of the Learning Sciences; see www.isls.org/icls.html

ISPI: International Society for Performance Improvement; see www.ispi.org

ISTE: International Society for Technology in Education; see www.iste.org/home

NSTA: The National Science Teachers Association; see www.nsta.org/about/positions/ngss.aspx

SALT: Society for Applied Learning Technology; see www.salt.org/salt.asp?ss=l
WERA: World Educational Research Association; www.weraonline.org

Appendix C: Journals and Trade Magazines

Peer Reviewed

Asia Pacific Education Review: www.springer.com/education+%26+language/journal/12564

British Journal of Educational Technology: http://onlinelibrary.wiley.com/journal/10.1111/(ISSN)1467–8535

Computers and Education: www.journals.elsevier.com/computers-and-education

Computers in Human Behavior: www.sciencedirect.com/science/journal/07475632

Distance Education: www.tandf.co.uk/journals/titles/01587919.asp

Educational Computing Research: www.baywood.com/Journals/PreviewJournals.asp?Id=0735-6331

Educational Researcher: www.aera.net/pubs

Educational Technology Review: www.aace.org/pubs/default.htm

Educational Technology Research & Development: www.springer.com/education+%26+language/learning+%26+instruction/journal/11423

Educational Technology & Society: http://ifets.ieee.org

Evaluation and Program Planning: www.sciencedirect.com/science/journal/01497189

Journal of Applied Instructional Design: www.jaidpub.org

Journal of Computers in Education: www.springer.com/education+%26+language/learning+%26+instruction/journal/40692

Journal of Computing in Higher Education: www.jchesite.org

Journal of Higher Education: www.ashe.ws/?page=186

Taylor & Francis Online: www.tandfonline.com/toc/hlns20/current#.U4FUMHKSx8E

Innovative Higher Education: www.uga.edu/ihe/ihe.html

Instructional Science: www.springer.com/education+%26+language/learning+%26+instruction/journal/11251

Interpersonal Computing and Technology Journal: www.helsinki.fi/science/optek

International Journal of Computer-Supported Collaborative Learning: www.springer.com/education+%26+language/learning+%26+instruction/journal/11412

International Journal of Designs for Learning: http://scholarworks.iu.edu/journals/index.php/ijdl/index

International Journal of Teaching and Learning in Higher Education: www.isetl.org/ijtlhe

Higher Education: www.springer.com/education+%26+language/higher+education/journal/10734

Performance Improvement Quarterly: www.ispi.org

Quarterly Review of Distance Education: www.infoagepub.com/index.php?id=89&i=58

Review of Research in Education: www.aera.net/pubs

Simulation & Gaming: www.unice.fr/sg

Smart Learning Environments: www.slejournal.com

Technology, Instruction, Cognition and Learning: www.oldcitypublishing.com/TICL/
TICL.html

TechTrends: http://link.springer.com/journal/11528

Nonrefereed Journals and Trades Magazines

The Chronical of Higher Education: http://chronicle.com/section/Home/5

Educational Technology: www.bookstoread.com/etp

Education Week: www.edweek.org/ew/index.html

Rethinking Schools: www.rethinkingschools.org/index.shtml

NEA Today Magazine: www.nea.org/home/1814.htm

Syllabus Magazine: syllabusmagazine.com

THE Journal: www.thejournal.com

See also combined listings such as those found at these URLs:

http://lrs.ed.uiuc.edu/tse-portal/publication/dans-journals.html

https://docs.google.com/spreadsheet/ccc?key=0AtQrhYg4UkE_cGNyT1lXbk1XNHR
zVmpxS1gwaEM2QXc&usp=drive_web#gid=1

www.onlinenewspapers.com/magazines/magazines-education.htm

Glossary
of Terms

Abduction: a pragmatic and naturalistic form of reasoning that begins with a person's intuitions that leads them to make targeted observations and draw preliminary conclusions; it is in contrast with deduction (reasoning at establishing conclusions with certainty as in mathematical proofs) or induction (probabilistic reasoning that is pervasive in social science reasoning).

Affordance: that which is made possible by a technology.

Andragogy: theories and approaches to learning and instruction specifically aimed at adult learners.

Assessment: a process to determine how well an individual is progressing or has progressed in a program of study; assessments may be formative and aimed at improving learner performance and understanding or summative and aimed at reporting an individual's level of performance and understanding.

Badges: in academia and education, a badge is associated with a specific competency that a learner can reliably and consistently demonstrate, thereby earning the appropriate recognition and certificate.

Behaviorism: a learning theory that only considers that which can be directly observed (e.g., human actions and the events surrounding those actions) in explaining and predicting learning.

Cognition: mental processes involved in learning and acquiring knowledge (e.g., awareness, attention, judgment, reasoning, etc.).

Cognitive apprenticeship: an instructional design framework that proposes that as learners gain competence and confidence they require less and less explicit learning support.

Cognitive developmental theory: the theory that as a person matures he or she naturally passes through progressive stages of development (see Piaget, 1929, 1970).

Cognitive load theory: the theory that short-term memory limitations are a primary consideration in designing effective instruction; while intrinsic cognitive load is inherent in a learning task and cannot be manipulated, extrinsic cognitive load due to unnecessary distracters ought to be minimized.

Cognitive social mediated theory: the theory that social and cultural factors, and especially language, play a key role in cognitive development (see Vygotsky, 1978).

Cognitivism: a learning theory that takes into account how humans are believed to process perceptions and information in order to explain and predict learning.

Communication theory: theories, models, principles, and formats for representing, transmitting, receiving, and processing information.

Competency: a related set of knowledge, skills, and attitudes that are associated with successful performance of a task or job function.

Complex cognitive skill: a task involving problem solving and higher order reasoning that is likely to be challenging for those new to that task domain.

Concept map: a representation of the relationships among a set of ideas.

Constructivism: a naturalistic epistemology that argues that individuals create internal representations to make sense of their experiences.

Critical theory: a perspective on education that challenges many standard and established educational practices as fundamentally dehumanizing or oppressive.

Culture: the common practices and values of a group of people.

Design-based research: a systemic approach to the planning and implementing of innovations that emphasizes an iterative approach to design with ongoing involvement of and collaboration with practitioners.

Diffusion of innovation: the speed and ease with which a new technology is adopted for widespread use within an organization.

Education: processes involved in improving knowledge, performance, and understanding through systematic and sustained efforts.

Educational technology: the disciplines application of technology for the purpose of improving learning, instruction, and/or performance.

Environment: the physical and psychological components that comprise the context in which learning and instruction take place.

Evaluation: a process aimed at improving or determining the value and quality of a program; evaluations may be formative and aimed at improving the program or summative and aimed at providing an overall judgment about the value of the program.

Experiential learning: a four-cycle theory of learning involving experience, observation, and reflection, concept and rule formation, and transfer to new situations (see Kolb, 1984).

Formal learning: instruction that typically occurs in association with a recognized educational institution or training organization that involves structured/designed courses and programs of instruction.

Formative assessment: a process typically involving timely and informative feedback to a learner so as to improve the learner's performance and understanding.

Gamification: the inclusion of aspects of a game in a learning environment of situation; examples include a game-like activity to promote interest or adding a competitive aspect to a learning activity.

Humanism: an educational perspective that emphasizes individual freedom and the value of the individual.

Incidental learning: learning that takes place without conscious effort, goals, or plans (a.k.a. nonintentional learning).

Informal learning: learning that occurs outside the context of a formal setting; examples include field trips, museums, and incidental learning in the context of everyday activities; some informal learning environments are designed to complement or supplement a formal learning environment.

Information theory: principles and models involving messages, encoding, transmitting, receiving, and decoding by machines and humans.

Instruction: that which facilitates and supports learning.

Instructional design: the planning, selection, sequencing, and development of activities and resources to support targeted learning outcomes.

Instructional design theory: a comprehensive account of how to design effective instruction; an example of such a theory is cognitive apprenticeship which involves an instructional scaffolding strategy that recommends strong and explicit learning support for novices and greatly reduced support for more advanced learners.

Instructional events: the notion that specific kinds of events and activities promote learning; for example, Gagné (1985) proposes the following nine events: gain attention, inform learner of the objective, stimulate recall of prior learning, present content, provide learning guidance, elicit performance, provide feedback, assess performance, and enhance retention and transfer.

Instructional principle: a simple statement intended to guide the design, development, or delivery of instruction, such as 'minimize extraneous cognitive load' or 'when providing a definition provide both examples and nonexamples.'

Instructional strategy: an organizing framework for a unit of instruction that involves one or more instructional principles; for example, an expository strategy is one in which explicit statements are made to learners to explain learning content; such statements should follow the relevant instructional principles (provide examples and nonexamples for any definitions involved in the exposition).

Instructional theory: accounts for how learners move from states of not knowing and not being able to do something to states of knowing and being able to do something.

Intelligent tutoring system: an instructional computing system which contains and maintains a model of the learner and what he or she knows and does not know about a particular domain, a knowledge model of the task domain, and an instructional model of how to select and sequence instructional units for individuals depending on what they know and/or misunderstand.

Intentional learning: goal-directed learning; learning that is planned and purposeful.

Interaction: the give and take between one or more learners and an instructional system or environment that may include human tutors and teachers as well as technology-facilitated components.

Learner characteristics: relevant differences among learners, including age and gender differences, cultural and language differences, levels of prior knowledge, learning preferences, and styles, etc.

Learning: involves the development of understanding and ability, and is characterized by stable and persistent changes in what a person (or group) knows and is able to do. It is a process that results in stable and persisting changes in a person's abilities, attitudes, beliefs, knowledge, mental models, and/or skills.

Learning analytics: the collection and analysis of large sets of data to enable and support evidence-based decision making on the part of administrators, curriculum specialists, instructional designers, program coordinators, students and teachers; learning analytics can support personalized learning.

Learning styles: the notion that different learners learn best when information is presented in certain forms and activities structured in a particular way; for example, Fleming (1995) distinguished visual, auditory, read/write, and kinesthetic learners.

Learning types: the different kinds of things that can be learned, such as attitudes, concepts, motor skills, principles, rules, skills, etc.

Mental models: internal representations of experience that are created just when needed to explain unusual phenomena or to solve challenging problems.

Mindtools: technologies that are intended to extend what a person can do or support how a person can acquire expertise and develop understanding.

MOOCs: massive open online courses; these are typically offered to anyone with internet access at no cost without formal recognition of mastery of content or university content (except for those few who are paying regular tuition).

Motivation: the interest and willingness of a person to perform a particular task.

Nonrecurrent task: a task that is performed differently depending on specific variations in the task setting; examples include designing a department store display and developing a policy to preserve a limited resource; heuristics are developed to aid those confronted with nonrecurrent tasks.

Operant conditioning: a behavior that posits reinforcement between a stimulus condition and a desired response as the key mechanism involved in learning (see Skinner, 1954).

Participatory design: the practice of involving representative end-users on the design and development team of a project or effort.

Performance: an observable behavior or action that serves as an indicator of competence or mastery of a learning task.

Personalized learning: the dynamic configuration of learning activities, assignments, and resources to fit individual needs and expectations, based on an automated analysis of student profiles, past performance, current learning needs and difficulties, and what has worked for similar students with similar learning needs and difficulties.

Problem-centered instruction: an approach that places problem solving at the center of instructional planning; an approach that suggests that each lesson should be organized around one or more meaningful problem.

Recurrent task: a task that is performed the same way every time regardless of some variation in the task setting; examples include replacing the toner cartridge in a printer and solving a quadratic equation; checklists and step-by-step procedural guides are developed to help those solving recurrent tasks.

Replication study: a study that applies the same approach, methodology, and instrumentation of a prior study using a different population and/or a different context; replications studies are aimed at confirming or refuting prior findings and determining the generalizability of those findings.

Scale: the level of implementation of a project or effort; scaling up refers to taking a project up one level (e.g., from school to district); scalability refers to the effort required to take an effort from one level to another level.

Serious games: digital games that are intended to result in specific learning outcomes or develop understanding of complex phenomena.

Situated learning: a learning theory that posits that context, to a large extent, determines meaning and affects interpretation, with the implication that learning activities should occur, when possible, in authentic situations; legitimate peripheral participation in a community of learners is a key learning process according to situated learning theory (see Lave, 1988).

Social learning: a learning theory that emphasizes how people learn from others through observation, imitation, and modeling (see Bandura, 1977, 1986).

Summative assessment: a process involving a formal report of an individual's level of performance and understanding in terms of a set of established standards.

Systems perspective: a perspective that considers a holistic account of a complex system, which is a view that considers the key components comprising a system and their dynamic interactions.

Technology: the practical and purposeful application of knowledge.

Technology integration: the seamless and unobtrusive use of one or more technologies to support targeted learning outcomes.

TPACK (technological, pedagogical, and content knowledge): the integrated set of knowledge pertaining to learning content, instructional methods, and technology affordances required to ensure effective technology integration in learning and instruction.

Universal design: the practice of designing instruction that is free from most of the barriers that learners are likely to encounter with particular attention given to removing and minimizing barriers for those with disabilities.

User-centered design: the practice of emphasizing the roles and practices of those who will be using an innovation that is being designed and developed; this often frequent interaction with end-users during design and development and particularly at every stage of prototyping a new product.

Values orientation: an educational perspective that recognizes that different people have different values, and that recognizing and respecting different values is a legitimate goal for educational technologists.

Zone of proximal development (ZPD): the gap between what a student is able to do with and without the assistance of a more knowledgeable other, such as a teacher or a more experienced student; instruction should be aimed at this zone in order to be effective, according to Vygotsky (1978).

References

Abrami, P. C., Wade, A., Pillay, V., Aslan, O., Bures, E. M., & Bentley, C. (2008). Encouraging self-regulated learning electronic portfolios. *Canadian Journal of Learning and Technology, 34*(3). Retrieved from www.cjlt.ca/index.php/cjlt/article/view/507/238

Anderson, J. R. (1983). *The architecture of cognition*. Cambridge, MA: Harvard University Press.

Anderson, J. R. (1996). A simple theory of complex cognition. *American Psychologist, 51*, 355–365.

Anderson, L. W., & Krathwohl, D. R. (Eds.) (2001). *A taxonomy for learning, teaching and assessing: A revision of Bloom's taxonomy of educational objectives*. New York: Longman.

Andrews, D. H., & Goodson, L. A. (1980). A comparative analysis of models of instructional design. *Journal of Instructional Development, 3*(4), 2–16.

Andrews, D. H., & Wulfeck, W. H., II (2014). In J. M. Spector, M. D. Merrill, J. Elen, & M. J. Bishop (Eds.), *Handbook of research on educational communications and technology* (pp. 303–310). New York: Springer.

Argyris, C., & Schön, D. (1996) *Organisational learning II: Theory, method and practice*, Reading, MA: Addison Wesley.

Ausubel, D. P. (1963). *The psychology of meaningful verbal learning*. New York: Grune & Stratton.

Bandura, A. (1977). *Social learning theory*. New York: General Learning Press.

Bandura, A. (1986). *Social foundations of thought and action*. Englewood Cliffs, NJ: Prentice-Hall.

Barron, A. E., & Kysilka, M. L. (1993). The effectiveness of digital audio in computer-based training. *Journal of Research on Computing in Education, 25*(3), 277–289.

Becker, K. (2010). The Clark–Kozma debate in the 21st century. Retrieved from www.academia.edu/462857/The_Clark-Kozma_Debate_in_the_21st_Century

Berlo, D. K. (1960). *The process of communication: An introduction to the theory and practice*. New York: Holt, Rinehart, & Winston.

Bloom, B. (1984). The 2 sigma problem: The search for methods of group instruction as effective as one-on-one tutoring. *Educational Researcher, 13*(6), 4–16.

Bloom, J. W. (2006). *Creating a classroom community of young scientists.* New York: Routledge.

Blumenfeld, P., Fishman, B. J., Karjcik, J., Marx, R. W., & Soloway, E. (2000). Creating usable innovation in systemic reform: Scaling up technology-embedded project-based science in urban schools. *Educational Pscyhologist, 35*(3), 140–164.

Bransford, J. D., Brown, A. L., Cocking, R. R. (Eds.) (2000). *How people learn: Brain, mind, experience and school* (expanded edition with additional material from the Committee on Learning Research and Educational Practice). Washington, DC: National Academy Press. Retrieved from www.nap.edu/openbook.php?isbn=0309070368

Brown, J. S., Collins, A., & Duguid, S. (1989). Situated cognition and the culture of learning. *Educational Researcher, 18*(1), 32–42.

Bruner, J. S. (1966). *Toward a theory of instruction.* Cambridge, MA: Harvard University Press.

Bruner, J. S. (1996). *The culture of education.* Cambridge, MA: Harvard University Press.

Carr-Chellman, A. A. (2005). *Global perspectives on e-learning: Rhetoric and reality.* Thousand Oaks, CA: Sage.

Chermayeff, I., Geismar, T. H., & Geissbuhler, S. (2003). *Designing.* New York: Graphics.

Chomsky, N. (1967). A review of B. F. Skinner's *Verbal Behavior.* In L. A. Jakobits & S. M. Murray (Eds.), Readings in the psychology of language (pp. 142–143). Englewood Cliffs, NJ: Prentice-Hall.

Clark, R. E. (1994). *Media will never influence learning: Educational Technology Research and Development, 42*(2), 21–29.

Clarke, J., & Dede, C. (2009). Robust designs for scalability. In L. Moller, J. B. Huett, & D. M. Harvey, *Learning and instructional technologies for the 21st century* (pp. 27–48). New York: Springer.

Collins, A., Brown, J. S., & Newman, S. E. (1990). Cognitive apprenticeship: Teaching the crafts of reading, writing, and mathematics. In L. B. Resnick (Ed.), *Knowing, learning, and instruction: Essays in honor of Robert Glaser* (pp. 453–494). Hillsdale, NJ: Lawrence Erlbaum.

Collins, J. (2001). *Good to great: Why some companies make the leap . . . and others don't.* New York: HarperCollins.

Collins, J. (2005). *Good to great and the social sectors: A monograph to accompany good to great.* New York: Harper.

Compaine, B. M. (Ed.) (2001). *The digital divide? Facing a crisis or creating myth?* Cambridge, MA: MIT Press.

Corbett, T., Koedinger, K. R., & Anderson, J. R. (1997). Intelligent tutoring systems. In M. Helander, T. K. Landauer, & P. Prabhu (Eds.), *Handbook of human-computer interaction* (2nd ed.) (pp. 849–874). Amsterdam: Elsevier.

Cushman, D., & Whiting, G. C. (1972). An approach to communication theory: Toward consensus on rules. *Journal of Communication, 22,* 217–238.

Davis, F. D. (1989). Perceived usefulness, perceived ease of use, and user acceptance of information technology. *Management Information Systems Quarterly, 13*(3), 319–340.

DBRC (Design Based Research Collective) (2003). Design-based research: An emerging paradigm for educational inquiry. *Educational Researcher, 32*(1), 5–8.

Dede, C., Honan, J., & Peters, L. (Eds.) (2005). *Scaling up success: Lessons learned from technology-based educational innovation.* New York: Jossey-Bass.

Dewey, J. (1907). *The school and society.* Chicago: University of Chicago Press.

Dewey, J. (1916). *Democracy and education: An introduction to the philosophy of education.* New York: Macmillan.

Dewey, J. (1938). *Experience and education.* New York: Kappa Delta Pi.

Dick, S., Carey, L., & Carey, J. O. (2009). The systematic design of instruction (7th ed.). Boston, MA: Allyn & Bacon.

Dijkstra, E. W. (1972). The humble programmer. *Communications of the ACM, 15*(10), 859–866.

Dörner, D. (1996). *The logic of failure: Why things go wrong and what we can do to make them right* (R. Kimber & R. Kimber (Trans.)). New York: Metropolitan Books.

Downes, S. (2008). CCK08—*The distributed course: The MOOC guide*. Retrieved from https://sites.google.com/site/themoocguide/3-cck08—-the-distributed-course

Dreyfus, H., & Dreyfus, S. (1986). *Mind over machine: The power of human intuition and expertise in the era of the computer*. New York: Free Press.

Driscoll, M. P. (2005). *Psychology of learning for instruction* (3rd ed.). New York: Allyn & Bacon.

Eckel, K. (1993). *Instruction language: Foundations of a strict science of instruction*. Englewood Cliffs, NJ: Educational Technology Publications.

Edelstein, L. (1943). *The Hippocratic Oath: Text, translation, and interpretation*. Baltimore, MD: Johns Hopkins University Press.

Ellsworth, J. B. (2000). *Surviving change: A study of educational change models*. Syracuse, NY: ERIC Clearinghouse on Information and Technology.

Ellsworth, J. B. (2015). Early adopters. In J. M. Spector (Ed.), *The encyclopedia of educational technology*. Thousand Oaks, CA: Sage.

Ericsson, K. A., Krampe, R. Th., & Tesch-Römer, C. (1993). The role of deliberate practice in the acquisition of expert performance. *Psychological Review, 100*(3), 363–406.

Erikson, E. H. (1959). *Identity and the life cycle*. New York: International Universities Press.

Erikson, E. H. (1968). *Identity, youth and crisis*. New York: Norton.

Festinger, L. (1957). *A theory of cognitive dissonance*. New York: Wiley.

Fleming, M., & Levie, W. H. (Eds.) (1993). *Instructional message design: Principles from the behavioral and cognitive sciences* (2nd ed.). Englewood Cliffs, NJ: Educational Technology Publications.

Fleming, N. D. (1995). I'm different, not dumb: Modes of presentation (VARK) in the tertiary classroom. In A. Zelmer (Ed.), Research and development in higher education. Proceedings of the 1995 Annual Conference of the Higher Education and Research Development Society of Australasia (HERDSA), *18*, 308–313.

Foulger, D. (2004). An ecological model of the communication process. Retrieved from http://davis.foulger.info/papers/ecologicalModelOfCommunication.htm

Gagné, R. M. (1985). *The conditions of learning* (4th ed.). New York: Holt, Rinehart & Winston.

Gagné, R. M., & Merrill, M. D. (1990). Integrative goals for instructional design. *Educational Technology Research and Development, 38*(1), 23–30.

Gibbons, A. S. (2015). Instructional design models. In J. M. Spector (Ed.), *The encyclopedia of educational technology*. Thousand Oaks, CA: Sage.

Gibbons, A. S., Boling, E., & Smith, K. M. (2014). Design models. In J. M. Spector, M. D. Merrill, M. J. Bishop, & J. Elen (Eds.), *Handbook for research on educational communications and technology* (4th ed., pp. 607–616). New York: Springer.

Gibbons, A. S., & Brewer, E. K. (2005). Elementary principles of design languages and design notation systems for instructional design. In J. M. Spector, C. Ohrazda, A. Van Schaack, & D. Wiley (Eds.), *Innovations in instructional technology: Essays in honor of M. David Merrill* (pp. 111–129). Mahwah, NJ: Lawrence Erlbaum Associates.

Gibson, J. J. (1977). The theory of affordances. In R. Shaw & J. D. Bransford (Eds.), *Acting and knowing* (pp. 67–82). Hillsdale, NJ: Erlbaum.

Gogus, A. S. (2006). *Individual and situation factors that influence teachers' perspectives and perceptions about the usefulness of the graphing calculator on the New York State Math B Regents exam*. Unpublished dissertation. Syracuse, NY: Syracuse University.

Graf, S., Liu, T-C., Kinshuk, Chen, N-S., & Yang, S. J. H. (2009). Learning styles and cognitive traits: Their relationships and its benefits in web-based educational systems. *Computers in Human Behavior, 25*(6), 1280–1289.

Gustafson, K. L., & Branch, R. M. (2002). *Survey of instructional development models*. Syracuse, NY: The ERIC Clearinghouse on Information Technology.

Haberman, J. (1971). *Knowledge and human interest*. Boston, MA: Beacon Press.

Hamilton, J., & Feldman, J. (2014). Planning a program evaluation: Matching methodology to program status. In J. M. Spector, M. D. Merrill, J. Elen, & M. J. Bishop (Eds.), *Handbook of research on educational communications and technology* (pp. 249–257). New York: Springer.

Hartley, R., Kinshuk, Koper, R., Okamoto, T., & Spector, J. M. (2010). The education and training of learning technologists: A competences approach. *Educational Technology & Society, 13*(2), 206–216.

Hassard, J., & Dias, M. (2009). *The art of teaching science: Inquiry and innovation in middle and high school* (2nd ed.). New York: Routledge.

Hellman, M. E. (2003). Moore's Law and communications. Retrieved from www-ee.stanford.edu/~hellman/opinion/moore.html

Herbel-Eisenmann, B., & Cirillo, M. (Eds.) (2009). *Promoting purposeful discourse*. Reston, VA: National Council of Teachers of Mathematics.

Herring, M. C., & Smaldino, S. E. (2015). TPACK (Technological, pedagogical, content knowledge): Implications for 21st century teacher education. In J. M. Spector (Ed.), *The encyclopedia of educational technology*. Thousand Oaks, CA: Sage.

Horkheimer, H., & Adorno, T. W. (1972). *Dialectic of enlightenment*. New York: Seabury.

Jarvis, P., & Watts, M. (Eds.) (2012). *The Routledge international handbook of learning*. New York: Routledge.

Johnson-Laird, P. N. (1983). *Mental models: Towards a cognitive science of language, inference, and consciousness*. Cambridge: Cambridge University Press.

Jonassen, D. H. (2000). Toward a design theory of problem solving. *Educational Technology Research & Development, 48*(4), 63–85.

Jonassen, D. H. (2004). *Learning to solve problems: An instructional design guide*. San Francisco, CA: Pfeiffer/Jossey-Bass.

Jonassen, D. H. (2006). *Modeling with technology: Mindtools for conceptual change*. Columbus, OH: Merrill/Prentice-Hall.

Jonassen, D. H. (2007). Toward a taxonomy of meaningful learning. *Educational Technology, 47*(5), 30–35.

Jonassen, D. H. (2014). Assessing problem solving. In J. M. Spector, M. D. Merrill, J. Elen, & M. J. Bishop (Eds.), *Handbook of research on educational communications and technology* (pp. 269–288). New York: Springer.

Jonassen, D. H., Carr, C., & Yueh, H-P. (1998). Computers as mindtools for engaging learners in critical thinking. *TechTrends, 43*, 24–32.

Jonassen, D. H., & Grabowski, B. L. (1993). *Handbook of research on individual differences, learning, and instruction*. Hillsdale, NJ: Erlbaum.

Jonassen, D. H., & Land, S. M. (Eds.) (2012). *Theoretical foundations of learning environments: Theory into practice* (2nd ed.). New York: Routledge.

Kalyuga, S., Ayres, P., Chandler, P. & Sweller, J. (2003). The expertise reversal effect. *Educational Psychologist, 38*(1) 23–31.

Keller, J. M. (2010). *Motivational design for learning and performance: The ARCS model approach*. New York: Springer.

Kim, C., DeMeester, K., Spector, J. M., Kim, M. K., & Lee, C-J. (2011). Teacher pedagogical beliefs, technology integration, and student learning. Paper presentation at the Annual Meeting of the American Educational Research Association, New Orleans, LA, April 11.

Kim, C., & Keller, J. M. (2010). Motivation, volition and belief change strategies to improve mathematics learning. *Journal of Computer Assisted Learning, 26*, 407–420.

Kim, C., Kim, M., Lee, C., Spector, J. M., & DeMeester, K. (2013). Teacher pedagogical beliefs and technology integration. *Teaching and Teacher Education, 29*, 76–85.

Klein, J. D., Grabowski, B., Spector, J. M., & de la Teja, I. (2008). Competencies for instructors: A validation study. In M. Orey, V. J. McLendon, & R. M. Branch (Ed.), *Educational media and technology yearbook 2008*. Portsmouth, NH: Greenwood.

Klein, J. D., Spector, J. M., Grabowski, B., & de la Teja, I. (2004). *Instructor competencies: Standards for face-to-face, online and blended settings*. Greenwich, CT: Information Age Publishing.

Kleinman, D. L., & Moore, K. (Eds.) (2014). *Routledge handbook of science, technology and society*. New York: Routledge.

Knowles, M. (1984). *Andragogy in action*. San Francisco, CA: Jossey-Bass.

Koehler, M. J., & Mishra, P. (2015). TPACK (Technological, pedagogical, content knowledge). In J. M. Spector (Ed.), *The encyclopedia of educational technology*. Thousand Oaks, CA: Sage.

Kolb, D. A. (1984). *Experiential learning: Experience as the source of learning and development*. Englewood Cliffs, NJ: Prentice-Hall.

Kopainsky, B., Pedercini, M., Davidsen, P. I., & Alessi, S. M. (2009). A blend of planning and learning: Simplifying a simulation model of national development. *Simulation & Gaming, 41*(5), 641–662.

Kozma, R. B. (1994). Will media influence learning? Reframing the debate. *Educational Technology Research and Development, 42*(2), 7–19.

Kuhn, T. S. (1962). *The structure of scientific revolutions*. Chicago: University of Chicago Press.

Lage, M. J., Platt, G. J., & Treglia, M. (2000). Inverting the classroom: A gateway to creating an inclusive learning environment. *Journal of Economic Education, 31*, 30–43.

Larson, M. B., & Lockee, B. B. (2013). *Streamline ID: A practical guide to instructional design*. New York: Routledge.

Lasswell, H. (1948). The structure and function of communication in society. In L. Bryson (Ed.), *The communication of ideas* (pp. 203–243). New York: Harper & Row.

Lave, J. (1988). *Cognition in practice: Mind, mathematics and culture in everyday life*. Cambridge: Cambridge University Press.

Leacock, T. L., & Nesbit, J. D. (2007). A framework for evaluating the quality of multimedia learning resources. *Educational Technology & Society, 10*(2), 44–59.

Lebow, D. G. (2009). Document review meets social software and the learning sciences. *Journal of e-Learning and Knowledge Society, 5*(1), 171–180.

Levin, H. M. (2001). Waiting for Godot: Cost-effectiveness analysis in education. *New Directions for Evaluation, 90*, 55–68.

Lin, L. (2009). Breadth-biased versus focused cognitive control in media multitasking behaviors. *Proceedings of the National Academy of Sciences of the United States of America, 106*(37), pp. 15521–15522.

Lohr, L. (2007). *Creating visuals for learning and performance: Lessons in visual literacy* (2nd ed.). Cleveland, OH: Prentice-Hall.

Luschei, T. F. (2014). Assessing the costs and benefits of educational technology. In J. M. Spector, M. D. Merrill, J. Elen, & M. J. Bishop (Eds.), *Handbook of research on educational communications and technology* (pp. 239–248). New York: Springer.

McKenney, S., Reeves, T. (2014). Educational design research. In J. M. Spector, M. D. Merrill, M. J. Bishop, & J. Elen, (Eds.), *Handbook for research on educational communications and technology* (4th ed., pp. 131–140). New York: Springer.

McLuhan, M. (1964). *Understanding media: The extensions of man*. New York: McGraw-Hill.

Meindl, J. D. (2003). Beyond Moore's Law: The interconnect era. *Computing in Science and Engineering, 5*(1), 20–24.

Merrill, M. D. (2002). First principles of instruction. *Educational Technology Research and Development, 50*(3), 43–59.

Merrill, M. D. (2007). The future of instructional design: The proper study of instructional design. In R. A. Reiser & J. V. Dempsey (Eds.), *Trends and issues in instructional design and technology* (2nd ed., pp. 336–341). Upper Saddle River, NJ: Pearson Education.

Merrill, M. D. (2013). *First principles of instruction. Identifying and designing effective, efficient, and engaging instruction*. San Francisco, CA: Wiley & Sons.

Merrill, M. D., Barclay, M., & van Schaak, A. (2008). Prescriptive principles for instructional design. In J. M. Spector, M. D. Merrill, J. J. G. van Merriënboer (Eds.), *Handbook of research on educational communications and instructional design* (3rd ed.) (pp. 173–184). New York: Routledge.

Militello, L. G., & Hutton, R. J. (1998). Applied cognitive task analysis (ACTA): A practitioner's toolkit for understanding cognitive task demands. *Ergonomics, 41*(11), 1618–1641.

Miller, G. A. (1956). The magical number seven, plus or minus two: Some limits on our capacity for processing information. *Psychological Review, 63*(2), 81–97.

Mishra, P., & Koehler, M. J. (2006). Technological pedagogical content knowledge: A framework for teacher knowledge. *Teacher College Record, 108*(6), 1017–1054.

Moore, G. E. (1965). Cramming more components onto integrated circuits. *Electronics, 38*(8), 114–117.

National Center on Education and the Economy. (2007). Tough choices for tough times: The report of the new commission on the skills of the American workforce. San Francisco, CA: Jossey-Bass.

Newman, B. M., & Newman, P. B. (2007). *Theories of human development*. Mahwah, NJ: Erlbaum.

Norman, D. A. (1988). *The design of everyday things*. New York: Doubleday.

Paivio, A. (1986). *Mental representations: A dual coding approach*. Oxford: Oxford University Press.

Paivio, A. (1991). *Mind and its evolution: A dual coding theoretical approach*. Mahwah, NJ: Erlbaum.

Papert, S. (1980). *Mindstorms: Children, computers and powerful ideas*. New York: Basic Books.

Peirce, C. S. (1931). *The collected papers of Charles Sanders Peirce Volume 5: Pragmatism and pragmatism*. Cambridge, MA: Harvard University Press. Retrieved from www.textlog.de/peirce_pragmatism.html

Piaget, J. (1929). *The child's conception of the world*. New York: Harcourt Brace Jovanovich.

Piaget, J. (1970). *The science of education and the psychology of the child*. New York: Grossman.

Pirnay-Dummer, P., Ifenthaler, D., & Spector, J. M. (2010). Highly integrated model assessment technology and tools. *Educational Technology Research & Development, 58*(1), 3–18.

Plato (1987). *Theaetetus* (R. A. H. Waterfield (Trans.)). London: Penguin Books.

Pliner, S., & Johnson, J. (2004). Historical, theoretical, and foundational principles of universal design in higher education. *Equity of Excellence in Education, 37*, 105–113.

Popper, K. (1963). *Conjectures and refutations: The growth of scientific knowledge*. London: Routledge.

Popper, K. (1972). *Objective knowledge: An evolutionary approach*. Oxford: Clarendon Press.

Preece, J., Rogers, Y., & Sharp, H. (2002). *Interaction design: Beyond human-computer interaction*. New York: Wiley.

Prensky, M. (2001). Digital natives, digital immigrants. *On the Horizon, 9*(5). Retrieved March 15, 2011 from www.marcprensky.com/writing/Prensky%20-%20Digital%20Natives,%20Digital%20Immigrants%20-%20Part1.pdf

Quine, W. V. O., & Ullian, J. S. (1978). *The web of belief* (2nd ed.). New York: McGraw-Hill.

Quint, J., Bloom, H. S., Black, A. R., Stephens, L., with Akey, T. M. (2005). *The challenge of scaling up educational reform: Findings and lessons from first things first* (Final Report; ERIC Number ED485680). New York: MDRC. Retrieved from http://eric.ed.gov/?id=ED485680

Reigeluth, C. M. (Ed.) (1983). *Instructional-design theories and models: An overview of their current status*. Hillsdale, NJ: Erlbaum.

Reigeluth, C. M. (Ed.) (1999). *Instructional-design theories and models: A new paradigm of instructional theory* (Volume II). Mahwah, NJ: Erlbaum.

Reigeluth, C. M., & Duffy, F. M. (2008). The AECT Future Minds initiative: Transforming America's School Systems. *Educational Technology, 48*(3), 45–49.

Richey, R. C., & Klein, J. D. (2014). Design and development research. In J. M. Spector, M. D. Merrill, M. J. Bishop, & J. Elen (Eds.), *Handbook for research on educational communications and technology* (4th ed., pp. 141–150). New York: Springer.

Richey, R. C., Klein, J. D., & Tracey, M. W. (2011). *The instructional design knowledge base: Theory, research and practice*. New York: Routledge.

Rogers, E. M. (2003). *Diffusion of innovations* (5th ed.). New York: Free Press.

Rooney, D., Hearn, G., & Ninan, A. (Eds.) (2005). *Handbook on the knowledge economy*. Cheltenham: Edward Elgar.

Schunk, D. H. (2007). *Learning theories: An educational perspective* (5th ed.). New York: Prentice Hall.

Seel, N. M. (2004). Model-centered learning environments: Theory, instructional design and effects. In N. M. Seel & S. Dijkstra (Eds.), *Curriculum, plans and processes in instructional design* (pp. 49–74). Mahwah, NJ: Erlbaum.

Senge, P. (1990). *The fifth discipline: The art and practice of the learning organization*. New York: Doubleday.

Shannon, C. E. (1948). A mathematical theory of communication. *Bell System Technical Journal, 27*, 379–423 and 623–656.

Shannon, C. E., & Weaver, W. (1949). *The mathematical theory of communication*. Urbana, IL: The University of Illinois Press.

Shulman, L. S. (1986). Those who understand: Knowledge growth in teaching. *Educational Researcher, 15*(2), 4–14.

Simonsen, J., & Robertson, T. (Eds.) (2013). *Routledge international handbook of participatory design*. New York: Routledge.

Skinner, B. F. (1954). The science of learning and the art of teaching. *Harvard Educational Review, 24*(2), 86–97.

Sleeman, D. H., & Brown, J. S. (Eds.) (1982). *Intelligent tutoring systems*. New York: Academic Press.

Spector, J. M. (2000). Trends and issues in educational technology: How far we have not come. *Update Semiannual Bulletin 21*(2). Syracuse, NY: The ERIC Clearinghouse on Information Technology. Retrieved on March 15, 2011 from http://supadoc.syr.edu/docushare/dsweb/Get/Document-12994/trends-tech-educ-eric.pdf

Spector, J. M. (2001). A philosophy of instructional design for the 21st century? *Journal of Structural Learning and Intelligent Systems, 14*(4), 307–318.

Spector, J. M. (2005). *Innovations in instructional technology: An introduction to this volume*. In J. M. Spector, C. Ohrazda, A. Van Schaack, & D. A. Wiley (Eds.) (2005), *Innovations in instructional technology: Essays in honor of M. David Merrill* (pp. xxxi–xxxvi). Mahwah, NJ: Erlbaum.

Spector, J. M. (2010). Mental representations and their analysis: An epistemological perspective. In D. Ifenthaler, P. Pirnay-dummer, & N. M. Seel (Eds.), *Computer-based diagnostics and systematic analysis of knowledge* (17–40). New York: Springer.

Spector, J. M. (2012). Naturalistic epistemology. In N. M. Seel (Ed.), *The encyclopedia of the sciences of learning*. New York: Springer.

Spector, J. M. (2014a). Conceptualizing the emerging field of smart learning environments. *Smart Learning Environment, 1*(2), 1–10.

Spector, J. M. (2014b). Remarks on MOOCs and mini-MOOCs. *Educational Technology Research & Development, 62*(3), 385–392.

Spector, J. M. (2015a). Program evaluation. In J. M. Spector (Ed.), *The encyclopedia of educational technology*. Thousand Oaks, CA: Sage.

Spector, J. M. (Ed.) (2015b). *The encyclopedia of educational technology*. Thousand Oaks, CA: Publications.

Spector, J. M., & Anderson, T. M. (Eds.) (2000). *Integrated and holistic perspectives on learning, instruction and technology: Understanding complexity*. Dordrecht: Kluwer Academic Press.

Spector, J. M., & Davidsen, P. I. (2006). How can organizational learning be modeled and measured. *Evaluation and Program Planning, 29*(1), 63–69.

Spector, J. M., Johnson, T. E., & Young, P. A. (2014). An editorial on research and development in and with educational technology. *Educational Technology Research & Development, 62*(1), 1–12.

Spector, J. M., Lockee, B. B., Smaldino, S. E., & Herring, M. C. (Eds.) (2013). *Learning, problem solving and mindtools: Essays in honor of David H. Jonassen*. New York: Routledge.

Spector, J. M., Merrill, M. D., Elen, J., & Bishop, M. J. (Eds.) (2014). *Handbook of research on educational communications and technology* (4th ed.). New York: Springer.

Spector, J. M., Merrill, M. D., van Merriënboer, J. J. G., & Driscoll, M. (Eds.) (2008). *Handbook of research on educational communications and technology* (3rd ed.). New York: Routledge.

Spector, J. M., Polson, M. C., & Muraida, D. J. (Eds.) (1993). *Automating instructional design: Concepts and issues*. Englewood Cliffs, NJ: Educational Technology Publications.

Spector, J. M., & Wang, X. (2002). Integrating technology into learning and working: Introduction. *Education, Technology and Society 5*(2). Retrieved from www.ifets.info/journals/5_2/editorial.pdf

Spector, J. M., Yuen, H. K., Wang, M., Churchill, D., & Law, N. (2014). Hong Kong perspectives on educational technology research and practice. *Educational Technology, 54*(5), 35–41.

Spiro, R. J., & Jehng, J. (1990). Cognitive flexibility and hypertext: Theory and technology for the non-linear and multidimensional traversal of complex subject matter. In D. Nix & R. Spiro (Eds.), *Cognition, education, and multimedia* (pp. 163–205). Hillsdale, NJ: Erlbaum.

Sterman, J. D. (1994). Learning in and about complex systems. *System Dynamics Review, 10*(2–3), 291–330.

Stewart. C. M., Schifter, C. C., & Selverian, M. E. M. (Eds.) (2010). *Teaching and learning with technology: Beyond constructivism*. New York: Routledge.

Sweller, J. (1988). Cognitive load during problem solving: Effects on learning. *Cognitive Science, 12*, 257–285.

Sweller, J., & Cooper, G. A. (1985). The use of worked examples as a substitute for problem solving in learning algebra. *Cognition and Instruction, 2*(1), 59–89.

Taba, H. (1962). *Curriculum development: Theory and practice*. New York: Harcourt, Brace & World.

Tennyson, R. D. (1995). Instructional systems development: The fourth generation, in Tennyson, R. D. & Barron, A. (Eds.), *Automating instructional design: Computer-based development and delivery tools*, 33–78.

Tennyson, R. D. (1997). Instructional development and ISD[4] methodology. *Performance Improvement Quarterly, 38*(6), 19–27.

Tennyson, R. D. & Cocchiarella, M. J. (1986). An empirically based instructional design theory for teaching concepts. *Review of Educational Research, 56*(1), 40–71.

Tolstoy, L. (1882). *Confession* (Trans. D. Patterson, 1983). New York: Norton.

Tufte, E. R. (1997). *Visual explanations: Images and quantities, evidence and narrative*. Cheshire, CN: Graphics Press.

Tufte, E. R. (2003). *The cognitive style of PowerPoint*. Cheshire, CN: Graphics Press.

Tulving, E. (1983). *Elements of episodic memory*. Oxford: Clarendon Press.

van der Linden, W., & Hambleton, R. K. (Eds.) (1997). *Handbook of modern item response theory*. New York: Springer.

van Merriënboer, J. J. G, & Kirschner, P. A. (2007). *Ten steps to complex learning: A systematic approach to four-component instructional design*. Mahwah, NJ: Educational Tehcnology Publications.

Vygotsky, L. S. (1962). *Thought and language*. Cambridge, MA: MIT Press.

Vygotsky, L. S. (1978). *Mind in society: The development of higher mental processes*. Cambridge, MA: Harvard University Press.

Walvoord, B. E., & Anderson, V. J. (1998). *Effective grading: A tool for learning and assessment*. San Francisco, CA: Jossey-Bass.

Watson, J. (1913). Psychology as a behaviorist views it. *Psychological Review, 20*, 158–177.

Wejnert, B. (2002). Integrating models of diffusion of innovations: A conceptual framework. *Annual Review of Sociology, 28*, 297–326.

Wittgenstein, L. (1922). *Tractatus logico-philosophicus* (Trans. C. K. Ogden). London: Kegan Paul, Trench, Trubner & Co. Retrieved from www.gutenberg.org/files/5740/5740-pdf.pdf?session_id=bb209e50f65d 3ca148f096fe9bbb569e1024044b

Wittgenstein, L. (1953). *Philosophical investigations* (G. E. M. Anscombe & R. Rhees (Eds.), G. E. M. Anscombe (Trans.)). Oxford: Blackwell.

Zepeda, S. J. (2014). *Job-embedded professional development: Support, collaboration, and learning in schools.* New York: Routledge.

Index

learning and 31; management of 129–131; professional training 192–194; technology and 4–5, 51, 53, 134; theories of 74–75, 82–83; values and 16

children: teaching 44

Clark, Richard 208

classroom culture 24

classrooms: flipping 141, 190

cloud-based tools 51

CMSs see content management systems

coaching 114

cognitive apprenticeship 113–114

cognitive development 65–66, 67–69, 70

cognitive dissonance 67–68, 76

cognitive flexibility theory 21

cognitive interaction 22

cognitive load theory 81–82

cognitive skills: training 45–46

cognitive social mediated theory 69–70

cognitive traits 112

cognitivism 77–78

collaboration tools 194

communication 20–22; business/industry 182; defining 90–91; effective communication 215–216; governmental agencies 184; higher education 180; interaction and 178–179; matrix 96; models 92–94; NPOs/NGOs 186; technology integration 166, 170; theories of 87–98

communities: MOOCs 117

competencies: professional preparation 189; teaching 42–43; training 44

complex cognitive skills 45–46

computer generation 87–89

computers: emerging technologies 204–205; Moore's Law 135; problem-solving 123–124

concept maps 102–103

concepts: educational technology 8, 10, 12; instructional theories 101–104; learning types 110

conceptual replication studies 200

concrete concepts 103, 110

concrete operational stage, cognitive development 67

constructionist communication models 92–93

constructivism 21, 78

content knowledge 55

content management systems (CMSs) 51

continuing education 147

convergers 111

copyrights 148

costs: change management 129; technology 53, 126, 135, 171–172

Creative Commons 148–149

critical theory 78–79

cultural development 65, 66, 69

culture 24; business/industry 183; communication/ interaction 178; development 65, 66, 69; ethics and 17; governmental agencies 184–185; higher education 180–181; NPOs/ NGOs 186; technology implications 142–143; technology integration 166, 170; technology-supported learning 157–158, 160

Curie, Marie 66

D

data 87–89

declarative knowledge 101

Dede, C. 199

demonstration projects, scalability 197

deployment of technology 128–129

depth, scalability 199

design: educational entities 158–159; missteps 161–163; principles 159–160; scale and 199; technology integration and 167; technology-supported learning 155–165, see also instructional design

design levels, values 18–19

development: andragogy 45; education and 7; theories 65–73

Dewey, J. 79, 100

diffusion of innovation model 126–127, 129, 142, 199

digital communications 20–21

digital divide 140

digital media 161

digital natives 140

Dijkstra, Edgars 123–124, 129

Dijkstra, Sanne 46

direct replication studies 200

disabled people 53, 158–159

distance learning courses 147, 152

divergers 111

Dörner, D. 23

Dreyfus, H. and S. 36–37

dropout rate example 124–125

dual coding theory 21

dynamic relationships, systems perspective 61

E

early adopters, technology 126–129

early majority, technology 126, 129

V

values 16–19, 33, 100
van Merriënboer, J. J. G. 115
VARK system 111–112
visual learners 111
vocational training 149
Vygotsky, Lev 28, 69–70

W

Watson, J. 77
weak technologies 54–55
wearable devices 205, 212
Weaver, W. 90, 92
web-based learning management systems 156

what you measure is what you get (WYMIWYG) 35–36
what you see is what you get (WYSIWYG) 169
wisdom/data/information/knowledge relationship 87–89
Wittgenstein, L. 68, 76
word processing 169
worker productivity 157
workplace educational technology 146–154
WYMIWYG *see* what you measure is what you get
WYSIWYG *see* what you see is what you get

Z

zone of proximal development (ZPD) 28, 69–70